# Foolish Genius

## Changemakers for a Wise Society

David W. Mahan

Hevel Publishing

**Foolish Genius**
**Changemakers for a Wise Society**

Copyright © 2023 David W. Mahan
First Edition Paperback ISBN: 979-8-9887690-0-2
First Edition Hardcover ISBN: 979-8-9887690-1-9
First Edition Ebook ISBN: 979-8-9887690-2-6
LCCN: 2023918493

No part of this publication may be reproduced, stored in a retrieval system, or transmitted, in any form or by any means, electronic, mechanical, photocopying, recording, or otherwise, without the written prior permission of the author.

**Contact:**
team@FoolishGenius.com

Printed in the United States of America

## Dedication

*To my parents, David and Elese Mahan: Your grace, integrity, and nightly readings through years of intense sacrifice throughout my childhood taught me more than you could know. Your next read is on me. Love you both.*

# Contents

Acknowledgments ................................................................................... vii
Introduction ............................................................................................. 1
1 The Common Dilemma ...................................................................... 3
    Common Issues .................................................................................. 5
    Change versus Progress .................................................................... 7
    Wisdom and the Wise Society .......................................................... 9
    Path to Progress ............................................................................... 11
2 Change ................................................................................................ 12
    Changemakers .................................................................................. 12
    The Common Man ........................................................................... 14
    The Common Man Is… .................................................................... 16
    Four Inhibitory Factors ................................................................... 19
    The Four *I*'s of Change .................................................................. 27
    Today's Changemaker: The Foolish Genius .................................. 31
3 Age of Wisdom .................................................................................. 35
    The Goal: Quality of Life ................................................................ 36
    Barriers to Wisdom .......................................................................... 40
    Components of Wisdom ................................................................. 41
    Prerequisites For Wisdom ............................................................... 49
    Critical Thinking .............................................................................. 52
    Personal Responsibility ................................................................... 54
    Characteristics of Wisdom .............................................................. 56
4 Principles ............................................................................................ 66
    Benjamin Lay .................................................................................... 68
    Pitfalls of Lacking Principles .......................................................... 70
5 A Philosopher's Revolution .............................................................. 82
    Philosophers and Social Change .................................................... 83
    Rules of Engagement ....................................................................... 91
    Principles of a Wise Society ............................................................ 94
6 Purpose ............................................................................................... 96
    The Story of Viktor Frankl ............................................................. 97
    What Is Purpose? ............................................................................. 99

Process-Oriented .................................................................................... 101
Selfishly Altruistic ................................................................................. 103
Conceptual Components of Purpose ................................................... 105
A Sense of Purpose .............................................................................. 108
Creative Process of Shared Purpose .................................................... 114

7 Creativity .................................................................................................. 120
A Picture Worth a Thousand Warriors ................................................ 120
Social Change with Creativity .............................................................. 122
What Is Creativity? ............................................................................... 124
A Creative Deficit ................................................................................. 129

8 Overcoming the Deficit ........................................................................... 134
Individuality .......................................................................................... 134
Perspective ............................................................................................ 140
Boundaries ............................................................................................ 146
Excellence ............................................................................................. 149
Ethical Creativity .................................................................................. 151
Ethical Leadership ................................................................................ 155

9 Servants and Supers ................................................................................. 160
Principled Versus Traditional Leadership ............................................ 165

10 The Heart of Wisdom ............................................................................ 175
Community ........................................................................................... 175
Rosa Guamán ....................................................................................... 178
Learning Our ABCDs ........................................................................... 182

Afterword ...................................................................................................... 187

Endnotes ....................................................................................................... 189

Index .............................................................................................................. 197

About the Author ......................................................................................... 203

Bulk Orders ................................................................................................... 204

Collaborate with David ................................................................................ 205
In-School Leadership Mentoring ......................................................... 205
Organizational Consulting ................................................................... 205
What else would you like to see? ......................................................... 205

# Acknowledgments

To Claudia Gere for her guidance, insights, and willingness to go above and beyond. She was invaluable throughout the editing and publishing process, and I can't thank her enough.

To the gifted minds at Good Comma Editing. Their advice and meticulous work in ensuring clear and consistent messaging was pivotal in molding this final product.

To my good friend, Malik Daley, for his incessant questions and curiosity that led to the exploration of several new ideas and countless late-night conversations.

To Charity Butler for willingly exposing herself to my thoughts and writing, no matter how undeveloped they may have been. Her insights and serene strength have been a grounding force throughout this process.

To Andrew Ortega, a close friend and confidant, whose combination of discipline, character, and love for people has served as a valued example to me since freshman year of high school.

To Dr. Tom Edwards for his willingness to share his innumerable insights, and humility to partner with me, despite his impressive accomplishments and missional lifestyle.

To Michael Jenkins, the quintessential community leader. Columbus is blessed to have a man like you working on its behalf.

# Introduction

In 1929, a women's freedom march promoted a product that would eventually ravage the lungs of women around the world. Edward Bernays organized this women's march to promote his client's product. Make a profit and break down the many social taboos weighing on women in the 1920s? A social entrepreneur's dream. Unfortunately, his client was the American Tobacco Company. Bernays's march spun cigarettes as "torches of freedom" lighting the way for women's empowerment, which can accurately be described as the day "death sticks" were made commonplace for the almost half of American women smoking cigarettes only fifty years later. Bernays went on to define the American breakfast, destabilize governments, counsel presidents, and become the "father of public relations" in recognition of his PR genius. If I could sum him up in one word, it would be Changemaker.

Changemakers take an idea and embed it in the minds of the general population until that idea becomes unconsciously influential. Changemakers are driven by passion, a sense of purpose, what they believe are good intentions, and, most commonly, their own definition of Common Sense. Ultimately, they wish to do what few can: create lasting change. Unfortunately, as in the case of Bernays and his "torches of freedom," Changemakers are too often equipped to create change but not to steer it. The Foolish Genius can't tell the difference, leaving the blind to lead the blind. What good is a leader if they lead you to your own eventual demise?

Truthfully, Bernays was a man of conviction and regretted his decision to promote cigarettes. He became an activist of sorts, dedicating his time to fighting the monster he helped create. In his book *Propaganda*, he wrote, "Truth is mighty and must prevail, and if any body of men believe that they have discovered a valuable truth, it is not merely their privilege but their duty to disseminate that truth."[1] This was a man who had incredible knowledge and ability and tried to do what was best but couldn't always tell what best was. In the same book, Bernays admitted, "Men are rarely aware of the real reasons which motivate their actions."[2]

This book is about shaping leaders who can spark change, but more importantly, arming them with the tools and concepts to implement change *responsibly*. To be clear, this is not a book about how to create change. I won't go into detail about the strategy of any one social movement or break down

## Foolish Genius

the psychology of their leaders. While creating Changemakers is important, I believe that the development and character of those Changemakers should be regarded just as highly. As you read about how the Foolish Genius becomes a Wisdom-led Changemaker, you will notice five key concepts:

1. Wisdom: The anchoring concept in this book and the only thing that separates positive change from misguided change. Wisdom receives guiding force through principles.

2. Principles: The guideposts by which we can "discover a valuable truth." Learn how—through a firm understanding of principles—a strange social outcast converted his people from complacent allies into steadfast abolitionists, forming the first religious antislavery group in America. Principles can be grasped only by a Changemaker who also has a strong sense of purpose.

3. Purpose: A concept that drives not only the Changemaker but also the explosively creative innovation of groups.

4. Creativity: The most powerful tool in the Changemaker's toolbox. A tool that is commonly used by the devious (and also commonly creates the devious), but with the right approach, can be used to create positive change.

5. Community Development: The book concludes with the one concept that encompasses them all, striking at the very heart of wisdom. Read about a woman whose efforts and love for her community restored the self-respect and economic viability to people who, by her diagnosis had forgotten their culture and were dependent on the goodwill of others.

Ultimately, the goal of this book is to give aspiring Changemakers the proper tools to determine if the change they seek to create will truly lead themselves and their constituents to a rewarding and more equitable future. More than that, I hope you will see the significance your own personal development has on the society you are working to shape. That is, I hope reading this will equip you to overcome the Common Dilemma.

# 1
# The Common Dilemma

*Common sense is the most fairly distributed thing in the world, for each one thinks he is so well-endowed with it that even those who are hardest to satisfy in all other matters are not in the habit of desiring more of it than they already have.* – René Descartes

---

### Takeaways
- Common Sense is the accepted basis for creating change, but not the best one.
- Progress is directional change.
- Wisdom is the best guide for social change.

---

Given the choice between liberty and bondage, Common Sense mistakes the two, inevitably choosing the latter. I define Common Sense as the unconscious beliefs and practices of a group's general population. We identify with leaders who share the same definition of Common Sense. We agree with them and support them as they battle against the injustices in the world. Those who oppose our heroes are our so-called villains. At a glance, our villains are similar to our heroes, sharing many of the same traits and characteristics, but they represent everything that is wrong in the world. The villains, of course, believe they are right, but they obviously don't share our worldview. The only difference between the two, as it stands, are their differing definitions of Common Sense, not their strategy for creating change or even their character. We like to simplify our heroes and villains as people who have a different starting point, walk in straight lines, and at no point do their paths intersect and perspectives resolve. Their definition of Common Sense will always conflict with that of their opponents, and the only way for them to win over their opponent is to embed their definition into that of the culture.

These heroes (and villains) are what I refer to as Changemakers. They are the politicians, activists, community leaders, and impassioned citizens who pick a cause, raise support, and set their minds on changing society. Unfortunately, no great idea goes unpunished. Anyone who has tried to impact society eventually encounters the opinion of the general public. It seems that the greater the opposition, the greater the impact. Martin Luther King Jr. was sent to jail twenty-nine times. Twenty-nine! He watched some of his followers being hosed down, his family being harassed, and members of both political parties throwing slurs. Most would have quit when organizing a march consistently interrupted by honking traffic. His practices and ideology of civil disobedience may seem like Common Sense now, but it took a lot of courage to convince people not to swing back when beaten without cause. Even now, putting civil disobedience in practice is radical and not an intuitive response against injustice. But research on civil disobedience has shown how effective a tool it is,[3] and of course, Martin Luther King Jr. is one of the most celebrated individuals in American history. He redefined Common Sense. What would his legacy be if he hadn't?

Edison created something so innovative it became symbolic of the concept. But even the lightbulb faced opposition. A British parliament committee was quoted saying Edison's idea was "good enough for our Transatlantic friends…but unworthy of the attention of practical or scientific men."[4] In a world filled with candles, the lightbulb was hard to accept. Today, Edison is one of the few inventors whose work has touched the entire world.

Common Sense doesn't change unless creative revolutionaries take up the mantle and win over the hearts of the Common Man (the general population). If an idea succeeds at changing what is seen as Common Sense in that day, then that idea will endure. In the King and Edison examples, their ideas benefited society, so changing the Common Sense of their time ended positively. Unfortunately, change does not always benefit the population that accepts it. History is riddled with leaders who were elected for one reason, but once they reached power, they took a different turn. Think of dictators who enter government legally then muscle their way into position to dissolve the same process that facilitated their election. Think of well-intentioned inventions that have been readopted for malicious purposes. Charisma and marketing have been used repeatedly to change the definition of Common Sense, but that change does not always play to our favor.

Our sense of what is socially acceptable is not set in stone. Slavery was a common practice in Europe around AD 1000, and it took another eight hundred years for slavery to be outlawed by a single European country. Many cultures of the past viewed pedophilia as acceptable (and some today still do). In early America, it was common practice for people to duel in response to an insult, so much so that one of our presidents, an especially short-tempered one, killed a man in response to an accusation and insult to his wife. A Vice President even dueled a former Secretary of the Treasury. Government officials killed each other in the streets, and the public accepted it as if it were a celebrity boxing match. Dueling wasn't specifically deemed illegal until 1859, and even then it was fairly common in certain states. Clearly, Common Sense sways over time. Sometimes it aligns with people who advocate for a positive outcome, and sometimes to those who support a negative one.

## Common Issues

Between 2010 and 2014, a longitudinal survey (one that has repeated observations of the same variables over time) assessed what the Australian Common Man thought about climate change.[5] The study surveyed 17,000 people, with almost a third of them interviewed multiple times. This study exposed the three major issues with relying on Common Sense to direct your actions.

The first issue with Common Sense lies in our inability to say how common it truly is. The study's executive summary stated, "Every group estimated their own opinion to be the most common among the broader community. Those who thought climate change was not happening (7.9 percent of respondents from Figure 2) strongly overestimated the prevalence of their own opinion (49.1 percent). Those who thought that climate change was natural or human-induced were more accurate in their perceptions, slightly underestimating the broader prevalence of their own opinions. *Every* group overestimated the percentage of people who denied climate change was happening."[6]

The second issue with Common Sense is that most people feel as if they have it, but that may not be true. After providing their survey opinions, the respondents were asked why they believe what they believe. The possible answers were friends/family, politicians/government, news/media, historical events, the weather, Common Sense, and scientific research. When the minority group who believed global warming was not happening was asked what they based their opinion on, the most frequently selected response was "Common Sense." Common Sense was the second most selected answer to support their opinion among all the participants.

The third issue with Common Sense is that it is subject to change. "There is inconsistency in individuals' opinions over time. Nearly half (48.5 percent) of repeat respondents changed their opinion on climate change on at least one occasion."[7]

> Common Sense is more *common* than it is *sense*.

A popular quote from Voltaire states, "Common Sense is not that common," but I disagree. Common Sense is more *common* than it is *sense*. In Australia, the Common Man's opinion of global warming was agreed upon by the overwhelming majority, yet neither group had an accurate perspective of how dominant the popular opinion was. On top of that, both the unpopular and popular groups defended their positions by calling it "Common Sense." The Common Man struggles with judging what Common Sense is, who shares it, and if it is truly beneficial. Common Sense, which traditionally meant good judgment, points to being the opposite of that in several ways. Common Sense is common, but the Common Man doesn't have a good grasp of what it is or how it changes over time, so it certainly cannot be used to justify the validity of one's actions.

The most dangerous and potentially disastrous aspect of Common Sense (and, as a result, change) is that it is morally indiscriminate. It doesn't matter what your way of thinking is; if you can create an argument with enough emotional appeal and some string of logic, you can sway the opinion of yourself, other Changemakers, and potentially, the Common Man. As humans, we understandably tend to respect people who exhibit discipline and sustained initiative over time. So the Common Man is naturally drawn toward Changemakers. As Changemakers seek to create lasting change, they will experience some consensus, but as we've already established, they will also experience opposition. The greatest men and women in history (greatest here meaning their level of impact, not their moral aptitude) achieved that status by their ability to overcome opposition, not by their integrity or character.

Many social activists revel in their latest victory in the same manner serial killers revel when they avoid or beat the law.

## Change versus Progress

The problem with Changemakers is that the change they implement can be positive in the short term but disastrous in the long. We cannot grade a Changemaker's work as we can a physician's success in surgery; it seems more similar to the courtroom success of a lawyer. In the medical world, patients can be monitored, and if their health improves, we know the surgery worked. Success is tied to the immediate surgery as well as the patient's health afterward.

But in the legal arena, lawyers don't always know if their clients are innocent prior to trial. A lawyer's success can be evaluated by an absolute verdict before court is adjourned, and their work usually escapes reevaluation over time. Changemakers are like lawyers in the sense that they are praised immediately after they win the case. They changed the definition of Common Sense. Later, once the new definition of Common Sense is rooted, they are never again evaluated to the same degree as they might have been had they lost the case, that is, against a different definition of Common Sense. The Common Man assumes that the changes represent progress, when in reality, the change in definition could instigate a future much worse than the past.

But change is not all bad. Today truly is an amazing time to be alive. The Information Age, Digital Age, or whatever you'd like to call it (I call it the Age of Knowledge) is upon us, and we've never been so comfortable. Ours is like no other society the world has ever seen! In less than one hundred years, we have created ways to communicate across the globe instantaneously. Money is plastic and doesn't have to be manually counted. We work just as hard as before, but now we can do it half-dressed on online calls from the safety of our living rooms. We adapted to a rapid rate of change in a way that no society has ever done before us. We have revolutionized almost every industry. Almost. Yet, with all our advancements, our standard for what falls into our definition of Common Sense seems to be at an all-time low. I know you know what I'm talking about. The generation that can receive answers to almost any question instantly is desperately confused. Despite our progressive spirit, it's hard to objectively say that we are truly progressing.

## Foolish Genius

Example number one: We are social beings—always have been, always will be. Even introverts need social interaction, just presented in a different way or with fewer people. It's in our DNA. Social interactions benefit mental health, lower mortality risk, and help with overall well-being. Put simply, you are rewarded when you interact with people. Extrapolate this thought, and you would think social media would make us gods, since we can interact with a seemingly infinite number of people from across the world. But social media not only has been linked to a plethora of negative effects on our body, (loneliness and depression,[8] immunity,[9] etc.) it has shifted our paradigm of what social interaction is. It has, in many ways, replaced "old-fashioned" interaction. What's the point in meeting new people when you can add a friend at the click of a button? This example is cliché and a little bit of a cheap shot: it's easy to hate on the Zuckerbergs and Facebooks/Metas of the world. But as warranted as the critiques may be, aren't we the ones who made social media social in the first place?

The next example of change versus progress takes the focus off the errant business sector and onto something much more well-intentioned: the education system. Maybe you're the hardcore entrepreneurial type. You respect social media because of the benefits it can provide if you learn to control it. You can build an audience, jumpstart a business, and even start a movement if you know how to use it. To you, it all comes down to discipline. But something you can't control is the education you receive as a child. To you, one of the biggest breakdowns in Common Sense may take place in the classroom.

The public school system in the United States was originally founded to level the playing field. Before the 1830s, it was social elite who were provided a formal education. But with state-funded school systems, students of all backgrounds could be given the same opportunity, or at the very least a new standard of opportunity. Today, the focus has shifted, with schools trying to move away from a place of learning to a place of holistic development. A new mission in an old skin. Yet students can graduate with straight A's and still not know how to properly process information. We spend increased time in the education system only to rely on our parents longer!

If it's not enough to talk about how many students graduate from schools of higher learning with no idea how to file income taxes, or how we are addicted to the technology originally designed to streamline our busy schedules, let's talk about our GDP. The GDP of the United States easily outpaces every other nation, yet, for all our wealth and physical health, suicide is the tenth leading cause of death.

On paper, we seem to be closing in on perfection, but our internal issues are emerging dominant. No matter who you are or what your background is, I'm sure you can add to this growing list of issues. We are progressing rapidly, but we seem to be breaking down just as fast.

But there is hope! Although we may not all agree on what exactly causes these issues, we are generally well-intentioned and want life to improve. Change is a popular topic of our day, and the term has become a bit of a buzzword (and I'm not helping). It seems as if everyone wants to have an impact, join the nearest protest, and leave a non-environmental footprint. This is a beautiful thing, seeing more people wanting to have a positive impact on the world, and thanks to the internet, starting a movement has never been easier. Influencers are now seen expanding their reach by tens of millions in a matter of months; petitions are being signed by millions in a matter of days. For today's Changemakers, this sounds great: more exposure for their amazing ideas and technology. But for the future of the Common Man, this may prove to do more harm than good.

With the barrier to entry lowered to the cost of a cellphone, just about anyone can build an audience and promote whatever they like. The beauty of this is that truly anyone can have a voice. The ability to create change has been democratized significantly. The downside is that it's hard to distinguish which Changemakers will lead us in creating positive change and true progress. We have an abundance of people with entrepreneurial and creative spirits all relying on Common Sense to determine their impact.

## Wisdom and the Wise Society

So far, we've mentioned the roles Common Sense, the Common Man, and Changemakers play in creating lasting change, but both Changemakers and the Common Man can be unreliable in their judgment. Most people are well-meaning, but intentions can't determine whether something will ultimately affect society positively or negatively. An alternative, judging our actions by feelings, is equally unstable. Common Sense is the accepted metric right now, but it has been shown time and time again to be ineffective. If we want to be intentional about creating a better society for all parties, there has to be a system or metric that ensures an idea is truly good, not merely that its advocate is adequately charismatic. Does the Changemaker have good intentions? If so, why does that matter? Are they effective leaders, or are they simply attractive? The innovators and revolutionaries of old have proven that, in order to make a lasting change, you need to change what is seen as Common Sense, but they have also exposed that Common Sense is not a reliable metric for mutual betterment.

When we speak colloquially of "having common sense" in terms of good judgment, what we truly mean is Wisdom. Wisdom is rare. Common Sense, as defined in this book, changes with the times, but Wisdom continues consistent through the ages. Common Sense has no sound process associated with it. It's easy and takes no effort to form as we grow older. Einstein described it as "nothing more than a deposit of prejudices laid down in the mind before you reach eighteen." Wisdom, on the other hand, can pass us by forever if we aren't intentional about seeking it. Since Common Sense has no process and is heavily dependent on our culture, it can't be used as a guide for our actions. Wisdom, on the other hand, can be studied and broken down. We aren't born with it, but we can gain it as we grow older. Wisdom is what separates progress from every other form of change.

> Wisdom is what separates progress from every other form of change.

Wisdom-led change on a personal level—as opposed to Wisdom in the prior paragraph—is something we can identify in our day-to-day life. We know we should get the recommended hours of sleep, drive responsibly, and eat an apple a day. We use marshmallows to test delayed gratification,[10] read books on forming healthy habits, and attempt to learn best practices that will ultimately lead us to success. Much like Common Sense, personal Wisdom gets passed down from one generation to the next. It gets weaved into the myths of our culture and laced into the Common Sense of the day. Whenever we struggle with personal Wisdom, we know where to turn. We have self-help books, social media influencers, community resources, and mentors (if you are so fortunate) to help us become proficient and reach our potential as individuals.

But walking with Wisdom as a Changemaker is a much more difficult road. Unfortunately, the development of Changemakers does not receive enough attention in our society, and although there are some generally accepted dos and don'ts (for example: don't lie to your following, don't manipulate the Common Man, be honest and transparent, don't sleep with subordinates, etc.), there is little substantial discussion regarding why these rules apply and what qualifies as wise social change.

Changemakers, therefore, often rely on these general dos and don'ts, but those are regulated by the Common Sense of their time, which may or may not coincide with Wisdom. They are left to deal with a judgmental Common Man with little to no guidance. Changemakers have to then decide if they will speak openly about the ways they were unwise, or double down in their definition of Common Sense. This well-intentioned pride is the root of inequitable change and is the defining characteristic of the first and most common type of Changemaker: the Foolish Genius. This Changemaker creates change based solely on their own mental prowess and definition of Common Sense.

## Path to Progress

Although a Wise Society sounds appealing to the Common Man, they won't be the ones leading the way toward true progress. It will take an army of Changemakers to usher in the Age of Wisdom, but simply creating change isn't enough. Yes, Changemakers who hold the mindset of the Foolish Genius will still create change, but if they also create progress, that will be merely coincidental. In the same way that being well-intentioned does not predict positive outcomes, the Foolish Genius can either push society toward progress or away from it.

Creating change isn't enough; we have to create change toward a Wise Society. This task can be accomplished only by Changemakers who submit to the guidance of Wisdom, have the ability to identify and uphold the principles associated with Wisdom, embrace the motivational power of purpose, have the creative fortitude to develop a sense of purpose, and possess the leadership ability to instill all of these into the Common Man. This book is for the Foolish Genius or developing Changemaker who is trying to create the type of equitable change only possible when Wisdom is valued, understood, and pursued.

# 2
# Change

*Yesterday I was clever, so I wanted to change the world. Today I am wise, so I am changing myself.* – Rumi

---

### Takeaways
- The Common Man plays a significant role in creating social change.
- Personal change flows into social change.
- Every Changemaker starts as a Foolish Genius, but we can pursue Wisdom and build toward a better world.

---

## Changemakers

Changemakers influence every facet of the society we live in. The purpose of their influence is to impact others to reach a desired outcome. Selfishly inspired change positively impacts the Changemakers who spark it first and foremost. Altruistic change aids those potentially impacted by that change. In either situation, change is a human interaction: a contract between the so-called heroes and villains (both Changemakers) and the general public. Change is a contract that heavily influences both parties, but we'll start our review with those who spark the change itself: the Changemaker. Changemakers impact how privilege is given or withheld, the conveniences "average people" experience, and even our moral consciousness. What a great power to hold over a nation and even the world!

Change is the process of taking something that already exists and redefining or repurposing it. When a Changemaker wants to create a shift, they have to redefine what is seen as Common Sense, but creating a new status quo—a new stasis of what Common Sense is—is not an easy task. It's bound to come up against roadblocks, which can come in many forms:

## *The 'Right Cause, Wrong Strategy' Objection*

"When they first started speaking, I was on board, but the solution they are going with won't solve anything! In fact, it could make everything worse."

## *The 'Naive Idealist' Objection*

"What they want to accomplish is impossible. Give them some time, and they'll see it's just not practical."

These two objections are often heard from people who agree with your mission. In the political realm, these first two groups may be referred to as Saints and Savables: people who share your same definition of Common Sense, or one similar enough that they will hear you out. They may not be convinced that your strategy is the right one—or that you are the best person to carry it out—but with a little time and building of trust, they may become your biggest supporters.

But there's a third group, which some refer to as Sinners. Once we venture to persuade this group, a whole new set of objections arises. Here are three.

## *The 'Status Quo' Objection*

"Here are more revolutionists trying to make a change with no regard for the consequences. They want to replace the current system without a clear plan. 'Nature abhors a vacuum,' I guess. We know we aren't perfect, but they aren't working toward perfection; they want chaos. Right now we are comfortable, and who's to say their ideas won't make things worse? They're simply fighting against the status quo to make a name for themselves."

## *The 'Obvious Idiot' Objection*

"I can't believe they could ever think that would work. How stupid could they be?"

## *The 'Terrible Person' Objection*

"If they would oppose [insert your favorite cause], then they are a bad person. I can't believe what they say, support what they stand for, or bother myself with their dangerous ideology."

These are just a few examples. Every Changemaker has faced a seemingly insurmountable mountain of objections in the minds of the people they are trying to win over, and some of these objections might have merit. The task of the Changemaker is to make war with a group's objections and replace them with their ideas—that is, get the Changemaker's ideas accepted and incorporated into that group's updated Common Sense. And it *will* feel like a war. Fighting against other people's Common Sense is, in their eyes, like attacking the protagonist, which makes you the villain. And who's to say that you aren't?

History has no shortage of self-proclaimed heroes whom history later deemed villains. Ted Kaczynski authored a 35,000-word essay that summarized the thinking behind his mail bombing campaign.[11] His writings were initially accepted as rational, but his acts of terrorism were insane, unjustified, and unethical.[12] For almost every insane action there is a sane justification. If everyone is entitled to their own beliefs and worldviews, who's to say that what you are fighting for is truly what is best for society? And if you have identified a real issue in society, who's to say your solution won't make things worse?

Love them or hate them, Changemakers are here to stay, and more than that, we wouldn't be here without them. When we aren't complaining about what we don't like about them, we are praising them for their perspective, creativity, vision, and dedication to their craft. But what really differentiates Changemakers from the Common Man is their ability to proceed through all four steps of change, which we'll get to soon. First, let's discuss the most overlooked character in our story: the Common Man.

## The Common Man

Since change is a contract between two parties, the outcome of change has an impact that reaches far beyond the personal life of the Changemaker. Not only does the impact of change spread beyond the Changemaker, but the terms of change themselves extend well beyond their control.

Growing up I used to be quite a prankster. To appease my loved ones, I learned to contain myself (until April Fools' Day, of course). So now I indulge in my fair share of Joker quotes (gems from *The Dark Knight*) and binge-watch prank shows to keep me satisfied. Prank shows are all the same, and if you've seen one you know what I'm talking about. There is a hired team of actors who pull a prank off in public, and whoever has the misfortune of being there at the wrong moment falls victim to the prank. More than the prank itself, I always love watching the faces of the innocent bystanders thrust into social situations with no appropriate response to the break in decorum. While the prank is underway, the camera pans to all the onlookers, whose eyes keep darting from the victim of the prank to the rest of the crowd. I watch them and wonder how they are going to react: will they step in and stop the prank, get help, or intervene in some way?

The bystanders' reactions are the whole show. They are what the producers are going for. They want to capture a reaction of shock, and eventually, support from the people they are involving in their game. Some bystanders will act out of impulse or automatic thought and attempt to leave, some will be the leader of the group and step in, and others will follow and do whatever the first two did. The Common Man does all the above. What separates the Changemakers from the Common Man is that the Changemakers are the ones creating the moment, while the Common Man is simply reacting to it. Change isn't caused by the Common Man; it happens *to* them. While the Common Man doesn't actively spark social change, they are still part of it. They have power but don't fully realize it, so they remain passive to the process of change.

Coincidentally, this is where the power of the Common Man lies. They may not be the ones producing the next great idea, but they validate it. If a concept is not approved and perpetuated by them, it will not create a lasting change. Thus the Common Man still determines what is considered Common Sense. They may be passive about their decision, but their decision matters regardless. They are the reason politicians spend millions to campaign on TV and why advertisers buy Google and Facebook ads to increase revenue. The opinion of the Common Man matters, and everyone who wants to make a lasting change knows it.

Before we go further, let's deconstruct some negative connotations around the Common Man. The word *common* is NOT derogatory. Words like *common* or *average* are often heard pejoratively, but we all stand (and often remain) as a Common Man at one point or another. It's our default state. We find the Common Man, ever the supermajority, at every level of every industry, although their industry and occupation are irrelevant. They could just as easily be lawyers, doctors, influencers, or engineers. They are set apart by their mindset and approach to change, not their IQ level, political affiliation, or social status. The word *common* doesn't mean they are an insecure paper pusher or in any other undervalued job. The Common Man is much more "common" than that.

# The Common Man Is...

Before diving into the differences between the Common Man and Changemakers, here are some misconceptions about the Common Man that merit discussion. Once Changemakers start to make a real impact, they can lose sight of what they were like before their influence increased. They can forget what it means to be a part of the Common Man. So just to clarify, here are a few things that the Common Man is not.

## *Not Stupid*

When you see that your favorite presidential candidate didn't win the election or hear him or her being described as having "no true knowledge of reality,"[13] it can be easy to see the Common Man as stupid, but this is not the case. Your potential to create change is not dependent on your intelligence. Anyone can be a Common Man, and anyone can be a Changemaker. Sure, intelligence is helpful when creating a strategy for change and learning from your mistakes, but it's not necessary to take initiative, and it's certainly not essential to have an impact.

## *Not Lazy*

Winston Churchill is one of the legendary Changemakers known for his intense work ethic and drive to succeed. Churchill rallied his people during the most pivotal part of World War II with such inspirational influence that Great Britain bounced back victoriously. His ability as an orator places him alongside Mister Rogers, Dr. Martin Luther King Jr., and Nelson Mandela. What makes Churchill even more amazing is that he stuttered! It's believed he would practice his speeches for hours at a time, making sure to get his pauses and cadence just right. He became a poster child for what the impact of hard work and diligence can do. This was, of course, after a childhood of consistently disappointing his father due to laziness and lack of achievement. Winston was not a particularly good student, showed little initiative, and shied away from sports and other extracurriculars known for instilling discipline. His father, not liking what he was seeing, decided that a career in the military was what his son needed, but even then, Churchill didn't study hard enough to pass his first two officer training exams. Still, he shot from the bottom of his class to become one of the most influential people in history.

The belief that the Common Man is lazy is a popular one that gets bounced around in several circles, but especially with business owners and entrepreneurs. Yes, of course, there are some people that lack initiative, necessary to create real impact, but that shouldn't be extrapolated to describe the Common Man as a whole. What we associate with stupidity and laziness is often a lack of purpose or an unchallenged mind, such as was the case with Einstein, Darwin, and Churchill.

Churchill's school days were deeply frustrating. Later in life, he reflected on his childhood, saying, "I had hardly ever been asked to learn anything which seemed of the slightest use or interest, or allowed to play any game which was amusing. In retrospect those years form not only the least agreeable, but also the only barren and unhappy period of my life."[14] A perceived "laziness" doesn't mean a lack of purpose and potential. In fact, it can mean the opposite.

Another reason this misconception persists is because of the publicity Changemakers receive. When we watch the news or check our feed and hear Changemakers describe the importance of hard work and pulling yourself up by your bootstraps, we are tempted to believe that if we aren't making a similar impact, it must be because we aren't working hard enough. But many of the hardest working people on earth will never get a blog written about them or see their name in lights; they will, however, feed their families and manage their businesses, which brings us to the next misconception.

## *Not All Are Meant to Become Changemakers*

In the past, our culture has placed a person's value in whether they've left an impact on others. But that led people to believe their lives had no value if they couldn't see themselves leaving an impact. So to help people avoid those negative thoughts, society now encourages us to stop pressuring every person to leave an impact on others. But I think everyone does have an impact, whether they want to or not. Humans are too social for it to be any other way. We enjoy billions of interactions throughout our lives, each leaving a small imprint on another individual. Even if that imprint is forgotten, it remains meaningful. If you were able to sum all the imprints from your entire life, you would conclude you cannot truly fathom, much less measure, the totality of those impacts. On a more macro scale, change is a social contract between the Changemakers and the Common Man. Both play an important role, and both benefit the other. The role of the follower is often undervalued, but they are the validators of those they are following. The Common Man is always involved when social change is created, but it is not in their nature to spark it. That's okay. In fact, it's more than okay.

Derek Sivers demonstrated this point beautifully during his famous Ted Talk, "How to Start a Movement."[15] He played a clip of a standalone, shirtless man dancing wildly, but not disruptively, in public. At first everyone stared at the spectacle, but then, for whatever reason, someone else started dancing and became a part of the spectacle. By the end of the clip, there was a large group of people frolicking about and enjoying themselves. Sivers commented, "Leadership is over-glorified. Yes, it was the shirtless guy who was first, and he'll get all the credit, but it was really the first follower that transformed the lone nut into a leader. So…we're told that we should all be leaders; that would be ineffective."[16] Although I believe that everyone contributes to change and should therefore be cognizant of the change they are contributing to, not everyone is responsible for sparking change.

## *Not Any More or Less Moral than Changemakers*

Thomas Edison likely had ADHD and grew up with hearing problems, almost to the point of being deaf.[17] Needless to say, he was a difficult student and had a hard time sitting still. Despite his perceived limitations, he commercialized electric light, which is arguably the single most influential invention in the last millennium. Candy Lightner was a dental assistant turned real estate agent divorcee before she started a grassroots movement that would change forever how Americans viewed drunk driving. On the other side of the spectrum, at twenty-five years old, the Unabomber had been Berkeley's youngest assistant professor, whose intelligence and aptitude for knowledge suggested that his years were filled with promise. Stalin grew up in poverty with an abusive shoemaker for a father and a laundress for a mother. He showed signs of "rising above it" when he received a scholarship to seminary. He was studying to become a priest.

As cliché as these examples may be, the principles stand strong. Someone's backstory informs their future but does not predict it. Each of these people started out identifying with the Common Man. Nobody familiar with their pasts could have predicted the transformational movements they would eventually lead. Everyone starts out as part of the Common Man, and everyone has the potential to become a Changemaker or remain a part of the Common Man. But your decision to become a Changemaker or not does not define your morality. Becoming someone who strives for change can make you a great person, but it has nothing to do with becoming a *good* one. In the same way, the Common Man is not morally better only because their flaws are not shown for all to see. Power exposes the flaws we have, but they still exist regardless of how influential they are.

> ...your decision to become a Changemaker or not does not define your morality. Becoming someone who strives for change can make you a great person, but it has nothing to do with becoming a *good* one.

## Four Inhibitory Factors

As I've stressed, not all who are part of the Common Man can or should become a Changemaker. However, there are some people who want to be a Changemaker but fail to achieve that goal. There are several factors that contribute to their failure, many of which are not mindset-focused. We will address those factors later. But to start, let's discuss four of the most common mindsets and habits that inhibit people from becoming Changemakers.

### 1. *Ignoring Ignorance*

Both Changemakers and the Common Man are ignorant. I mean no disrespect by this; I believe ignorance is a human trait. To be clear, I do not mean we are all stupid; I mean that we all lack knowledge. We can know only what's presented to us. Though we are armed with Google, we lack the perspective to know what to search. If it doesn't make the news or gain popularity on Twitter, how are we to be aware of what's going on? And even when an event makes the news, we know only what the source is telling us, not necessarily the truth. The fact of the matter is, unless someone is omniscient, they are ignorant.

We like to ignore the truth that we lack knowledge; no one likes to be ignorant. But to put things into perspective, our lack must be better understood. No one has all the answers, and if two people disagree, it's more likely that neither is completely correct than one of them is completely so. We are actually arguing about who is *more accurate*, but once the reality of ignorance sets in, the pride of intelligence can subside and both parties can recognize the flaws in their positions.

As the old proverb goes, "Not to know is bad; not to wish to know is worse." Not knowing is human nature, but if one does not accept the fact that they are ignorant, they are also susceptible to looking down on others based on a difference in intelligence, specifically, a different *type* of intelligence. For example, a scientist may look down on a construction worker because the latter's job does not appear to require the same mental aptitude. Conversely, the construction worker may look down on the scientist because they have to hire a contractor to do basic carpentry in their house. We all start comparing ourselves as children, sizing up other students in school, seeing who can finish their math drills faster, who has the better athletic prowess (physical "intelligence") at recess, etc. Yes, some people may have less overall intelligence than others, but the difference on a macro level is minute when you realize that the difference between what you don't know and what you do is nearly infinite.

Ignoring your ignorance can also place you in an offensive state. If you ignore your ignorance, it's easy to fall into the trap of thinking you're always right, or conversely, thinking you're always wrong—both equally constrictive snares. The "always right" group has too much confidence, while the "always wrong" group has too little. Taking a black and white approach like this is counterproductive to problem-solving and conflict resolution.

## *2. Intentions over Actions*

Despite the all-too-common ignoring ignorance problem and a black-and-white approach to problem-solving, the Common Man is as well-meaning as they come. The fact that they have good intentions is an inherently good thing. The faith they put in these intentions is not.

# Change

Thanks to the persistence of lifelong activist Opal Lee, Juneteenth became a United States federal holiday in summer 2021, the first since Martin Luther King Jr., Day was instituted. This holiday was one of the black community's best kept secrets, so when it rushed to the forefront of national news, the world watched to see how predominantly white businesses would celebrate the occasion. Whenever news like this surfaces, there's always someone who becomes the poster child of what not to do, and IKEA became that poster child.

In the culturally rich city of Atlanta, Georgia, IKEA set out to celebrate the holiday by serving a meal to their employees "to honor the perseverance of Black Americans and acknowledge the progress yet to be made": a well-stated sentiment that, I'm sure, was appreciated by many of them. A small group within the company decided to create a special menu to celebrate the occasion and emailed it to their colleagues as another thoughtful move. Unfortunately the "special menu," as it was described, consisted of fried chicken, watermelon, mac and cheese, potato salad, collard greens, and candied yams.

Sometimes the jokes just write themselves. In honor of black emancipation, this group at IKEA played on some of the biggest black stereotypes there are. As you can imagine, the email was not well received. Twenty-plus employees called off work, which hurt the company, but the news coverage and public opinion hurt their image much more. Attempting to apologize, the store manager released a statement saying, "I truly apologize if the menu came off as subjective. It was created with the best of intentions by a few of our coworkers who believed they were representing their culture and tradition with these foods of celebration."

This specific branch had not demonstrated a history of racist behaviors, and the overarching IKEA brand has not either, at least not any more than most corporations its size. I believe the store manager and the few coworkers in charge of the menu acted goodheartedly. They wanted to create a celebration that was relevant to the people-group they were honoring, yet in all their well-intentioned actions, they did much more harm than good.

There are several issues with good intentions, the first that they are difficult to truly know, even for the person who owns those intentions. It's possible that the store manager was making a joke and thought he could get away with it. It's possible one of the coworkers suggested it with negative intent but the rest of the group was none the wiser. Intent can be difficult to prove

## Foolish Genius

in isolated incidents, but the impact is not. Having faith that you will do good and that the people you support will reap a positive impact simply because you have good intentions reveals a blind faith. If that IKEA branch had placed their trust in an effective approval process instead of good intentions, it likely would not have taken long to receive feedback on the offensive nature of the menu. Quotes on the danger of good intentions are numerous, but Henning Mankell wrote a particularly tasteful one: "Good intentions that are not clothed in reason lead to greater disasters than those actions built on ill will or stupidity."[18]

The combination of good intentions and the pride that can ensue from ignoring your ignorance results in dangerously strong convictions and self-righteousness. Change is a social contract. While both Changemakers and the Common Man are often well-intentioned, the Common Man typically relies solely on good intentions to create true progress. This can work, but usually doesn't.

## *3. More Mindset*

The way we think can be broken down into two types of processes: automatic and controlled. Controlled thinking is what you do when you try to answer what the square root of 430 is; it requires attention and determination. Automatic thinking is what you use to count to 10; it can be done without effort. Automatic thinking is what we use in our daily lives the most: waking up, driving to work, going to class, etc. These things are so habitual that controlled thinking is unnecessary. Maybe the first five times you drove to work or went to class you used controlled thinking, making sure that every turn was the correct one, but once you know your way, taking the right path becomes an autonomous task. The Common Man lives their life in an autonomous manner, but this does not mean they have a lower IQ or don't think as much. After all, automatic thought is still thought. A good example is one of my favorite toys.

In true prankster form, there is one simple toy that I've always enjoyed, even as an adult. The Chinese finger trap has always been a favorite of mine, confusing first-time users since its widely debated origin. If you haven't yet had the pleasure, the Chinese finger trap is a small woven bamboo cylinder that is open on both ends. The victim places one finger of each hand on opposite sides of the trap, creating a sort of finger bridge. The fun starts when the victim tries to pull their fingers out of the trap. The bamboo constricts and tightens onto the fingers during every pull. The harder one pulls, the harder the trap tightens. This is when the victim's eyes widen, and they realize they are stuck without a free hand to pull themselves free. The panic comes from your hands being stuck, but the embarrassment comes from being bested by a strip of grass. All this puts the victim in an automatic thought process, causing them to pull harder and harder, moving their elbows up and down in hysteria. A little bit of controlled thought would reveal that the way to escape the trap is to push your fingers deeper into the trap, loosening the grip on them. Automatic thought is reflexive and efficient, but when problems arise, it can lead to the "More Mindset."

To use the finger trap example, the automatic answer to your fingers getting stuck is to pull. When that doesn't work, you think you need to pull *more*. The automatic solution is pulling harder and harder when the actual solution is just the opposite of that. The "More Mindset" is a lazy way to problem solve and frame personal and systemic issues. For example, if a school is failing, the common response is to throw more money at the problem. When people fail, whether it be in business or day-to-day activities, the common response is more education is needed. This More Mindset is caused by half-truths. While adding resources is often needed, this mindset downplays the decision-making that created a failing system and diagnoses any loss as due to "insignificant resources."

It's not to say that resources could not help the situation. Schools in low-income areas do deserve to have more funding. Being able to give the students updated books, the teachers better pay, and the staff more training would likely increase the quality of the school. The More Mindset may fix certain issues, but it's more likely to clear the symptoms of an issue while still leaving the real problem unaddressed. Resources are often only half of the problem.

A school could struggle with nepotism, lack proper teacher training, or be led by a prideful principal. Personal failure could be due to a lack of diligence. Every business investor knows that you can't throw money at every good startup idea. Even if the business plan is flawless and the idea is groundbreaking, the timing of the product to market and the team's compatibility and capability matter just as much, if not more. Throwing money at a broken system doesn't guarantee positive outcomes and reform. The More Mindset pushes more knowledge as a solution to societal issues, without first conducting a proper audit. The same pride that comes from ignoring our ignorance shows its ugly face through the More Mindset. It is a one-dimensional approach to problem-solving that is born from reactive reasoning, inadequate thought, and a lack of creativity.

When a problem arises, the More Mindset fixates on the problem, not on the process that leads to a solution. But fixating on a single perceived solution too early can undermine the process by which we understand foundational issues. Once you've convinced yourself that you just need one thing (money, time, attention, etc.), you will find solutions that provide that one thing. But to solve a complex problem, you need complete analysis of those foundational issues, and that takes time. This is why the focus should be on end-to-end processes rather than one-off solutions. For example, startup founders go through hell in order to create a product and business model that are both sustainable and replicable. But if money had been thrown at their first idea, they likely would have forfeited the learning process that iterated and adapted the product to fit the market. Everyone has dreamed of winning the lottery, striking it rich, and living the rest of their years on easy street. For a select few, this dream is realized, at least in the short term. But the majority of lottery winners who have the opportunity to escape poverty and live life lavishly return to being broke within seven years.[19] Focusing on a single answer to a complex problem instead of on the process to get to a solution often leads to shortcuts and unstable "solutions."

Money is the most common but not the only object of the More Mindset; it could be a resource of any kind. Someone who struggles with depression may think if they only had more friends or medication, they would feel better. More healthy relationships or medication may be needed, but depression is a complicated issue; presuming the addition of any single thing will solve it would be disregarding the influence of the balance of the contributing factors. The More Mindset oversimplifies issues, which is why it can keep people from becoming Changemakers.

## *4. Plan of Distraction*

Distraction is one of the major reasons why the Common Man isn't viewed in the greatest light. Just as intellectuals often have an air of superiority around the formally uneducated, or as bearded men often judge men who can't grow facial hair, people of action often look down on the Common Man. Possibly the most famous of criticisms of the Common Man comes from the great Athenian philosopher, Plato. When arguing why true democ-

# Change

racy would not work, Plato described the Common Man as having "no true knowledge of reality, and no clear standard of perfection in their mind to which they can turn."[20] Plato could be a bit of a downer sometimes, but his words do hold weight.

The Common Man's approach to change is simple: they don't do it, not intentionally at least. They go through the motions and move when the crowd moves. They have beliefs and values just like everyone else, but they are more rooted in their cultural background and emotions than critical thought. Their values may even be self-contradictory. The Common Man is not likely to be able to defend their values since they don't quite understand the underlying principles that form them. Their inaction and distaste for change is not due to a lack of awareness about injustice; they see the same things that everyone else sees. But Changemakers assign themselves responsibility to do something about the injustice, as the following illustrates.

Candy Lightner is a mother of three, and in 1980, she tragically lost one of her children when her thirteen-year-old was hit by a drunk driver. She quickly learned that the perpetrator had a history of drunk driving and had even been arrested for it within the same week. He was given a mild reprimand. Four days after her child was killed, she started Mothers Against Drunk Driving (MADD). What started out as a few people around a kitchen table expanded to over three hundred chapters around the country in under a decade. She went from being an unregistered voter to serving on the National Commission on Drunk Driving by request of President Reagan. Her impact helped decrease alcohol-related fatalities in the US by over thirty-five percent from 1980 to 2000. Ms. Lightner was originally a Common Man, but the moment she assessed her convictions and owned them as her responsibility, she became a Changemaker.

Ms. Lightner dedicated herself to her vision of a world safe from drunk drivers, a vision that demanded enormous creativity to communicate effectively. Her seemingly normal upbringing, her measure as a mother, and her traumatic experience gave her the perspective that enabled her to touch the hearts of millions of mothers, and in turn, the entire nation. Drunk driving was not a new phenomenon of the time. Anybody could have done what she did, yet they didn't. Something about Ms. Lightner was different—a something that impelled her to not only wish that drunk driving would decrease but also spurred her to immediate then constant action. She didn't simply vote for someone who advocated for justice for the victims of drunk driving, although that would have been an appropriate and common response. She birthed an entire movement with no experience or historical indication that she could pull off something of such magnitude. Ms. Lightner didn't just wish that the future would be different; she envisioned one that was. Her vision was distinct and clear, yet relatable enough that she could convince others to support her vision. And she eventually reached the president of the United States!

Plato's criticism was not an attack on the intelligence of the Common Man but on their lack of perspective and vision. It's not that the Common Man is blind. They see the same injustices that the Changemakers see. It's not that they are bad people or lack an emotional attachment to social causes; they simply cannot see, for example, a future where it's possible a social cause is no longer necessary. At least, they cannot see it clearly enough to make that vision their own. In order to garner support and redefine Common Sense, the vision has to be so clear and well-communicated that the general population can see themselves supporting it.

The Common Man has just as much potential to enact change as Changemakers, and when they see the issues in their time, they want to contribute, but instead of working toward a plan of action, they settle for a plan of distraction. When you can't produce a plausible plan of action, the natural next step is to ignore the issues as best you can. When you do not have a clear vision of a hopeful future, the alternative is accepted as inevitable, and hope seems to serve no purpose other than to delay a coming pain. So the Common Man lives their lives surrounded by entertainment, whether that be in the form of social media, "situationships," or other distractions. They might retweet something or attend an occasional protest, but they don't assign themselves responsibility for the change. Instead, the Common Man returns to whatever keeps them from having to think about hard topics.

If this sounds like an accusation, it is one that we all are guilty of, even those who have gone on to make palpable change. Again, the Common Man is our default state. Pain is constantly in our face, and to be honest, it gets tiring. It can be testing to cope with every incident on our Twitter feed: this week's police shooting, the social movement of the day, etc. Entertainment is an easy getaway. But even that can only help you ignore symptoms. The core of the issues, the questions we don't have answers to, will always find their way back into our thoughts.

Once you're in your plan of distraction, there are two options. The first is the easiest and, without a doubt, the most favored of the two. Simply keep doing what you are doing. This takes no decisive action or thought. It shifts responsibility from the individual to the system and does not ask the individual for anything out of the ordinary. Life will continue along the same trajectory, and the issues of the Age of Knowledge will continue to compound, both on personal and societal levels. It may not be what we want out of life, but it is comfortable, and just like people from all epochs, "doing what's always been done" is the most common choice. The difference in our time is that the rate at which our problems compound is far speedier than any other time in history; that is, inaction comes at a greater price than action.

The second option is triggering and committing to cultivate lasting change. The Common Man could willfully emerge from their plan of distraction and create change, on both social and personal levels, but they almost never do. They don't accept responsibility for solving problems or improving things, which keeps them from becoming Changemakers.

## The Four *I*'s of Change

Lasting change is difficult to create, but it doesn't have to be hard to understand. Every one of the great Changemakers (both heroes and villains) followed a simple process of personal change in order to impact society. To create change on both a personal and social level, all you need are the four *I*'s.

### *1. Initiative*

New Year's is a beautiful time. It's a time to start fresh, enjoy loved ones, and consider a hopeful future. Every year, millions of Americans evaluate their lives to determine what changes they want to implement. It's certainly encouraging if you think about it: so many people have good intentions to improve themselves and their livelihoods. The first week in January, everyone is off to the races, doing what they set out to do. Gyms are packed, weight loss shakes and cleaning supplies fly off the shelves, cigarette packs are thrown out. Week two is more of the first, but this time, there might be a cheat day thrown in. After all, you did so well the first week, you deserve it. By the end of the month more than seventy-five percent of those who set out with a goal abandon it. Only about eight percent go on to reach their goal.[21] I don't think I have ever contributed to the eight percent, and clearly, most of us haven't.

Those who keep their resolutions understand the first step toward change: initiative. Oftentimes, people write their resolutions, show initiative for a couple of weeks, then slowly decline after that. One-time initiative is great to impress someone in a conversation and can be valuable for a quick self-esteem boost, but this type of activity does not create change. Resourcefulness is an intentional and daily choice. The discipline to take the initiative every day is what sets true Changemakers apart from those who take a momentary interest in creating change. Nowadays, it's not hard to find people who are ninety-five percent talk. They know the social value that comes with ambition so they vocalize their goals and dreams, but they never seem to put forth any sustained effort. However, I'm not knocking self-promotion. When followed up with daily creativity, sharing your goals with others and building community around the platform you create can help you reach your goals faster. And, of course, if you have lofty goals, like changing a city or culture, failure will be a part of that process. But failure due to lack of sustained effort does not yield the same (often hidden) benefits as failure that occurs despite that effort. *Daily* initiative sets you apart as an individual and is the first step to becoming a Changemaker.

## *2. Intimacy*

The second "I" stands for intimacy. When I hear this word, I often think of romantic relationships or even close friendships. When people enter intimate relationships, several interesting things happen. First, they begin to sacrifice a significant amount of time and effort to maintain that relationship, which, most of the time, doesn't feel like a sacrifice. They appropriate time from everything they once deemed important before the relationship started, and they believe it's worth doing so. Second, and interestingly, people in an intimate relationship often begin a sort of blending: personalities start to mix, habits align, and worldviews begin to fuse. This is why parents care about who their children associate with. They want their children to be aware of whom they are becoming because there is real transformative power in intimacy.

But let's expand the definition of intimacy to go beyond interpersonal relationships. When a kid watches Lebron James or Sue Bird play and decides they want to become a ball player too, they just hatched a resolution. Next comes daily initiative, when they are hooping after school every day, even when their friends decide to play football. This level of dedication is represented by the first "I": initiative. But after a while, if a genuine love for the game doesn't develop, the sacrifice they have been making will no longer seem worth it. If they do not grow intimate with the sport (learning the plays, watching older players, knowing the names and stats of every player on their favorite team) then even a disciplined child will eventually give up on their resolution.

> In fact, intimacy, as it is used in this book, is measured by the level of impact something else can have on you. The deeper the intimacy, the greater potential for transformation.

The same thing happens to teens, college students, and full-time working adults. If you do not develop an intimacy with whatever you are trying to grow in, be it a career, a partner, even a religion, it will not have the impact necessary to create lasting personal change. In fact, intimacy, as it is used in this book, is measured by the level of impact something else can have on you. The deeper the intimacy, the greater potential for transformation. It is when the discipline that comes from daily initiative is combined with the relationship that comes from intimacy that lasting change begins to develop. And that is rarely done without people taking notice.

## *3. Influence*

Those who reach the third "I," influence, are privileged to make a deep impact on people whom they may never meet personally.[22] Influence is rarely achieved quickly, and when it is, it is rarely significant. To have a lasting influence and create change, you need to first change yourself, then change others. This is why the first two I's are based solely on personal development. Oftentimes the process of graduating from personal change to social influence happens cyclically. We change ourselves, then those around us notice the change and become inspired to do the same, thus pushing us to continue in our growth. This is the essence of influence. When we begin to live our lives in a way that is consistent with a single philosophy, people take notice. That type of consistency is always countercultural. Attracted to that, they tune into our story and allow themselves to be inspired or moved to action.

On a micro level, this could look like changing your diet and setting an example for your family members to change theirs. It could be making music for six years that no one listens to but striking gold with great hits in your sixth year. Or it could be getting in shape and training your body five times a week for three years, then creating a successful fitness program for other people to follow in only two months. Or fighting for social change for several years and finally seeing legislation change twenty-five years later. No matter what the influence, its impact is heavily determined by your dedication to the process and your ability to appeal to the Common Man. If they believe what you're doing isn't beneficial enough to substitute for some part of their current lifestyle, then your influence will not be widely effective.

Every good parent, friend, and mentor wants to see the people they care for undergo these first three I's. They want to see you intentionally and autonomously work toward your own self-development (initiative), fall in love with your craft (intimacy), and become so consistent and successful that your story becomes an example to others (influence). These three stages apply to personal change and result in an individual becoming a leader. If someone took an interest in real estate, worked daily in the mastery of it, and wrapped their life story around that pursuit, it would be no surprise, a few years down the line, when people started asking them for advice on their real estate projects. For most, this is where the process of change stops. We may have proven to ourselves and to others that we have what it takes to undergo personal change, but we have yet to experience the fourth and final "I" in the process.

## *4. Incarnation*

The last "I" arises from the beliefs that 1) every culture's definition of Common Sense stems from a combination of ideals, worldviews, and philosophies, and that 2) the Common Man will embody those ideals and beliefs in their day-to-day life, whether intentionally or otherwise, by making decisions based on their definition of Common Sense. We are no longer talking about a light-hearted influence that can fade with the memory of it. The fourth "I" deals with change on a much deeper level, so deep that, ironically, its impact may not even be noticed by those impacted by it—yet it can sway generations. The fourth "I" is incarnation.

Incarnation, as it is used throughout the book, has nothing to do with a religious practice, a deity, or any particular belief. It is simply the embodiment of an ideal, which can only be realized on a large scale when it becomes a part of a culture's Common Sense. Incarnation, then, is not something that happens occasionally. It is a daily occurrence. We all embody something: a set of ideals, or some combination of philosophies and principles. We all are the incarnation of something, yet Changemakers—and only Changemakers—have the ability to modify instantiations of incarnations the Common Man had earlier embraced. It is the goal of every Changemaker to inject their ideals into the definition of Common Sense and have them played out for generations, and hopefully for the betterment of all potentially affected. This is achieved when a belief or piece of knowledge that was once considered odd, unusual, or nontraditional becomes part of the Common Man's daily life. Only those who completely go through this fourth process create lasting change—a change that will outlast any one Changemaker.

## Today's Changemaker: The Foolish Genius

Change is beneficial only if it is moving toward true progress, which is the path of Wisdom. Wisdom is the consistent practice of sound judgment toward a high-quality life. It is made up of three ingredients: knowledge, experience, and principles. The first ingredient in Wisdom is knowledge, something we have in abundance. It's what defines our time. Every society has some way to receive knowledge, but in today's digital age, the Internet sets us apart. With smartphones and local libraries providing computer access, virtually everyone has an unlimited number of resources at their disposal. A wide range of knowledge isn't accessible only to the educated elite; it is available to any with a willingness to learn.

When armed with Google, who isn't a genius? The mass spread of knowledge has created a new form of Changemaker: the Foolish Genius. They confuse knowledge and understanding with Wisdom: a costly mistake for those who are looking for change. For example, let's pick on Facebook again. Some people use it very well, growing their network, fostering connections, growing a business, expressing themselves, whatever it may be. For those people, Facebook is a positive thing. But for many others, it's a breeding ground for negative thoughts and unhealthy practices.

The Foolish Genius logs on daily to a site they know has a negative impact on them. (Now, I don't fault the Foolish Genius too much. We all have our vices, and a social media addiction can be one that is especially hard to

## Foolish Genius

beat, even for Changemakers). But after scrolling and scrolling and winding up feeling down, a Foolish Genius blames Facebook for the impact it has on his or her life and moves to action on the first problem their mind settles on. Often this problem is one that places blame on another party or whoever has more perceived power (or money) in that situation. Whether it is Facebook's fault is debatable. One can argue people aren't forced to log on, so it's their fault if they do. On the other hand, you can argue that social media is largely designed after slot machines and casinos, making Facebook addictive in nature, so the Foolish Genius is a victim. Both arguments have merit, but neither truly matters, at least not in and of themselves. Arguments are battles of fact and knowledge. The problem with the Foolish Genius doesn't lie in which stance they take, but in the steps taken, or not, following the argument. The Foolish Genius will experience a problem, pick a side, back up their resolve with as much information as possible, then create a one-sided solution based on confidence in their own answer and frame of mind.

It's important to note that the Foolish Genius identified a problem and stuck with a solution long enough to see it through. Both actions are commendable, but how disappointing is it to see the result of their hard-fought idea causing almost as many issues down the line as the original problem? As someone who is incentivized to go against the grain, to double down on your own capabilities, and to attempt to do the almost impossible, you may think it's unnecessary or even inhibitory to force yourself to demonstrate humility by adopting a perspective considerate of contradictory views.

When the Foolish Genius argues, they are looking at things via a black and white prism: there exists only right and wrong. As someone who grew up loving to debate, I find myself falling into this trap frequently. This is the same phenomenon that happens when someone is using the More Mindset. When it comes to finding solutions to the numerous issues we deal with, black and white doesn't cut it. True, knowledge is needed for Wisdom and indeed is its first ingredient, but focusing too much on knowledge puts us in a state of right and wrong, black and white. Unfortunately, not every question can be answered with a simple answer, nor should it be. Doing so is counterproductive and can even be dangerous.

Surface level facts about situations cannot paint an accurate picture of real-life. No one gets more flak in the US than the middle-aged white man. They are the picture of privilege and a constant reminder of oppression once (or still) endured by several minorities. Given that these men typically are an educated group, get jobs pretty fast, struggle less financially, have a decent family unit, and have a long list of privileges at their disposal, they get truly little sympathy in our culture. Let's face it, there are a lot of other groups worse off. Or are there? With all their advantages and privilege, the middle-aged white man is more likely to commit suicide than any other group. This is not to say that they have things the hardest, but pain from internal struggles hurts as much as that caused by external situations. Who am I to compare and criticize them? The fact of the matter is their issues are much deeper than what meets the eye. In our Age of Knowledge, we have learned how to deal with so many of our external issues that the internal ones are bubbling to the top at a much faster rate. Innumerable people are looking for finite solutions to unanswerable questions and are left feeling confused and hopeless. The questions that will help us progress past this age will not be as intellectual as they are philosophical. Intellectuals deal with facts, while philosophers deal with truth. The truth that is unveiled through asking unanswerable questions hold much more value, especially today, than anything that can be solved through a few taps on the screen, and the pursuit of those answers will lead to more growth than any finite solution ever could. Facts inform wisdom, but so does truth. When looking to create sustainable solutions to intricate problems, relying fully on intellectual prowess alone will leave you with band-aid solutions to long-term and consequential issues.

As you gain experience and move through the four *I*'s of Change, ask yourself how congruent your own characteristics are with each. Do you still hold on to some of the discussed misconceptions or pitfalls? Most people who are being honest with themselves see areas where they are weak. Are you process-focused? Are you holistically empathetic? You may not dislike an entire ethnic group, but do you have bias against people from a particular religion or political affiliation? Ask people who know and care about you. Take implicit bias tests. Is there something inhibiting you from viewing others' perspectives and harming your ability to reach them? Are you compassionately empathetic, or do you lean too far on the emotional or cognitive sides of empathy (to be covered in the next chapter)? If you want to become a Changemaker, each characteristic of Wisdom should be your own, and if it's not already, you should be intentional to improve in that area. This is how Wisdom will become your guide.

No matter how close you are to Wisdom, you will never embody it fully. There will always be a little bit of a Foolish Genius in you, as there is in me, and that's okay. The intent of this book is to present these ideas in a way that we can compare ourselves to Wisdom instead of comparing ourselves to each other. We all are born using Common Sense as our basis for decision-making, and my goal is to show you how we can learn to replace Common Sense with Wisdom, whether we're a Changemaker or otherwise.

# 3
# Age of Wisdom

*The fool doth think he is wise, but the wise man knows himself to be a fool.* – William Shakespeare, *As You Like It*

---

### Takeaways
- Wisdom is a concept that we can build intimacy with.
- Ego is the enemy of Wisdom.
- Wisdom never changes, because the foundation of Wisdom is built with principles.

---

We recognize people by their characteristics. When you first meet someone, you recognize them by mostly physical characteristics: hair color, height, perfume, etc. But as you get to know that person more deeply, you start noticing their personality traits, even to the point of seeing traces of him or her in other people.

Think about the last time you had to buy a gift for your best friend. Maybe you were at the mall, walking up and down the aisles, thinking, *Would so and so like this?* You could instantly answer *Yes, they'd think this is hilarious* or *No, they wouldn't find this useful.* Gift giving for best friends is a fun exercise because it's filled with going over all the shared memories. You know them so well that you can move on from memories and accurately picture them in other possible scenarios. You end up smiling to yourself in the middle of the aisle, thinking of the reaction you're sure they'll have.

Now remember the last time you had to pick out a gift for someone you didn't know very well. Suddenly it's not so fun anymore. You're stressed because you're not sure if they'll like what you get them. You likely play it safe with a gift that most people would appreciate because a custom gift would be too difficult, and there's nothing worse than giving an unappreciated gift.

But when you know someone well, you get to the point where you don't even have to ask them something to know what their answer is. You know how they'll think, how they'll respond, and how their face will look when you ask them the question because you've walked with them for a while. You've learned to understand their personality, and that can make your decision-making easier.

Intimacy with concepts works the same way. The closer you get to concepts, the more you'll be able to make decisions based on them. You'll wonder, *Would Wisdom agree with this?* And be able to tell yourself, *No, Wisdom wouldn't entertain this idea* or *Yes, Wisdom would agree with this initiative, but only if it were done this way.* The more intimate you are with the concept, the more nuanced and detailed those answers become. For the purposes of this book, think of Wisdom as a character pushing you toward a first-rate life. Once you recognize its characteristics, you'll start to see how those traits can guide you in your decision-making.

## The Goal: Quality of Life

Take a moment and imagine what success looks like to you. Is it a nice house, job security, financial freedom, or internal peace? Answers vary, but the most common response I hear is "happiness." Everyone wants to be happy, and we have done a good job of letting everyone know that. A quest for happiness is in our movies, is talked about by our favorite influencers, is in our self-help books, and has even made its way into the scientific community. With all this talk of happiness, you would think we would be closer to achieving it, but seeing as that is not the case, several studies have started to explore the reason why.

In 2011, sixty-nine people were recruited for a study to determine what happens when people value happiness.[23] In the prebrief, the participants were told that the topic of the study was television programming. Then all participants watched a fairly neutral film clip to get their emotions on the same plane. The next part of the experiment required half the group to read this excerpt that promotes the value of happiness:

People who report higher than normal levels of happiness experience benefits in their social relationships, professional success, and overall health and well-being. That is, happiness not only feels good, it also conveys important benefits: the happier people can make themselves feel from moment to moment, the more likely they are to be successful, healthy, and popular.... In fact, recent research suggests that people who are able to achieve the greatest amount of happiness.... can experience long-term beneficial outcomes....[24]

The second group read the same paragraph, but instead of the word *happiness* appearing, the phrase "making accurate judgments" showed up in the text. After each group was finished reading, the participants were again randomly assigned to watch either a happy video or a sad video, then complete a survey to measure their emotional state. In the summary debrief, the study team wrote "valuing happiness can lead to less happiness, precisely in a situation that should give rise to it, namely a happy emotion induction. Supporting the reliability of this finding, this pattern was obtained using both an explicit and an implicit measure of emotion."[25] In other words, the conclusion showed that the participants who watched a happy video after reading the happiness paragraph expressed less happiness than the other participants.

This conclusion does not mean we shouldn't value positive feelings. Neither does it mean that valuing happiness is completely futile. We should value positive feelings and happiness. But we should also know where our priorities lie.

In our attempt as a culture to promote happiness, we are setting ourselves up for crushing failure. Pursuing happiness does not lead to happiness, so the goal of pursuing Wisdom cannot be happiness. If the goal of Wisdom is happiness, then pursuing it would be self-defeating. It seems paradoxical until you take happiness out of the equation entirely. Happiness was never supposed to be our main focus, and when we try to make it that, we wind up prioritizing an *aspect* of fulfillment rather than fulfillment itself. Similar to falling into the More Mindset, pursuing a piece of the solution as the answer will result in a state that is worse than where we began. Happiness is not a bad thing, and wanting it is not either, but a lifelong, focused pursuit of it is. Pursuing Wisdom will naturally lead to happiness, but the *goal* of Wisdom is much more fulfilling. It is a high-quality life.

This is what the goal of the Wise Society is and what every Changemaker should work toward: a widespread, high quality of life. A high quality of life is much more encompassing than happiness. Its traditional definition is the standard of health, comfort, and happiness experienced by an individual or group[26]. However, a high-quality life can be measured through a multitude of factors, with three rising to the top: wealth, health, and meaning in life.

## *1. Wealth*

Wealth is often what determines our comfort level, but even this statement cannot be made without a caveat. Having wealth is a good thing, but in order to be helpful, it has to be paired with a healthy perspective. Wealth is relative. To a former billionaire who lost their fortune and now has a net worth of "only" twenty million, he is broke. To just about everyone else on earth, to call twenty million broke is preposterous. For some people, making six figures is the goal, and anything under that is not wealthy. For others, sixty thousand dollars a year is great as long as they can make their income passively. What I count as wealth is having enough money to be able to focus on the unanswerable questions of life.

If you have two hundred thousand dollars in your bank account but your lifestyle is extremely demanding and you can do nothing but work to maintain your income, then the resource has become the product. Money is a resource; it is potential. If you are too focused on your potential to the point of inaction, then that potential will not be realized. Your definition of wealth is determined by your living conditions and your needs. If you have an unhealthy perspective, you may fall into the trap of placing wants into the "needs" category, something that is extremely common in our comfortable society.

This is why many of the Common Man do not become Changemakers. Sometimes, the Common Man wants to become a Changemaker, but they are not able to focus on changing the world because of more pressing responsibilities. This is often the case in low-income communities. Kids in higher income communities aren't born more intelligent than kids from low-income communities. They aren't born with more ambition or a birthright to success. What they are born with is the ability to focus on the higher tiers of Maslow's hierarchy of needs. They have a safety net to take risks. If you are constantly in survival mode, you will not care about problem-solving for anybody besides you and your immediate circle.

If buying more things and having a higher social status is why you want to build wealth, then Wisdom's advice may not be for you. Wisdom suggests that building true wealth means making money the product just long enough until it can take its rightful place as potential.

## *2. Health*

The world changed when the COVID-19 pandemic hit. No one knew how to adjust, but the school systems especially had to change their strategies. Suddenly, teachers tasked with covering standardized curriculum went off-book to make sure their students were safe. Material in most common core classes was no longer seen as that important, at least not urgently so. Schools, which used to be tasked with instilling students with knowledge, were now focused on much deeper needs. Were their students healthy? Were they home alone all day while their parents worked? Were the students who were receiving free meals at school still being fed consistently? These questions took priority in the minds of school administrators, and appropriately so.

In times of crisis, we realize what really matters, and health is always near the top of that list. For the Changemaker, there are three types of health that should be protected closely: physical, mental, and social.

Change is not a quick or easy process, and while Changemakers are deciding what direction the world should proceed, they might wrongly prioritize their mission over their health. When it comes to physical health, this could mean avoiding exercise or eating quickly so they're able to get back to work. In terms of mental health, this could look like inadequate rest or relaxation. Socially, Changemakers might begin to isolate or under-prioritize time with the special people in their life. As simple as it sounds, to achieve a high-quality life, the importance of prioritizing your health cannot be overstated.

## *3. Meaning*

Meaning is something we crave on such a deep level that our search for it is often unconscious. Our questions of identity (*Who am I? Why am I here?*) are all questions of meaning. Even statements of love are basically stating that you have value or *meaning* in that person's eyes outside of your work and accomplishments. We look for significance in everything we do and feel a deep dissatisfaction when we toil without it, which is why meaning is necessary for a high-quality life. We find rest in it. We work and build wealth, not so we're able to do nothing for the rest of our lives, but so we can do the things that bring us fulfillment and meaning. We take care of our health so we can be with those who mean the world to us. Without meaning, there is no point. Meaning informs our priorities: it's the *why* behind every *what*.

Wisdom seeks to integrate these three components into your daily life. The Common Man may not have the urge, wealth, or health to focus on them, so the Changemaker should use their gifts, privilege (both earned and unearned), and discipline to boost the quality of life for the Common Man and themselves.

## Barriers to Wisdom

Just like any form of growth, learning Wisdom will require dissatisfaction with the current state of affairs, a careful strategy, and education. Our instinctual avoidance of personal responsibility is partly why wisdom is so scarce, but there are other factors that play into it. The first reason is that attaining knowledge, and only knowledge, is more convenient. Plain and simple, the More Mindset is easy. If the solution to every problem is simply adding more of something, then we need not be concerned about analyzing alternative paths.

The second reason is that Wisdom often arises from adversity. It doesn't have to come this way, but we are stubborn creatures. No matter how many times our mom told us that the stove was hot, we still had the urge to touch it to test her theory. As soon as she told us, we had knowledge. As soon as we touched it, we had experience. It wasn't till we started using mitts and potholders around the stove that we had Wisdom. The adversity that came with burning our hand was the motivating factor for buying a potholder.

Pain and failure bring more Wisdom than any other teachers, but I don't have to cite a study to tell you that we naturally try to avoid pain. In our urge to skip failure, however, we sometimes miss the motivation and grit required to turn our knowledge into Wisdom. If the stove was hot and burned our hand but we didn't feel the pain, we wouldn't be motivated to buy the potholder. Remember that Wisdom is consequential, and unless we can attach a consequence to our knowledge, we are not likely going to convert that knowledge into Wisdom.

Beyond the ease of knowledge and aversion to adversity, ego is the greatest inhibitor to Wisdom. I cannot stress this enough. Ego leads to excessive risk tolerance; ego goes against the characteristics of Wisdom *and* the principles of change. It's off-putting, it restricts perspective, and it stunts personal growth. With knowledge comes pride, but with humility comes Wisdom. Ego is the enemy of Wisdom. It feigns Wisdom, but over time its differences become clear. Ego debates when humility discusses (because why discuss when you are certain you are right)? It takes humility to broaden your perspective and seriously consider someone else's point of view.

> Ego is the enemy of Wisdom. It feigns Wisdom, but over time its differences become clear. Ego debates when humility discusses (because why discuss when you are certain you are right)?

Unless one is careful, it is easy to become prideful through knowledge. Scholars are famously snobby people, and although rules shouldn't be made based on stereotypes, they can be helpful in identifying trends. Knowledge usually comes with status, and with it, ego. Ego doesn't acknowledge flaws in itself, but it will readily point out flaws in others. Ego is always certain; Wisdom understands that there is a variable of uncertainty in nearly every situation. Ego controls; humility trusts. Ego cannot coexist with Wisdom and doesn't attempt to.

Humility isn't discussed much in our current society, and it really is a shame. It's often perceived as somehow being tied to insecurity, but this isn't the case at all. Humility is confidence with true perspective, and a nonnegotiable trait when one seeks Wisdom as their guide.

## Components of Wisdom

People walk through life accumulating a unique combination of experiences that help shape who they are (their characteristics and thought patterns), and those characteristics and thought patterns help create a difference in perspectives. Experiences, however, are also shaped by a person's traits and characteristics.

Concepts don't have experiences, but they do have components. As we go through this book, core concepts will be described by their characteristics as well as their components. Think of the components as essential pieces, or ingredients, of the concept. If you lose a component, you no longer have the concept. Wisdom has three essential components, the first being knowledge.

## *Knowledge*

When I first started to consider the Wise Society concept, I thought about how it would impact the seven pillars, or mountains, of society: Religion, Government, Media, Business, Arts & Culture, Family, and Education. Each pillar influences society in its own way, but when it comes to implementing lasting change, one stands alone. When debating which pillar proves the most useful in shaping long-term, widespread change, it's hard to refute the argument for education. Religion is also a top choice, given how deeply tied it can be to an individual's meaning and purpose. But if you look into one of the biggest religions in the world today, you'll find what Christians call the "Great Commission."

> Then the eleven disciples went to Galilee, to the mountain where Jesus had told them to go. When they saw him, they worshipped him; but some doubted. Then Jesus came to them and said, "All authority in heaven and on earth has been given to me. Therefore go and make disciples of all nations, baptizing them in the name of the Father and of the Son and of the Holy Spirit, and teaching them to obey everything I have commanded you. And surely I am with you always, to the very end of the age" (Matt. 28:16–20, NIV).

Make disciples (disciples here can also be translated into pupils) and teach them to obey: there are four action items in the Great Commission, the principal responsibility for all Christians, and half of them are directly tied to education.

Making an impact within any pillar requires education. The role of the government is solidified through education. The definition and view of family can be changed in a single generation through education.

Every concept and skill discussed in this book requires work and effort to attain, but the beauty is that everyone can attain them—through education. Creativity is a skill everyone can learn to hone and incorporate into their life. Identifying principles is a skill that proves invaluable. Learning to love your community is a skill, and it's likely more challenging than learning creativity and principle identification. But everyone benefits from a servant leader who learns to love each person through teaching. Education, the process of learning, is the agent of lasting change.

Knowledge produces change, but it doesn't necessarily bring progress. Wisdom is the only thing that generates progress. Knowledge is blind. It has no say in what it is used for or what agenda may back it. If the mind were a car, knowledge is the fuel. It guarantees the potential for movement but has no influence on direction. It brings indiscriminate change. Progress is positive change, but since knowledge can be steered in any direction, good or bad, it cannot be relied on to bring consistently positive growth.

Out of curiosity I Googled the "top 10 wisest people in the world," and suffice to say, I was pretty disappointed when my search results displayed "Top 10 Most Intelligent People on Earth" and "The 30 Smartest People Alive Today." With the exception of one post, it wasn't until the third page that results on Wisdom started popping up.

The confusion between knowledge and progress stems from four main points.

1. Knowledge is developed over time and can be easily charted and quantified. Knowledge can be found in the number of facts you know (think of them as roads in your mind), while Wisdom is found in the intersection of those facts.

2. Knowledge is discovery; Wisdom is application. Wisdom finds the relation between new knowledge and all pre-existing concepts. Knowledge can be new, but Wisdom is timeless: it doesn't change, making it one of the constant and unyielding pillars of life. It can be defined as the practical application of knowledge. The operative word practical gives direction to knowledge, so Wisdom deals more with the colloquial definition of Common Sense than rocket science.

3. This exposes the third reason why knowledge is often prioritized over Wisdom: pride. As previously touched on, with knowledge comes pride, but Wisdom accompanies humility. Before one can encounter Wisdom, they must first acknowledge the limitations of their knowledge. Our pride leads us to assume that our decisions and actions must lead to progress. What pride would admit it's moving in the wrong direction?

4. A deeper reason why more knowledge is commonly mistaken for progress lies in the opinions people have of human nature. One of the most well-known philosophical debates is whether mankind is good or not. If you are inherently good, then adding fuel

(knowledge) to your intentions should theoretically lead to a positive outcome. Many societal issues could therefore be solved by simply increasing the amount of widespread knowledge. Since knowledge does generally increase, but societal issues seem unaided, I believe people like to convince themselves that they are good more than they truly are.

If the idea that we are naturally good stems from a need for self-reassurance, and not, in fact, human nature, then we are left with the notion that humans are either 1) naturally evil, or 2) born with the same capacity to do evil as to do good. With either assumption, more knowledge in and of itself will not create progress and will create more problems than it solves.

While knowledge isn't proof of Wisdom, it is still a prerequisite for it. Throughout this book, I write a lot about how Wisdom should be prioritized above knowledge (so I will likely hear from some upset scholars) but it's important to note that I do value knowledge greatly. Education is the first step to solving any problem, and one cannot have Wisdom without it. All the problems we address in our society and the solutions we propose couldn't even be addressed if there hadn't been centuries of scholars and intellectuals before us shaping what we understand today to be Common Sense. I have a great appreciation for the intellectuals of the world, and they should always play a major role in our society. Without the Age of Knowledge, we couldn't have dreamed of entering the Age of Wisdom, but now we have entered a stage in our development where a Wise Society is actually plausible. A point of this book is to demonstrate that although you can't solve problems or implement solutions if knowledge is deemed the final step, it must nonetheless always be the first step.

## *Experience*

My family and I went camping at least once a year when I was a kid, packing up all our sleeping bags and fishing gear to rough it for a couple days in the woods. To this day, camping is still one of my favorite things to do when I want to get out of my head and take a break from my laptop lifestyle. As a child, many of my favorite moments happened after all the events of the day, when everyone was slowing down, dinner was caught, and it was time to make the fire.

Most people in America could start a fire if given five dollars, but it takes a certain skill and finesse to make a contained fire that is large enough for six people to sit around and stable enough to last at least an hour. Anyone can start a fire, but it takes a different type of knowledge and skill to keep it going.

This is the relationship between explicit knowledge and tacit knowledge gained by experience. In our digital age, social movements can be started and supported by millions in a matter of days, yet they can die out just as quickly. To start something, all you need is passion, a little motivation, and Google. But to keep it going and growing, you need something else entirely.

Experience can exist outside of knowledge. I can enter one hundred relationships and repeat the same mistakes in every one of them. Experience often brings knowledge, but knowledge, as I am using it here, is static. Experience is dynamic, exposing flaws in knowledge as well as sometimes revealing the beautiful and creative nature of life. Experience and learning are social, but knowledge undergoes an interpretation by the individual. Experience does as well, but it is more social in that interpretation. Knowledge is potential, while experience is the actualization of that potential. Or, hearkening back to eighth grade science, knowledge is potential energy while experience is kinetic energy.

In my camping example, the difference between book knowledge (understanding how to start a fire) and experience (being able to do it) may seem minute at times. After all, it doesn't take long to learn the skill of starting fires. But in other spheres, the difference between knowledge and experience is significant, even worth fighting for.

Every fall, anxiety hits the new round of college seniors as they apply for the open positions in their dream companies. They read the job descriptions and quickly realize only one bullet point mentions a degree. And it's often not even a specific degree; the descriptions list three to four different majors they will accept. *Great*, they think. *Four to six years of nonstop schooling just to cover one bullet point.* After a mini panic attack and a few angry tweets, they apply for minimum-wage and even unpaid internships just to give them the one thing every employer wants and few degrees guarantee: experience. This isn't every story, but it isn't an uncommon one either. Knowledge is 2D; it exists on a lower plane than experience. Experience takes knowledge and gives it an application. Of course, employers aren't the only ones who know this.

I'd bet that the most common question in the minds of middle school math students has nothing to do with equations or proofs. More than likely that question is, *When will we ever use this?* They question when—really, if—this knowledge will ever transition to experience. Experience is desired over knowledge because it has a physical function. So as long as knowledge becomes functional, we're happy with it even if that function isn't practical. (How many times have we smiled because we learned how to do something essentially meaningless, like how to roller skate backwards or how to flip a half-empty water bottle and stick the landing?) Experience takes knowledge and places it on a plane that we can understand and appreciate, even if that understanding has no long-term significance.

Wisdom does in fact require experience, but how can it be that someone with very little life experience is also wise? As an undergrad, I served as a teacher in an after-school program. Every now and then I would run into a student whose understanding of life stood out from the rest. Of this group of particularly clever students, some of them were fast learners and some struggled with classes, but they all seemed to understand human nature and life in a way that isn't common until your mid-twenties. How could this be?

It may have had something to do with the number of stories they had encountered. While experience is needed for cultivating wisdom, it doesn't have to be firsthand. Stories, or secondhand experiences, ever abound. Social media, entertainment, and marketing all thrive off our obsession for stories, and if we relate to them enough, they can move us to action. A well-crafted story can make us laugh hysterically, binge-watch a show for six hours, donate half of our paycheck to a charity we haven't researched, or radically change our lives. Some stories can consume us so much that they no longer feel like stories.

For example, some people get so caught up with a character in a TV show or movie that they will visit the actor's house announcing, "I know you don't know me, but I just had to meet you in real life." (As if real life isn't the only way to meet someone.) These same people are unlikely to talk to a neighbor five doors down from their own because they are "strangers," meaning simply that they don't know or resonate with their story.

Just as personal experience amasses more stories for future reference, secondhand experiences do too. A story good enough that you can see yourself in its narrative can shape your life and decisions. But the number of stories my students consumed couldn't be the only factor that determined how much Wisdom they had. If that were the case, all movie junkies and old people would be full of Wisdom. Something else must exist to qualify how much those experiences contribute to Wisdom, and that is explained by the next component.

## *Principles*

Wisdom is timeless. No matter what is going on in the world, what technology is being developed, or what is being taught in the classroom, Wisdom never changes. The same Wisdom that guided the first successful monogamous relationship has been available to guide every generation of teenagers since. Just as nothing created is ever truly new, Wisdom of old still applies to every aspect of life today. This makes it one of the great equalizers, which is what I call concepts that include unanswerable questions, which I further define as concepts that no one person can fully understand, such as love, peace, purpose, and yes, Wisdom.

Since they lie outside of time, wealth, or circumstance, great equalizers offer everyone the same opportunity to become wiser. An observant employee at Kroger could be wiser than a well-established politician. (And based on our current political state, that may even be likely.) This is not generally the case with knowledge. Yes, even individuals in low tax brackets can pick up a book in what little free time they may have to expand their knowledge, but it goes without saying that the wealthy can afford a higher quality of education and have the luxury to call off work to study their hobbies if need be.

Part of what makes Wisdom a great equalizer is its third component, which is timeless, unwavering, as consequential as good judgment, and unbiased in nature: principles.

Principles are conventionally defined as "fundamental truths or propositions that serve as the foundation for a system of belief or behavior or for a chain of reasoning."[27] They are how you determine what is good judgment and how you grade what is practical. Principles are timeless. Since they are at the core of belief, they do not change over time.

Easily the most forgotten aspect of Wisdom, principles are arguably the most important. They bestow long-lasting fulfillment and meaning to your experience; they anchor all your decisions and give purpose to your actions. If knowledge is the fuel, principles steer the car. Principles are conscious.

Everyone is alive, but not everyone is conscious. Great leaders are known for taking up a cause, not backing down to adversity, and leading the charge into a brighter future. Where do they get this conviction, steadfastness, and overall fortitude? They hold on to their principles. A prevalent misconception of leadership is that in order to be a leader you cannot be a follower. This cannot be further from the truth. Everyone follows something.

## Foolish Genius

The difference between leaders and everyone else is that they know what they are following: principles.

Leaders follow with intention and conviction because they are holding on to principles that extend much deeper and last much longer than themselves. This applies to both heroes (socially accepted leaders like Martin Luther King Jr., Benjamin Franklin, Winston Churchill, etc.) and villains (morally deviant leaders like Genghis Khan, Vlad the Impaler, etc.). Even the worst of the great leaders have a code, and that code aligns with their principles. The moment they publicly stray from these principles, their followers recognize the leader's failure and lose faith in them. In the same way that everyone has equal access to Wisdom, everyone can be a leader. Leadership is a by-product of Wisdom, and it is determined by your ability to identify principles, evaluate them, and consistently follow them.

When you watch a movie, principles are the rules that keep the protagonist on track. Their dedication to those rules separates them from the rest. Anyone who has lived through the fourth "I," Incarnation—implementing and embedding change at its deepest level—employs a set of principles that guide their behavior. By observing one's actions, you can track what guides their choices. The ability to identify and evaluate principles is essential to anyone who makes choices, and even more so for people who make choices for others. We can use principles to evaluate Changemakers and decide if the changes they wish to make are truly based in Wisdom and will lead to true progress.

We can try to hash out why we, as a society, are not in the Age of Wisdom, or why we cannot seem to have widespread quality of life. It would be a noble endeavor to think about a question so big, but it's an intimidating question, to say the least. Society is so complex. To understand that question, you would have to be able to understand the intricacies of group dynamics, group motivation, collective action, and a plethora of topics that, frankly, becomes far too complex to yield concrete, widely agreed-upon solutions.

But what we do know is that 1) personal change is connected to social change, and 2) Wisdom can be dissected and studied to apply to our daily lives. So our focus should turn from "Why isn't our society walking in Wisdom?" to "How can we walk in Wisdom to change our society?" That walk always starts with a humble gait toward improving the three requirements for Wisdom: perspective, critical thinking, and personal responsibility.

# Prerequisites For Wisdom

## *Perspective*

Perspective is the lens through which you see the world, and it has great influence on defining your principles. Your opinions on human nature, your religion, your upbringing, and all your past experiences determine your perspective. Being conscious of your perspective is the first step in understanding your principles. Everyone thinks, but not everyone thinks for themselves. Whether you think for yourself can be determined by how well you know and understand your perspective.

Since principles hold such a large stake in Wisdom, you cannot truly be Wisdom-led if you do not understand your own principles. When identifying which ones resonate with you, you must be conscious of your perspective, or your worldview. But many people are grossly unaware of or indifferent to how their worldview shapes their thinking.

During my first professional speaking engagement, I spoke to a small group of engineers on the process of identifying and pursuing purpose. With a worksheet as a guide, I divided the process into four or five steps they could follow to get started on that journey. The first two steps contained questions entirely about them. For most people, these two sections proved to be the hardest. *Why?* you might be thinking. *Shouldn't answering questions about yourself and your life be the easiest thing to do? After all, who is a better expert on you than you?* That's also what I thought going into this presentation—the engineers would be able to answer the questions effortlessly and move on to step three. I was wrong.

Therapists get paid a fair amount of money to do their job, but what are they getting paid to do? They aren't fixing your problems like a traditional doctor. Traditional doctors identify a problem you're having, prescribe medication or operate on it, and work to ensure it doesn't return. You're all better. But this isn't the case with therapists. Their job isn't to heal you; their job is to help you identify what is hurting or limiting you. The therapist takes care of the first step, but the task of healing rests entirely on the patient. Therapists coax out what has shaped you just enough that you can begin the process of reshaping yourself. That is the power of being conscious—something the engineers I encountered discovered they were not.

If you are to live a life of purpose, become a leader, or become wise, you have to consciously identify what your perspective is and how it relates

Foolish Genius

to the perspectives around you. This is not easy to do, because the easiest person to not be critical of is yourself. Yet it remains a necessary and extremely beneficial exercise to repeat.[28]

## *Perspective and Justice*

Perspectives should grow as we do. Our brains naturally build schemas, which are basically categories to interpret information. For example, when we see a Toyota Camry drive by, we understand it's a car. The visualization and characteristics of the Camry fit our schema for what a car should look like. As we grow older, our schemas change.

A toddler might see an airplane taxiing on a runway and try to place it in the car schema. Why not? It has wheels, it moves fast, it's loud, and it's a means of transportation. In due course, he or she will eventually realize that airplanes are not supersized cars but are completely different machines entirely and deserve to be placed in a schema of their own. As children mature, their schemas get more specific, and their perspectives broaden.

What happens when we stop adjusting our schemas? We reap stereotypes and incorrect generalizations. If, as a child, your schema placed all black people in the same group, and you watched the news and saw a black man committing a crime, unless you change your schema over time, you could become extremely prejudiced. That prejudice might lead you to clutch your purse or cross the street every time a black person walked by.

Although everyone has a perspective, not everyone widens their perspective as they grow. This is why not every older person is wise. There is no point in having experience if you don't learn and grow from that experience, and Wisdom can grow only as much as your perspective grows. Even as I write this book, I understand that thirty years from now I will look back and want to amend it as my understanding of Wisdom deepens. If this is not the case, then I never understood Wisdom in the first place.

Perspective is power. The first step of any strategy is information. When war breaks out, job number one is to gain Intelligence, then create a strategy based on it. When a businessperson has a brilliant idea, their first step is to conduct market research. The reason for the Intelligence and the market research is to gain an accurate perspective of the situation.

When Steve Jobs was developing the Apple store, he wanted his customers to experience the best possible service in the industry. He thought of different companies who were known for their hospitality, and the Ritz-

Carlton stood out. The Ritz-Carlton's customer service is unmatched, even among other high-end hotel chains, so Jobs sent a team to be trained in the Ritz-Carlton training program. After going through the entire training, the group came back and got to work. They modeled their overall service process after the Ritz-Carlton hotel, even modeling the Genius Bar after the Concierge Desk. Everyone who has walked inside the Ritz can see their customer service, but Jobs knew that to run his store the same way, his employees would have to have the perspective of a Ritz employee. It worked. Per square foot, the Apple store is the highest-grossing retailer in the world.

Have you ever worked on an awful project with your coworkers, gone through a tragic loss as a family, or enlisted in the military? Then you'll know that going through something difficult alongside someone else bonds you. The job or environment may not be doing it intentionally, but fraternities used to haze their new recruits in a group and soldiers go through hell week in a group. Even gangs know this and will initiate a single individual by jumping them with a group. Why is that? It not only is more efficient, but it builds comradery among the survivors. Simply knowing that someone else went through something we went through brings comfort to us.

Perspective allows us to do this without getting hazed or jumped. It allows us to better understand someone else by identifying their experiences and emotions and comparing them to our own. Without perspective, we wouldn't be able to relate to one another or empathize with them in some way. Since you cannot hate someone you empathize or identify with, perspective is loving in nature.

Wisdom is unbiased, and perspective facilitates this characteristic. At the core, humans are all the same, so if a principle contains bias, the belief system built upon it would inevitably contain contradictions. Since perspective is the cure for prejudice and bias, and perspective in its truest form sees all sides of each situation, perspective is required for justice. Every weekday for twenty-five years on TV, Judge Judy heard ridiculous cases, one after the other. Her job, as with any judge, was to hear both sides of the case, view the evidence, and make a decision. This is our society's best process for gaining perspective.

As humans, our perspectives are extremely limited, which is why the closest we can get to justice is determined by a process outside ourselves. Definitions of justice differ among people, which is why we have law to define the rules of justice and a process to determine if the law was broken.

Foolish Genius

Cases like Brock Turner's, in which the well-off Stanford University student received only a light sentence for his rape conviction, occur when bias comes into play. The results are disastrous, and they reiterate the fact that Wisdom and justice cannot coexist with bias. But even as we discuss ideas for obtaining true justice, it is important to stress needed reform must occur within the constraints and mechanisms of the system. Since justice outside a system relies on the perspective of a few, it cannot be true justice. Justice reached through unjust means is no justice at all.

# Critical Thinking

Martin Luther King Jr. once said, "Rarely do we find men who willingly engage in hard, solid thinking. There is an almost universal quest for easy answers and half-baked solutions. Nothing pains some people more than having to think." In a similar way that everyone is alive, but not everyone is conscious, everyone thinks, but not everyone thinks critically.

Critical thinking is the truest form of thought; every other form is inconsequential. Critical thinking allows for weighing different options, and it accounts for the good judgment mentioned in the conventional definition of Wisdom.

Consider these critical thinking challenges. If critical thinking and perspective were embodied as parents, perspective would be the fun-loving, happy parent while critical thinking would be the disciplinarian (but still loving) one. While perspective brings the accepting and "nicer" aspects of love, critical thinking brings its disciplinary and tougher attributes. It is all still love, although one without the other makes it more difficult for Wisdom to take root.

Without critical thinking, you would still have the open-mindedness necessary to grow your perspective, but you wouldn't be able to decipher how someone else's principles differ from yours or analyze why they differ. You would be able to recognize what principles people have but lack the ability to choose your own. Without perspective, critical thinking would be harsh and rarely seek to understand before arriving at conclusions. It would also be ineffective: you cannot analyze or make well-informed decisions without truly understanding multiple points of view, especially your own. It would be like a judge deciding a case before hearing it.

## Age of Wisdom

American society is seemingly becoming more sensitive every year. This isn't entirely a bad thing. Some people are reconsidering how their words affect other people, breaking down schemas, and widening their perspective. But our hostility toward differing opinions has created several issues within our society. In an attempt to become more inclusive, we have ironically become exclusive to opinions that strongly differ from today's now-favored opinions. The reason for this can be summarized by a lack of effective communication among groups, and hence, a lack of perspective.

As a nation, we have forgotten that you can support an individual without supporting all the decisions and morals of that individual. For example, if a man has a brother who is badly strung out on crack, not supporting his addiction is a loving act. It is also loving to separate himself from the brother as long as the brother refuses to change or get help for his lifestyle. All this does not undermine the love he has for his brother; in fact, it proves it. Coddling someone who has detrimental habits and beliefs is not healthy for either party involved.

This example is simple because it is a widely accepted idea that crack is bad, but what about more nuanced ideas? What if your principles are not held by many others? First, it is your responsibility to honestly hear out their point of view. Consider their point, not to highlight a flaw, but to learn something from it. After this, you are free to reject as much of it as you'd like. In fact, rejection is just as necessary as consideration. You cannot have a belief system that encompasses all beliefs. By upholding a principle, you are inevitably rejecting several others. Wisdom lies in having the critical thinking ability to challenge and reject certain principles while still being accommodating enough to consider and adjust your own.

I listed critical thinking after perspective because that is the order in which Changemakers should absorb information. If you enter a new culture or are confronted by an opposing point of view, approaching with a critical eye first may preclude any benefits of a wider perspective. You will identify the areas where those different from you are hypocritical, biased, or factually wrong, and you will miss the spirit behind their words and the reasoning behind their way of life. They may be all those things, but if you come to the table without a willing and open mind, you will fail to widen your perspective. Be willing to listen, then think critically to ensure only the ideas you want to incorporate seep into your definition of Common Sense.

## Personal Responsibility

One of the most famous philosophical questions of all time is *Why are we here?* or *What is our purpose?* Everything in nature seems to follow the trend of having a purpose or playing a role in a larger ecosystem, so what is ours? The question of purpose is a heavy one, and whenever someone finds their purpose, it comes with an equally heavy responsibility. Purpose is another one of the great equalizers.

If you dive into any one of the great equalizers, you'll find yourself learning about the others. For example, you cannot be wise without having some knowledge about love and purpose. You cannot understand love without obtaining Wisdom along the way. With principle comes direction, and with direction comes purpose. The purpose of a car is to reach a destination, and like I mentioned earlier, if knowledge is the fuel, your principles steer. In a similar way that you as a new car owner must drive it safely, when you identify your principles, you are personally responsible to uphold them.

Responsibility is in some part the reason why so much of our knowledge fails to transition to Wisdom. More accurately, the avoidance of responsibility is. Unless blame or responsibility can be forced upon us, we will, more times than not, avoid both. This phenomenon is called the diffusion of responsibility, and the term was coined after an experiment completed by John Darley and Bibb Latané.

Darley and Latané wanted to see how bystanders would act in emergency settings if they were in a crowd. The study found that "when we don't feel responsible for a situation, we feel less guilty when we do nothing to help.... Eventually, when the subjects thought that four other people had heard the call [request for assistance] too, just 31 percent took action."[29] The Common Man falls into this trap quite often, opting out of action due to a rejection of responsibility. But Changemakers can fall into this trap as well.

Changemakers accept some responsibility for their actions. They have to if they are to create change in whatever realm they are enthusiastic about. Some personal responsibility is necessary to successfully work through all four P's of Change. For the Changemaker, though, diffusion of responsibility can look like creating change while in reality it might be taking shortcuts to save money, intentionally skirt humane practices, or not own up to mistakes they caused.

A common saying is that it takes a village to raise a child, but what if that child turns out to be a menace to society? If a village can be responsible for raising a child, can it not also be blamed for raising a child poorly? Responsibility and blame are linked, and we naturally try to avoid both. This introduces conflict within us. We have a natural urge to find meaning in our life, but we also have a seemingly natural aversion to the responsibility required to develop a sense of purpose. That is, we want purpose and meaning but don't want the responsibility that comes with them. We must give up on one of those ideas in order for the other to grow.

I don't agree with many of his opinions, but George Bernard Shaw hit it right on the head when he stated, "We are made wise not by the recollection of our past, but by the responsibility for our future." Responsibility is the glue. Without it, everything else falls apart. It applies to every section and attribute of Wisdom. We have a responsibility to change and grow our perspective. We have a responsibility to examine ourselves and not say "That's just me" to explain away ignorance or character flaws. We have a responsibility to think critically; without it, we couldn't hold our principles (or any opinion for that matter) to any standard of criticism. We have a responsibility to expand our knowledge and our experience, and to uphold our principles.

You can have confidence in your principles only if they have been tested and you believe you have the responsibility to uphold them. Without responsibility, you are left with empty words, finger pointing, and false courage. Since there can be no Wisdom without practical application, you are responsible to apply whatever knowledge you gain. Last, because your principles are the foundation of your belief and will eventually require something of you, it is important that your principles are ideas that you can stand on. Your responsibility is to do just that: stand.

Without perspective, the change we create will be unjust. Without critical thinking, the only form of consequential thought, we couldn't create it at all. Think of these as the technical skills are necessary for Changemakers to start following the steps laid out by Wisdom. Once that journey begins, Changemakers can look for the characteristics of Wisdom to see the fruit of their labor.

# Characteristics of Wisdom

Having understood the goal of Wisdom, the three main components of Wisdom, and the prerequisites for walking with Wisdom, some of you have everything you need to move forward and lead a Wisdom-led life. Not me. Whenever I start a new project, initial questions I ask are, *What are the metrics? How do I know that all my work and effort won't be going to waste?* A static definition is nice, but it's hard to jump into an application with only a definition. So to aid in your pursuit of Wisdom, I've compiled a list of Wisdom metrics, or characteristics, you can measure yourself against. The longer we pursue Wisdom, the more we should reflect these characteristics.

## *Consistent*

The characteristic of consistency comes straight from the definition of Wisdom. Everyone makes both foolish and wise decisions, but a person's character is defined by what they do consistently.

Remember the New Year resolutions? Staying consistent is easier said than done, but as difficult as it is in application, its importance cannot be stressed enough. Consistency is a requirement for success in every lifestyle, and for the Changemaker, remaining consistent is a requirement for enduring change. Changemakers have to choose to fight for their cause or passion every day. To neglect reliability is to forfeit the fight. Wisdom hates shortcuts, making it less rewarding in the short term. But the benefits of seeking Wisdom compound over time. Starting the pursuit of Wisdom may require a shift in relationships, a change in mindset, or completing an important thirty-minute activity every day, but if you do not back your actions with dependable effort, your activity will not drive lasting change. Motivation is the spark, but consistency feeds the fire.

## *Intentional*

Wisdom is not in the nature of the Common Man or Changemakers, whereas nothing is as intuitive or simple as Common Sense. Common Sense takes no effort to build over time. As long as you're conscious, you will be inclined toward actions approved by Common Sense. Wisdom, on the other hand, requires much more of us, and if our pursuit of it is not intentional, we never even make it out of the gate.

## *Empathetic*

Wisdom is compassionately and holistically empathetic. Empathy has become a buzzword as of late; whenever that happens there are always cases when the word is used incorrectly or its meaning is misconstrued. To clear things up, I'm going to break down empathy into two basic types. The first is affective or emotional empathy.

Have you ever sat by a friend and could tell they were "off" emotionally, but you didn't quite know what to do? When this happens, I usually volunteer, "You good?" a couple of times, but I don't poke the bear too hard. Then, if we are truly friends (or if the person has just hit rock bottom) odds are the emotional walls will eventually break and tears, combined with an explanation, will flood the room. I might be taken aback for a couple of seconds, but then I start to feel my friend's pain and sit with him or her, maybe even volunteering a few tears of my own. This is affective empathy. It is the emotional response we have to others' emotional states. When we think of empathy, emotional empathy comes to the forefront of our minds, severely tipping the scales against an equally important form, cognitive empathy.

Cognitive empathy is understanding another person's point of view. Continuing from the example above, imagine that your friend explains he was just in a car accident. No one was harmed, but his car was completely totaled. You feel bad for him because you do not like to see him in distress (affective empathy), but you can put yourselves in his shoes and get perspective on the situation (cognitive empathy). You know that with his financial condition, he can afford another car, and you know his good health is the most important factor in this situation.

The Foolish Genius will appeal only to emotional empathy because adding the perspective needed for cognitive empathy will not benefit their cause in any way. Since emotional empathy is not about understanding the other party, a holistic perspective isn't necessary. You can make feelings the basis for a movement, which isn't bad until it is time to fashion an actual solution to the problem.

For example, children who want their parents to buy them more candy could run a campaign showing babies crying every time they are denied sweets. This would appeal to the emotional empathy of the Common Man because no one wants to see a baby in distress, no matter the reason. With this campaign, the children's proposed solution could very well be to give them the sweets they desire whenever they want. This solution (based solely on emotional empathy) would alleviate the distress of the children, at least in the short term, and give a sense of gratification and accomplishment to any adult who granted the children's request. This gratification will make those adults believe that they have empathy (because they share the distress of the children and wish to end it). But to any adult who understands the danger of giving your children everything they desire, the proposed solution would be nonsensical. Refusing to support the children's solution does not mean that these adults don't have emotional empathy; they likely have more than the children, and they also have a more holistic perspective. The adults' solution to the problem will consider the truths of life as well as the emotional needs of the children. With an appeal to cognitive empathy as well as emotional, the adults' answer would not only alleviate the problem, but would also create an opportunity for long-term progress based on a holistic perspective.

Here's an example regarding adults. A slimy salesman will appeal only to the emotional empathy of a customer, making them feel like they need something more than they actually do and leading them to pay more than they can afford. Social movement organizations, startup founders, and non-profits often do something similar, but use their respective causes as their selling points. People want to feel they contribute positively as an individual or as a member of an important group. So, for instance, founders will exaggerate the importance of their group's cause in order to provide that sense of purpose. But just as perceived injustice is not always an injustice, a solution to a perceived injustice that's not based in reality can result in the acceptance of a false reality devoid of coherent principles. This false reality can be used to modify the definition of Common Sense, and often succeeds. But, it does not lead to progress: it is based in a lie.

Another reason why appealing solely to emotional empathy can be dangerous is because it can affect our view of morality. The decision of whether something is right or wrong should be absolute. If you cut someone off on the road and cause an accident unintentionally, you will be deemed as wrong in the situation. Now, if you have a pregnant woman in the back and are rushing to the hospital, people might show you more grace. But that does not mean the actual action of cutting someone else off is any more right or wrong. (It just means the reason for doing it is more understandable.) But by appealing to emotion only, people can twist the facts of right and wrong, leading others to change their definitions of morality and correctness.

Appealing to emotional empathy instead of both emotional and cognitive empathy will result in short term solutions supported by people who are blinded by the perceived injustices and anecdotal evidence.

This is not to say that affective empathy is not important. Appealing to cognitive empathy alone will result in action that favors the majority, as there is little nuance in strictly cognitive-based decisions. Your emotions should help inform your perspective and relate with those around you. Sometimes all your friend may need is someone to sit by them while they cope, cry, and talk through his or her problems, not someone who instantly starts talking about the bigger picture. But after those moments, when it is healthy to continue, seeing the bigger picture is best for determining the next steps forward. The reason I maintain Wisdom is inherently *compassionately* empathetic is because in order to judge well, it is essential to balance both emotional and cognitive empathy, especially for Changemakers who are making decisions for entire communities. Compassion implies the appropriate balance is struck.

Even bigger, more than just being compassionately empathetic, Wisdom is holistically empathetic. To be holistically empathetic is to be understanding of everyone's side of an issue, no matter what their feelings or beliefs are. In the last example, it was a friend we were intently listening to, but what about people we don't have a good relationship with? Again, you can be understanding without necessarily sympathizing with them. We must combat the ignorance with which we are blessed or cursed; being informed on how all sides perceive a problem can only improve the potential quality of an effective decision.

## *Balanced*

Over the last century, there have not been many evangelist Changemakers that can be mentioned with the likes of Billy Graham. A young Billy converted to Christianity at the age of sixteen and started his ministry thirteen years later. His ministry became his movement, and an impactful one at that. Over the next fifty-five years, he preached to more than 215 million people. He was able to preach in 185 countries (to put that in perspective, there are 195 countries in the world today). He counseled twelve presidents and has even been described as the greatest Christian evangelist since the Apostle Paul. He was obviously driven, obsessed with his cause, and determined to lead people toward what he believed was the answer to their unanswerable questions. He was intentional, empathetic, and effective, yet with all these

# Foolish Genius

positives, "America's Pastor" was left with two notable regrets at the end of his ministry.

When Billy Graham's name comes up, people who love him rave about his ministry, influence, and in-depth passion for the gospel, whereas those far less impressed typically bring up his questionable political advice and annoying passion for the gospel. The first regret he had was about the latter: he stated that if he could do it again, he would stay out of politics. However, what his fans and detractors rarely surface is his greatest regret in life: how he fulfilled his roles as husband and father.

For Graham, it was love at first sight. He met his future wife Ruth in college, and in a couple of years, the two were married. Two years after that, their first child was born. Virginia Graham was the oldest of five children, and the only one to be born before Billy started his ministry in 1947.

Billy was a man on a mission, and, from his perspective, it was a holy one. Yet, after his successful ministry preaching to virtually the entire world, the people he wished he had served more were the ones back home. Changemakers tend to evidence tunnel vision at times, and often this serves to their benefit. They are focused and driven by their purpose, yet in all of it, they often forget to maintain balance. Balance can take a few forms; for Billy, he realized his work–family life balance tipped too far to one side, and it stung. Changemakers also fall into an unbalanced lifestyle by neglecting mental health. Pursuing change of any kind can be a difficult and isolating process; immersed in the grind and picking ourselves up by the bootstraps, we can easily forget the journey is a long one. That is, the compounding effect that comes with consistently unhealthy habits can match if not exceed the consistent practice of healthy habits.

The goal of Wisdom is not "more" of something. It is not concerned whether you bought a Lamborghini by thirty or how many friends you accumulate, although it can help you achieve both. The goal is a high-quality life. Balance is the process of finding the right mixture of wealth, health, and purpose to lead a life worth living.

## *Loving*

This may sound like a purely emotional statement, but in Wisdom's true form, it is both an emotional and logical one. Take a moment to imagine what Wisdom looks like. What images come to mind? I first think of old, bearded monks. Some might picture a woman personified as Wisdom, like the one depicted in the Book of Solomon. I'm sure many others would take the fantasy route with images of Yoda, Gandalf, and Dumbledore. Now take a few seconds to clear your head.

Next, picture what love looks like. I'm sure there are a lot of hearts or images of mothers in your mind. The point is, Wisdom and love are not often personified in the same way. Saying that Wisdom is loving in nature may seem like a stretch at first, but when you consider the other characteristics of Wisdom, you realize that this one encompasses all the others. From a communal standpoint, it makes sense. When you do better, others around you do well. This feeds into the selfishly altruistic aspect of Wisdom. Thankfully, however, when we dissect Wisdom as a process in our daily lives, we uncover the greatest portrayals of love. When I think of human love in its purest form, I always think of seasoned married couples. Imagine being joined with someone more than double the amount of time you existed as a single person. As frail as they may look, they possess a love so strong and so rare that a lifetime of challenges and hardships couldn't break it. That is a concept only fully comprehended by those who have experienced it, but it can still serve to teach everyone who cares enough to let it.

Anyone who has the honor of experiencing a successful marriage will tell you that they don't *like* their partner all the time. As humans, we are too complex to like everything about anyone. Liking is temperamental; it comes and goes. Think about all the arguments that seasoned couples have shared—all those times when their vices and insecurities pressured the relationship. In those moments, the word *like* goes out the window. The relationship will remain strong not because of how much partners like each other but how much they're willing to empathize with and consistently and intentionally love one another in spite of their insecurities and faults. Love takes work and effort over time. Couples learn to balance their own needs and interests with the needs and interests of their partner. They do this so well that they become a single unit. Sure, there is give and take, but overall they move in unity: they've achieved a true balance. As love takes work over time to arrive at true unity, Wisdom learns from and walks that same path.

## Foolish Genius

> Love and Wisdom are inseparable concepts. One cannot exist outside the other: to move in Wisdom is to move in love, and vice versa.

Love and Wisdom are inseparable concepts. One cannot exist outside the other: to move in Wisdom is to move in love, and vice versa. If a husband loves his wife, he is acting in Wisdom. (Is it not wise to love your spouse?) The more Wisdom couples exhibit, the better their relationship becomes, and the more their love deepens. This is also true outside of romantic relationships.

Questions of love and Wisdom become more difficult to answer when the outcomes are not associated with positive feelings. In 2015, the National Institutes of Health estimated that one of every ten Americans will suffer from a drug use disorder at some point in their lives. They also stated that 75 percent of them will not receive any form of treatment.[30] Thus for many people, someone in their family will have a drug problem for which they will not seek treatment. For those families, it can be difficult to gauge what it means to love those with the drug use disorder. You want to be there for them, but you don't want to coddle them. You want them to seek help, but you don't want to make decisions for them or make them feel you are trying to control them. If they are a possible threat to the family and refuse to seek help or be intentional about their growth, the wise and loving thing to do is respectfully create boundaries that consider the needs of all involved, safeguard against abusive relationships, and maximize the family's quality of life.

In the context of change, your motivation for it needs to be derived from love if it is to be Wisdom-led. Love is more than good intentions and heartfelt sentiment. It needs to be proven over time, just like Wisdom. Anyone can say they are Wisdom-led, but their actions need to back it up. Many people think they understand love but struggle with a constant cycle of shallow or toxic relationships. That is, you cannot claim either Wisdom or love without the track record to back them up. Changemakers will have action backing their motivations, which means their intentions will carry more weight.

Since change is a social contract that affects both the Changemaker and the Common Man, the motivation for that change affects both parties. Changemakers can create change out of love, apathy, or hate. When they create change out of love, that love is directed toward the Common Man; the

## Age of Wisdom

opposite is true for hate. But when Changemakers create change out of apathy, they aren't thinking about the Common Man at all. The Changemakers are not focused on the Common Man's needs or worried about how they will be affected—they are focused solely on looking out for themselves. This happens quite often, especially in our individualistic society. When someone wants to create change, many times they are looking to solve a problem with the simple motivation of making a profit. But if a Changemaker's intention is monetary gain, then problem-solving will go no further than sales and profit. A Changemaker's motivation for change affects the choices made throughout the change, not just its beginning, affecting the lives of both the Common Man and the Changemaker.

I can hear the critique already: "Weren't you the one to say that good intentions don't necessarily create good outcomes? Why then does a Changemaker's motivation matter?" Intentions prime your solution, but they don't create them.

Motivations matter when the structure of change comes into play. For example, if I create a business out of a love for single mothers, their well-being will be directly incorporated into my business plan. If I'm apathetic, then I don't truly care about their well-being, and I'll do just what is needed to look good to the press. An apathetic business is profit-centric, not people-centric, and the difference can be monumental. A business of any kind needs profit, but an apathetic one prioritizes the profit over the people they service. In terms of Wisdom, creating change out of apathy is not as effective as creating change out of love. Even if you amaze with your marketing and PR game, true colors will emerge in times of struggle.

Summer 2020 was pure chaos, and no one knew what to do. COVID-19 was running wild, keeping everyone in their homes until a video was released showing a police officer kneeling on the neck of a black man who was begging for air. This gut-wrenching video spurred months of protests and riots all across the globe. Our nation was in an uproar and corporate America did not know how to react. Some companies took a side and were rewarded for their stance. Others took the same stance but were reprimanded because their approach was inauthentic. Many companies tried to appease both sides and lost all respect in the process. The last two types of companies revealed they didn't hold a stance either way and only wanted to be *seen* doing the politically correct thing instead of taking a genuine stance on justice and truth. They cared for people as long as those people brought in sales, but apathy will shine through when love for the Common Man is not built into your structure. Apathetic change does not experience the same longevity and does not touch the hearts of the Common Man as easily as change motivated by love.

As for change motivated by hate, it is a strong motivation and can be convincing. Hate can either be directed toward a people group or toward an ideal. Hate, when applied to a concept, is the byproduct of love for people. (For example, a hatred of racism is, at the core, a love for mankind.) But hate, when applied to people, is the byproduct of ignorance.

If hatred is directed toward a person or people group, it is usually born of unfamiliarity. This is because there is always something in an individual that you can relate to yourself: no two people have nothing in common. Hatred of an individual is a consequence of generalization and a lack of understanding and perspective. Humans cannot be the embodiment of any one concept, so even if someone were mostly evil, to say you hate them is to say you hate all of them, including the aspects that aren't evil. Acting out of hatred is self-defeating. It attacks the Changemaker just as much as it does the Common Man. Hate is best suited in a scorched earth strategy, a strategy that has no place in the daily lives of the Common Man or in the Wise Society.

From communal, personal, and motivational perspectives, Wisdom is shown to be loving in nature. Love and Wisdom share the same characteristics and work together in tandem. Neither can exist outside a set of boundaries. If you cannot remember these characteristics, at least recall that Wisdom is loving.

## *Process-Focused*

The characteristics of Wisdom may be simple to grasp, but they are much harder to apply. Each one takes work and practice. Empathy is learned. Balance can be hard to achieve and even harder to maintain. Consistency is fought for over time. Love takes effort and intention. Our knowledge of Wisdom will not help us achieve it unless we are willing to get our hands dirty and start pursuing it. So, this last characteristic of Wisdom is its process-focus. With concepts like Wisdom and love, there is never a final destination. No one will ever become fully Wisdom-led or fully loving, but the most foolish mistake the Common Man or a Changemaker could make is to abandon the journey for the want of a finish line. The pursuit of indeterminable concepts are the only ones that will lead to incalculable growth. The pursuit of

Wisdom trains us to live a life that will benefit us as well as the lives of everyone we touch—a life that is guided by the principles we subscribe to. Change on that level is immeasurable.

# 4
# Principles

*An army of principles can penetrate where an army of soldiers cannot.* – Thomas Paine

---

### Takeaways
- Identifying principles is an essential skill.
- A lack of principles is dangerous for both the Common Man and Changemakers.
- The wrong principles, or a lack of them altogether, distinguishes the Foolish Genius from the Wisdom-led Changemaker.

---

There is something beautiful about a social movement, a group of people representing different walks of life uniting under a single cause to change society. What's more powerful than people standing up against authority or social norms in a democratic way to rectify the sins of the past and move the world into a better future?

Today it seems like social movements are sprouting up left and right (apparently, there are quite a few sins to rectify), often times seen championed by impassioned Gen-Zers. This generation of "social justice warriors," of which I am a member, has turned a critical eye on past generations and are calling out leaders and symbols that represent the shortcomings of the past. This trend seemed to hit a peak during summer 2020, when statues around the nation were being torn down because of the racist behavior displayed by the people they represented. These people had achieved great things but had also gone along with or participated in atrocities like slavery and other issues so obviously abhorrent today. Questions like *Why did slavery last so long?* are valid when slavery was seen as acceptable, but the practice is rejected without a second thought today. How can issues like this transcend past generations without being questioned by the Common Man or most Changemakers?

As you know, slavery is not unique to America or to white people, nor was the abolition of it an original American idea. Slavery's roots date as far back as the Sumerian civilization, the first civilization known to man. In fact, when we look back on major societies of the past, it's hard to find one that didn't view slave trade as a common and acceptable practice. Today, we see slavery as an injustice that outweighs the economic benefits, but this has not been the case for the vast majority of human existence. It was often seen as a part of natural law and necessary to the growth of a society.

But as there is today, there were people who spoke out against the popular opinion of the day and stood firm in their belief of the contrary. Whenever someone chooses to take the path less traveled and sacrifice a life of comfort, I wonder what motivates them. When a social movement starts, often it is initially spurred by members who have personally experienced the relevant injustice, and sometimes this is enough. In Haiti's case, the first nation to permanently abolish slavery, the motivations were obvious. When the Haitian Revolution began in the 1790s, the rebels had been slaves themselves. Their motivations for freedom were both righteous and selfish in nature. They were fighting for freedom of their own land, a land in which they were a majority. But often this is not the case.

Many social movements can't accomplish what they set out to do today without appealing to the humanity of others, specifically, people who don't experience the relevant injustice firsthand. In these cases, the motivations of the supporters vary widely. The fight for the abolition of slavery in the US was progressed by people who had experienced slavery, like the abolitionists Harriet Tubman and Sojourner Truth, but the black population was not large enough to fashion the type of impact that was necessary. Even today, African Americans make up less than fifteen percent of the population.

In order to create lasting impact and change the definition of Common Sense on this topic, there needed to be a collective effort made by people who would fight against slavery regardless of their personal connection to it. If people supported only the issues that touched them personally, change would occur only when something inconvenienced groups with greater power or larger numbers. In the case of slavery in the US, the victims had neither. Understanding how change occurred from these circumstances helps Changemakers today learn how to take a stand and fight against injustices that don't have a direct effect on them. Thankfully, there were quite a few revolutionists that advocated the abolition of slavery although they had no obvious personal connection to it. One of the earliest was a man by the name of Benjamin Lay.

# Benjamin Lay

People were settling into their seats. In true Quaker fashion, individuals were speaking in a popcorn style with no set speaker or assigned leadership. The Philadelphia Yearly Meeting was a major event, and Quakers from several regions had come to connect with their community and hear the news and announcements. It was 1738, and Quakers still allowed slave owners to attend their meetings. Everything was proceeding normally, with people speaking as they felt, when a small man standing four feet, seven inches and wearing a plain cloak called for the attention of the room.[31]

Out of this small man came a commanding voice explaining the incompatibility of their beliefs with the institution of slavery. At the climax of his speech, he threw open his cloak, revealing military garb, a sword, and a book (some believe it was a Bible). Through the gasps of the crowd, he declared, "Thus shall God shed the blood of those persons who enslave their fellow creatures." He then took the book, held it over his head, and stabbed it with a sword. Out of the puncture came a red liquid gushing out, as if the book were bleeding, and spraying onto the slave owners in the crowd. Havoc ensued as women passed out, screams filled the room, and panic engulfed the meeting. The man sat peacefully, just as he had before his speech, until he was thrown out, going willingly with the enforcers.

This small man, Benjamin Lay, also known as the "first revolutionary abolitionist," was unique to say the least. He was a Quaker; Quakers were early leaders in the fight for abolition. But even among this nonviolent sect, Benjamin stood out. He was born in England in 1681. At twenty-one, he became a sailor, and it was during this time he started to form his opinion on slavery, when he would hear stories told by sailors of the slave trade. He joined the Quaker community around 1717 when he was engaged to Sarah Smith, a popular Quaker preacher who was also a dwarf. Despite Sarah's kindhearted character, Benjamin quickly gained an unpopular reputation for his radical and theatrical stands against slavery and his willingness to call out any Quaker who reaped the benefits of the slave trade.

Theater wasn't the only art form Lay used to express his beliefs. His work entitled "All Slave Keepers That Keep the Innocent in Bondage, Apostates"[32] was one of the first antislavery essays in North America that attacked the notion of slavery with the same fervor he expressed in Quaker meetings. While his book was being printed by Benjamin Franklin, Lay continued to badger the Quaker community, and in 1758, twenty years after his escapade at the Philadelphia Yearly Meeting, the Quakers finally banned slaveowners from attending their meetings. On hearing the news, Lay reportedly said, "I can now die in peace." He passed away the following year.[33]

Until the book titled *The Fearless Benjamin Lay: The Quaker Dwarf Who Became the First Revolutionary Abolitionist*[34] was released in 2017, Benjamin Lay was not widely recognized for the role he played as an abolitionist or in convincing Quakers to stand against slavery. Two hundred and fifty years after his death, the Quakers of North London released a statement stating the Quakers of his time were wrong for disowning him as they did. His influence was immeasurable, but it didn't begin to manifest itself until a year before his death. Benjamin Lay was undoubtedly a Changemaker, but he would not likely have been labeled one during his lifetime.

Benjamin Lay had no apparent social or personal incentive to take the stand that he did. He was not a former slave, he was not married to a former slave, and he did not hold the guilt of previously owning a slave. Not only was he merely four feet, seven inches tall, he also had long, wiry arms and legs, an oversized head, and a hunched back that led his peers to describe him as a troll. He had very little formal education and lived in a cave, denounced by his own religious sect. Yet, despite the rejection and lack of external incentives, Lay unceasingly lived his life guided by his principles, not by the norms of the day or the expectations of his peers.

"He could see basic injustices in society which were seen as normal and dragged the injustices into the light."[35] In

> A focus on principles calls Common Sense into question and allows us to compare issues in a conceptual space outside of time and norms.

this quote, Quaker writer Tim Gee used the plural form of "injustice" because abolitionism wasn't the only cause where Lay was ahead of his time.

He opposed the death penalty about two hundred and fifty years before Furman v. Georgia, he was a feminist a century before the term was coined, he was a vegetarian before the first vegetarian society formed in 1847, and his aggressive yet nonviolent tactics were groundbreaking. He took his beliefs, found their roots, and used them to form his opinions on other topics. A focus on principles calls Common Sense into question and allows us to compare issues in a conceptual space outside of time and norms. Principles at the apex of a person's thinking evoke a conviction to uphold a set standard regardless of the opinions of the day.

The importance of principles stretches far past choosing which social movements to take part in.

## Pitfalls of Lacking Principles

Many of the biggest pitfalls that the Common Man and Changemakers fall into include the inability to identify and adhere to principles. Of these pitfalls, there are seven the telltale signs of a Foolish Genius that I observe occurring over and over, both from watching others and from looking back at my own life.

### *Pitfall #1. Continuing Harmful Traditions*

We live our day-to-day lives in a combination of routines and traditions. They may change from time to time, but overall, they stay fairly consistent, begetting security and comfort in a seemingly random and hectic life. They bring meaning to otherwise trivial activities, but even trivial traditions serve a purpose.

This may be the most "hater" statement in this book, but I'm not too fond of Santa Claus. It's not because he sneaks into homes. I get that, and I was fond of him as a kid. It started in my early years as an undergrad, I remember going home to visit the family, viewing Christmas lights, singing songs in the car, and inevitably being coaxed by my parents to sit on a bearded man's lap to take a picture with him and my three siblings. The tradition started when my sisters and I were too young to walk, and it was always a joyous time. The car ride was fun, and there were free cookies and hot chocolate to dip them in. The longer the tradition persisted as we grew older, the stronger it became. By the time I was twelve, it was a necessity. It wasn't Christmas without taking a trip to see the lights and getting a picture with the good Saint. The tradition became a symbol of wonder, family unity, and Christmas itself.

# Principles

In my family, the oldest sibling is eight years older than the youngest, meaning that feelings toward Santa evolved at different times. As we grew up, the older siblings first noticed how odd it was to sit in a grown man's lap as a young adult. The two younger siblings were suspicious but were still willing to go along with the tradition for tradition's sake. My parents were still all for it since they remembered the past and knew how important the tradition had become to the family. The older we grew, the more my sisters and I detached from the tradition, while our parents remained fond of it. When the youngest was sixteen and the oldest twenty-four, my parents finally gave in, and we abandoned the "Santa's lap-sitting" tradition. Initially, seeing Santa every year was a tradition that served a purpose. It delighted the family with unity and charm. But at some point the tradition became the purpose, and its original intent was lost.

Now here's an example of a harmful tradition with no family interests contributing to its unfortunate flourishing. First and foremost, your waiters! They have to deal with some of the most irritating people day in and day out, and the majority do it for much less than what the trouble is worth. When I first learned that all waiters and waitresses were not compensated in the same manner as other employees, I was confused. The model for how they are paid didn't make any intuitive sense to me, so I looked into the history. As it turns out, tipping has a deeper history than what meets the eye.

Its origins take place in Europe, where masters would tip their servants if their work was satisfactory. In the nineteenth century, the practice made its way across the pond and became popular in Reconstruction America. When it first arrived, it was met with a lot of backlash from individuals who saw it as a way to demean the personhood of the waiter, as if they were a slave or servant. Despite those efforts, tipping became popular after the Emancipation. The practice took on a new form of abuse when restaurant owners saw tipping the new wave of black employees as a way to avoid paying the newly freed slaves. If tipping was the norm, restaurateurs wouldn't have to spend a dime on their wages. Since those days, little progress has been made to change this horrible system. The "tippable minimum wage" is more than five dollars less than the standard minimum wage, although the law requires that employees need to take home at least the standard minimum wage with tips included. Despite the fact that poverty, sexual harassment, and wage violations abide in this industry more than most, we justify this system based in racism and sexism because, at the end of the day, they are still paid the minimum wage. Tipping used to be in addition to what was owed, like the word implies, but now is used to as a substitute for base pay.

A custom that was created as a genuine show of gratitude became a way to avoid paying livable wages. But tipping is so ingrained in our system it would take years of persistent work and lobbying to rectify it. Still, that need not stop Changemakers.

If you fail to see the underlying principles behind a common custom or tradition, you lose the ability to judge it properly and make well-informed decisions on whether to continue them. The Santa tradition in my family ended when the principle of the matter was evaluated. Tipping in America has never had the same purpose that it did in Europe, yet because we fail to understand the principles and purpose behind it, we are easily persuaded to continue the harmful custom.

## *Pitfall #2. Repeating History*

The first pitfall occurs when Common Sense isn't questioned and principles are ignored. The second pitfall occurs when history is forgotten alongside the principles. You may have heard philosopher George Santayana's popular aphorism: "Those who cannot remember the past are condemned to repeat it," and Mark Twain's: "History doesn't repeat itself, but it often rhymes." I'd argue that those who cannot identify principles and adhere to principles are doomed, regardless of memory. A society that remembers history but fails to grasp the principles within that history will not understand the warning signs. Mark Twain hit it on the nose: history will never precisely replicate itself, so the warning signs will not look exactly the same as before, but they will look similar. When comparing current events to those of the past, it is useless to do so without understanding the principles at play in both scenarios.

## *Pitfall #3. Surface-Level Identity*

The third pitfall is different from the others, but stick with me.

When we are in a certain group, we play the part that fits that group—not in an attempt to be fake (we are still honest and being ourselves), but how we interact with people changes with the environment. When I see my hometown friends, they know me as an extroverted, joking, and active person. But when I was in college, I was around extroverted and athletic people, and I found myself being quieter and more introspective. My significant other and closest friends have seen both versions of me and know my individualities alter based on my mood, thoughts, and environment. And to varying degrees, so do everyone else's.

A friend of mine was talking about a conversation he had with a prior roommate. The prior roommate is a kind person, but he talks in a forceful way, is loud, and struggles with a stutter. While my friend was describing the conversation to me, he relayed the roommate's tone as harsh and forceful, but he relayed his own words in a smooth and more suave tone of voice. Later on I was able to watch both of them interact, and my friend carried on this trend in real time. When he was around his old roommate, he would become slightly calmer and more relaxed, as if to balance out the kind yet abrasive personality of the roommate. It was an unconscious shift but noticeable all the same. Would I say that he's fake? Absolutely not! We create bonds with people partly because of who they are and partly because of who we are because of them. People are multifaceted: they can be serious, silly, thoughtful, funny, heartfelt, and unfeeling, all at the same time and without being fake or disingenuous.

I'm always disappointed when I hear people take pride in a show of immaturity and explain it away with "That's just how I am," or "There are two versions of me: nice me and me with an attitude." If someone has only one opportunity to evaluate you as a person, they will likely infer a lack of depth or a fake face. I'm certainly not saying that exhibiting consistent behavior means you lack depth, but if you don't have the self-awareness to know what your principles are, you'll focus on the surface-level attributes and leverage them as your main "selling points." As long as your core principles don't shift or change, isn't everything beyond that just an expression of them? People are meant to communicate with different people and groups, all with different traditions, customs, love languages, and methods of expression. If you are to be truly effective in expressing your values and core principles to a multitude of people in a multitude of situations, you'll need depth. The more secure you are in your principles, the less the expression of your surface-level attributes matters and the more the expression of your core principles matters. You can be like an artist who switches mediums: they aren't fake or disingenuous for changing how they express themselves as long as that expression is coming out of a place of honesty and self-awareness. The alternative is art removed from interpretation. The focus should be on your principles and ideas in who you are and what you do, not the outward expression of them. Those always follow naturally and should not merit undo attention.

## *Pitfall #4. Over Reliance on Values at the Expense of Principles*

History is filled with examples of powerful Changemakers taking advantage of and oppressing other people: dictators rising to power, dynasties ruling with an iron fist, etc. But whenever a new dictator or harsh dynasty arises, one must ask how they came to be. No one can rise to power without the support of a substantial group of people. Hitler came to power legally and without (much) force. Once a dictator, we all know what happened, but many psychologists wondered how. How did a failed art student rise to power and, once there, inspire a whole nation to be on board with his genocidal lunacy? This aspect of conformity is what Stanley Milgram investigated in his well-known "Obedience to Authority" experiments in the 1960s.

A group of participants were recruited, all being told that they had the equal opportunity to be either a "learner" or a "teacher." Teachers would dispense electrical shocks to the learners when they answered a question incorrectly, with shock values labeled between 15 and 450 volts. Alongside these labels were words expressing how much shock the learner would experience, ranging from "slight shock" and "moderate shock" all the way to "intense shock," "extreme intensity shock," and the ever-so-dramatic "XXX" label. In reality, all the recruited participants were assigned the role of teacher, while the learners were actors (who were never actually shocked). Though the actors never felt any pain, they were instructed to show signs of distress at shocks labeled as low as 75 volts. The point was to see if the participants would obey the directions of the experiment administrator, the authority in the situation.

The experiment was gruesome. The actors delivered grunts at 75 volts but would escalate their expression of discomfort as the learner flipped another switch. They began to ask to leave the experiment at 150 volts, and by the time 300 volts was reached, the actors would let out chilling screams and express heart pain. After 330 volts, the actors were silent. As the "teacher" participants delivered the shocks, they became hesitant fairly early, looking to the administrator for guidance, who would direct them to continue. You can imagine the stress the participants were under, thinking they were harming other randomly selected individuals, listening to their desperate cries for mercy and blood-curdling screams, while under constant pressure to continue from the onlooking experiment leader. Not all "teachers" made it to the last voltage. In fact, 35 percent of the participants stopped before reaching that point. But that left 65 percent of participants who heard all the cries, begging, and pleading, yet chose to continue, releasing the last 450 volts (labeled "XXX") under the pressure and coercion of the administrator.

After debriefing the participants, analysis began. Milgram divided his participants into three groups: Justified and Obedient, Guilty and Obedient, and Rebels. The first group were those who completed the experiment but blamed their actions on the administrator. The second also completed the experiment but blamed themselves for the continued compliance. The third group was the most interesting. These rebels, the ones who refused to complete the experiment, believed there was a deeper principle that overrode the experimenter's authority, namely, not to harm another human being.

Everyone has values, whether conscious or not. If I am a selfish person, I may value personal success much more than any interest outside of me. I assume, since you are reading a self-help book, that you value human life and personal development to some extent. If our values don't progress toward principles, those values will fall into the pit of useless good intention. Ray Dalio put it succinctly: "Principles are what allow you to live a life consistent with those values. Principles connect your values to your actions."[36]

Have you ever yelled at someone you truly care about, knowing while you were blowing up that you were doing something wrong? Your values and actions were not acting in tandem, and you probably felt compelled to stop and apologize because you knew that was not the person you want to be. As soon as you realized that your actions were contrary to your values, you had three options: 1) keep going because they deserve it or to prove your point, 2) stop because that's not who you are, or 3) keep going and apologize afterward. Unfortunately, values are not directly tied to action, and our minds, as powerful as they are, can create justifications for whatever path we choose. After yelling, you may have felt compelled to apologize, but after thinking about it, you could have decided that they deserved it. The first group in Milgram's experiment essentially did the same thing. Although they knew something wasn't right, rather than acting counter to the administrator's commands, they went the easiest route, which was to explain away their actions. The second group didn't try to explain their actions; they opted to continue and feel the guilt of it. Guilt is interesting because although it feels bad, it can validate that your values are in the right place. So no matter how much damage we cause, feeling bad about it can make us feel more human afterward. The third group, the Rebels, complemented their values with principles as they stood together against the administrator's instructions, allowing them to perform against the current. The Rebels respected authority, but once one of their more important principles was contradicted, they could no longer be a part of the experiment. Neither the experiment administrator's words nor the presumed importance of the study took precedence over the Rebels' principles.

## *Pitfall #5. Group Polarization, Groupthink, and a Breakdown in Collaboration*

The extremes of polarization, groupthink, and a breakdown in collaboration are most severely seen in political debates. Politics hits home for so many people because it sets the standard for how a nation is to live and behave. We know intuitively that our political parties should work together to achieve better outcomes, but we also shy away from discussion with members of the other party. This is a barrier to success, whether that success is defined as collaboration or domination. If one country is at war with another and seeks to dominate them, their first step is to understand how they think and what their next moves will be. Espionage is alive and well, whether it be corporate, economic, nation-state, or otherwise. Also, for any two groups to collaborate, some line of communication has to be open. Whether the goal is collaboration or domination, one party must understand the other.

Take the debate of the death penalty. Both sides of the argument value justice, and both value human life, but a slight difference in prioritization can cause a large difference in principles. A principle of one who opposes the death penalty could be that "human life should be preserved," while a principle for the supporter could be that "human life should be preserved unless it has taken human life." The core values are very similar, if not identical, yet the principles or rules associated with them show a great divide. A stronger value for justice will act differently than a stronger value for human life. Wisdom teaches you to get to the core principles in order to create actionable solutions to complex problems. If we don't pay attention to principles and simply assume that "good people" share "good values," we will only achieve poor communication among groups and the resulting one-sided solutions.

## Principles

Earlier in the book, you read about the shortcomings of intellectual pride, and how we can only place so much trust in it or those who appeal to it. As a collective nation, we as individuals have grown accustomed to a high level of self-arrogance. We believe we are right, and we hate anyone who disagrees, believing that their disagreement is somehow rooted in a deep, fundamental issue with their values. We think we couldn't possibly disagree on an issue and share the same deep-rooted values. We think we couldn't possibly both be victims of the same form of manipulation. We think Milgram's participants must have all been conservative because a liberal would never hurt someone, or we think they must have all been liberal because a conservative wouldn't have listened to the administrator and budged on their principles. We have abundant confidence in the words fed to us by one-sided thinkers as we listen to them bash the misquoted lines of others—others who in turn think their one-sided solutions will also lead to the benefit of the "greater good" despite being the polar opposite of "our" one-sided thinkers.

Abandoning a dedication to principles in favor of a group alliance such as just described almost always happens unintentionally. We first stand on a principle, find that we agree with a group's stance on that issue, and begin to defend that issue with that group. But over time, the defense of that issue can turn into the defense of an individual leader or the group itself that champions the cause. We can get into a habit defending a person or group, forgetting to stop and think about what we are defending.

I'm not saying political affiliations are bad, and I'm not undermining the positive effects of a group identity, but principles go deeper than party lines. Tying yourself to a group of any kind without anchoring to a certain set of principles will inevitably lead to the group members moving much like driftwood, lost in a sea of feel-good statements, party rhetoric, unifying speeches, and possibly the most blinding of all, good intentions. Everything people in your group say may sound good, but if honest you will soon find yourself supporting contradictions. Without knowing how to identify your principles, how could you possibly know when they are eroding over time? You'll end up in one of the first two groups of Milgram's experiment, either blaming yourself or the relevant authority for your actions. Or perhaps you'll find yourself in a fourth group: those continuing the experiment with no end, because when the Common Man sacrifices their principles, they also sacrifice their power.

Foolish Genius

Everyone who is willing to place trust in someone or something is susceptible to being manipulated, but those who are able to identify their principles are the ones able to take calculated risks in this arena. Everything else is blind dedication as opposed to carefully placed faith. The Foolish Genius does not mind blind dedication because it does not question, but Wisdom knows blind dedication doesn't promote individual growth. The Foolish Genius and the Changemaker have fundamentally different goals and, because of that, fundamentally different strategies. The Foolish Genius can create lasting change without the empowerment of the Common Man; Wisdom cannot. The Wisdom-led Changemaker not only knows how to identify their principles and live consistent with their convictions, but they can also instruct the Common Man to do the same.

## *Pitfall #6. Creating a Foundation on Charismatic Leadership*

Charisma is a powerful tool for any leader, and I would encourage all Changemakers to study it. But just like any other impressive tool, it can do more harm than good if not used properly. Like many of the other pitfalls, this is a two-sided danger. It's hard to say how influential leaders like Barack Obama, Martin Luther King Jr., and Winston Churchill would have been without leveraging their charismatic skills, or if they would have earned a public voice at all. At the same time, one must agree that many dictators, corrupted cult leaders, and all-around psychopaths would have failed to grow a following if charisma were not on their side.

For the Common Man, charisma can replace principles in the decision-making process. You hear someone speak, and if they seem kind and personable, you naturally begin to trust them. This blind trust is why politicians focus just as much on polling data as they do policy: personality (as revealed in polls) matters much more when principles are not in play.

You put your organization at risk when you lay a foundation of charismatic leadership. Although charisma is a great tool for gathering an audience and creating a sense of group identity, you run the risk of attaching that identity to yourself and not your cause. We see this all the time with businesses and religious organizations. Members join because they like the head of the group, but as soon as the leader leaves for whatever reason, half the membership leaves with them. The Foolish Genius may not mind this exodus because they may not be fighting for a cause that will outlive them. But this is

Principles

never the case for Wisdom or its followers. Building a foundation on principles will ensure longevity for the movements you create, whether charisma is a factor or not.

## *Pitfall #7. Passive Manipulation*

Manipulation is power's dirty mistress. It seems like every day we are fighting to hold those in power accountable for abusing their influence, but those in power often don't start with the intent of manipulation. They begin an effort married to their convictions and to the people they are leading, but as with any relationship, the temptation for more power can corrupt and ruin. Dominance, however, implies more work and responsibility than is advertised. The instant those in command begin to dislike the people they are leading or tire of the burdens of responsibility, manipulation arrives to tempt and offer an easier path. Sometimes the cheating takes place out in the open, like when dictators control their people by force with no regard for finesse or discretion. But most of the time, the fornication happens behind closed doors.

History is replete with examples of "passive manipulation." Many times it's intentional, for example, when big corporations use language they know will not be understood by the people they are asking to sign their terms of agreement. In a similar way, the Changemaker can create change only when the Common Man signs off on the contract. Unfortunately, the Common Man often undervalues the contract as if it were unimportant, clicking "I agree" before doing the necessary due diligence. After the terms are accepted, the Common Man waits patiently to see how the fine print affects them, and when it results in a negative outcome, accuses the Changemakers for not making their intentions clear. This is an example of intentional passive manipulation or knowledge-based manipulation. It can be sneaky, but it is much easier to spot than its counterpart: principle-based manipulation.

Have you ever been in a room where someone was caught in an affair? The room erupts, but what's instantly on everyone's minds are the five questions: what happened, with whom, when, where, and why. The first four can be answered pretty quickly, leaving the cheater to fumble through why. Some answers are bold like, "it doesn't matter why; are you staying with me or not?" or "I wasn't happy and wanted to try something else." These are the answers of an intentional cheater. But sometimes you'll hear a response along the lines of, "I don't know how it happened," or my personal favorite, "It was an accident." These responses are interesting because they appeal to the

## Foolish Genius

humanity of the victim. If you show yourself to be a victim, as lost and confused as the person you cheated on, you may be able to induce empathy. And to the cheater's defense, most people aren't sure what leads to breakdowns in relationships. Sometimes it can be hard to pinpoint the moment where everything went south. The same can be said for principle-based manipulation.

Changemakers often begin with the hope that the change they create will come with the full participation and agreement of their followers, but every leader eventually has a difficult time dealing with the same people they are trying to serve. The reality is that your specific cause may not be championed by many of the people you will try to woo. Once Changemakers realize this, they have the choice to forfeit some decisional power to their membership or go over their heads to find ways to get them to "sign off" and concur without thorough knowledge of what they are signing. Creating change without proper education about that change is intentional passive manipulation or knowledge-based manipulation. Unintentional passive manipulation, or principle-based manipulation, takes place when people are educated but they remain unaware of the core principles shaping that education.

When an idea is taught without an expression of the founding principles, it becomes an absolute. If people disagree with the idea, they are wrong. If they agree, they are right. Whoever creates the curriculum will embed their principles into it, likely without trying. Only those who understand the founding principles and assumptions will be able to question the curriculum and the worldview behind it. This is how worldviews spread without the intention of the teachers spreading them and how Common Sense is passed down from one generation to the next.

> You can't stop people from having opinions, but you can control which opinions they consider. The Foolish Genius will do this by expressing their opinion as fact, and when others accept it as so, principle-based manipulation is inevitable.

You can't stop people from having opinions, but you can control which opinions they consider. The Foolish Genius will do this by expressing their opinion as fact, and when others accept it as so, principle-based manipulation is inevitable. They don't do it purposefully. But if you neglect to empower your followers with the ability to question your perspective, they will accept

Principles

your perspective as the truth. The only way to evaluate a worldview properly is to understand and question the principles that it is built upon. This is the role of a philosopher.

# 5
# A Philosopher's Revolution

*You never change things by fighting the existing reality. To change something, build a new model that makes the existing model obsolete.* – Buckminster Fuller

---

### Takeaways
- Principles are the basis for our worldviews and philosophies.
- Anyone can be a philosopher and evaluate principles.
- We have a responsibility to uphold our principles and should criticize them more than the people who oppose them.

---

When you think of the word *revolutionist*, what comes to mind? Do you think of someone old or young? Are they physically fit? I picture them organizing protests, giving speeches, and rallying support in the streets to fight for a cause. I think of people like Toussaint L'Ouverture, Nelson Mandela, and Rosa Luxemburg: people who, victorious or not, risked their lives against an oppressive system. The more conflict they overcame, the greater the impression on me.

Now, think of the word *philosopher*. For me, and I imagine for you as well, it's a different image. I think of an old man with white hair, sitting alone in a traditional Queen Anne's chair by a fire staring inquisitively into the blaze. Or maybe an irritating group of smart friends gathering together and playing mind games with one another. Imagine how infuriating Socrates must have been, only answering a question with another question, or Zeno of Elea, trapping curious people in an impossible paradox. Imagine trying to chill with a group of philosophers. Every time you tried to relax, someone would ask a headache-inducing question. And let's not forget how low a view many of them had of the Common Man. Overall, I don't picture the philosopher doing much; the only action I imagine philosophers taking would be speaking, pacing, or scratching a pen across a page. Yet, philosophers have inspired many of the greatest revolutions in history, all from the comfort of a chair.

## Philosophers and Social Change

"We hold these truths to be self-evident, that all men are created equal, that they are endowed by their Creator with certain unalienable rights, that among these are life, liberty, and the pursuit of happiness . . ." and so on. These principles, although they were written in 1776 and are still realized today, were not based on a philosophy created by the signers of the Declaration of Independence. They had been influenced, consciously or not, by the mind of John Locke. In his book, *Origins of the American Revolution*, Professor J. C. Miller writes,

> If any one man can be said to have dominated the political philosophy of the American Revolution, it is John Locke. American political thinking was largely an exegesis upon Locke: and patriots quoted him with as much reverence as Communists quote Marx today. Indeed, it is not too much to say that during the era of the American Revolution, the "party line" was John Locke.[37]

This was not to say that every American Revolutionist had read the writings of John Locke, or even that they knew his name, yet each one risked their life on the basis of his work. The same occurred in the Russian Revolution with the influence of Karl Marx, and the French Revolution with Jean-Jacques Rousseau. The philosopher's revolution is, at first, a quiet one. It starts like a snowball at the top of a mountain, stirring in the minds of the first adopters. Then it takes hold in the minds of future leaders, and a leader's vision becomes the manifestation of their philosophy. Philosophers create the worldview, and Changemakers attempt to realize that view through social activism. From there, the view continues to garner support and inspire conviction until it has the sweeping force of an avalanche. It is at this point that the philosopher is no longer just a thinker but also a silent revolutionist.

Karl Marx, a man whose controversial theories have placed him in the ranks as one of the most influential men of all time, stated, "Philosophy can only be realized by the abolition of the proletariat, and the proletariat can only be abolished by the realization of philosophy."[38] Philosophy and the Common Man share a symbiotic relationship. Philosophers do not become

Changemakers until their philosophy is picked up and adopted by the Common Man. Without them, philosophy would lack gravitas, and without the consistency of a philosophy, the Common Man couldn't exercise his associated power effectively. An inability to identify principles and apply philosophical thought allows those already in power to remain there to exercise their existing power without accountability.

The "goal" of philosophy is widely debated, but I don't believe it has to be tied to social change. I don't believe it has to be tied to any tangible goal at all. The philosopher should seek to find truth for the sake of truth. Changemakers can then use the philosopher's findings to push society forward, or what they believe to be forward. Ireland's President Michael D. Higgins stated "The dissemination, at all levels of society, of the tools, language and methods of philosophical enquiry can, I believe, provide a meaningful component in any concerted attempt at offering a long-term and holistic response to our current predicament."[39] The Foolish Genius does not need to have the mind of the philosopher because, to them, the direction in which society moves is not as important as the movement itself, nor is their thinking long-term or holistic. They will attach to a philosophy like anyone else, but they don't need to evaluate it with the same scrutiny. The philosophy (or, more often, the combination of philosophies) they attach to will be the one(s) that align most closely with their definition of Common Sense, and they will defend that philosophy with a conviction that does not match their will to understand it (Pitfall #5, groupthink). Since Wisdom always steers toward true progress, those who follow it must be able to question the worldview and principles of the philosophy they attach to, build upon their findings, and teach the Common Man to do the same.

Our ignorance coupled with a massive number of facts makes decision-making difficult. Facts, whenever possible, should of course be used, but when given the choice of prioritizing those facts in a way that is helpful, you need a baseline for interpretation. Philosophy is the search for truth, and it evaluates and communicates those truths in the form of principles. The cornerstone of every Changemaker is a principle that they believe is truth. If both Changemakers and the Common Man are without an understanding of principles or an elementary understanding of how to evaluate them, the principles they build on will not only be harmful and untrue but they will also be accepted as truth by the Common Man. The philosopher's role is to evaluate principles, select those they believe represent truth, and build a framework by

## A Philosopher's Revolution

which we can evaluate whether something is fact or fiction. The end result is a framework or worldview that is built solidly on principles. This worldview is then adopted by those who subscribe to it, and it informs their belief of what is right and how they should behave.

The worldviews they construct are what shape the definition of Common Sense. When two groups fundamentally disagree, they are operating out of two different philosophies. And our philosophies affect the decisions we make in every area of our lives. Although the word *philosophy* literally means the "love of wisdom," I would argue that philosophy in application would better be described as the study and evaluation of principles. You question what beliefs are held and break them down into principles, the smallest units of perceived truth. Once defined, you apply the principles in real life.

Since principles are so foundational, they are generally not constricted to a single sector of thought. The best philosophers often contributed massive and timeless works that were and are impactful outside of the realm of philosophy. Where would our current societies be without the influence of John Locke, Karl Marx, Adam Smith, Rene Descartes, or David Hume? How often are art and philosophy integrated? Where would our STEM fields be without Aristotle, Pythagoras, Darwin, Hobbes, Galileo, and Newton? And the list goes on. Think about it: why was arguably the greatest strategist and warrior of all time, Alexander the Great, mentored by Aristotle, a man who would sit and talk all day?

I couldn't care less about philosophy as a profession, but as a mental process, it is essential. It allows people to create real change and adapt to their surroundings. A philosophical mind is flexible. It can switch industries if needed, using principles as a guide to navigate the new terrain. Philosophers identify principles, consider and evaluate them, then sculpt their worldview with principles as the building blocks. Philosophy may seem complex because of the impact it has had on society (for better or for worse) but there is a real sense in which we all could be, and should be, philosophers.

It was once argued—and still is in certain circles—that only the most intelligent of thinkers could think like a philosopher. This thinking continues by some today since it seems only the most intelligent of our society often opt to challenge and create the philosophies that shape our perspectives. But this doesn't mean that philosophy is incomprehensible for the average adult. One man took that belief even further, arguing that the mind of children as young as four years old could think similarly to the philosophers of old.

## Foolish Genius

Professor Matthew Lipman was born in 1923 in Vineland, New Jersey, and like many other kids, he was a mischievous one. By his own account he was a class clown, walking the halls while "emitting wolf howls between classes and sundry practical jokes."[40] Lipman was ahead of the curve and wasn't challenged by his high school coursework. While his classmates were spending their energy absorbing material, he found himself bored. That boredom eventually boiled over; he was expelled just weeks before graduation for being too loud in the school library.

With college not an option for young Lipman, he volunteered for the Air Corps but was denied; later, he was drafted as an infantryman in 1943. After enlistment, the Army allowed him to pursue a degree in engineering, where he drew near to a professor who opened his mind to the world of philosophy. After a stint in the infantry, he saw combat, earning two Bronze Stars. Lipman then pursued a career in philosophy. He received his B.S. at Columbia University, went on to earn a doctorate there too, and become a professor. While teaching, he reached the conclusion that you also may have considered: people don't know how to think. He believed that his students had underdeveloped reasoning skills and sought to alleviate that problem by teaching logic.

At that time, the belief was that children under the age of eleven did not have the ability to think critically, but Lipman disagreed. He thought back to his childhood and concluded that children could be taught reasoning skills if they were presented in a new way. After teaching at Columbia for almost two decades, Professor Lipman paired up with Professor Ann Margaret Sharp to establish the Institute for the Advancement of Philosophy for Children (IAPC) at Montclair State College. They developed a method to foster independent thought in children called Philosophy for Children, or P4C. Lipman was a fan of Dewey's Community of Inquiry and was the first to implement it in the classroom. Lipman's first task was to get the students to start asking questions—thoughtful questions that dealt more in truth than in facts.

Every innovative thought can be traced back to an original question, which is often forgotten as your thoughts develop, and the innovations you think of will only be as good as the questions you ask. In grade school, we were always told to ask questions, and often, the best students did. Western philosophy wouldn't exist if the art of asking questions had not been established by one of the most well-known philosophers of all time, Socrates.

## A Philosopher's Revolution

The famous Socrates was certain that he knew nothing and, in that spirit, decided not to give answers but to ask questions instead. He served as a guide, helping people map out their own thoughts and principles. His style of questioning helped draw out implied assumptions and biases. The Socratic method is used heavily to educate law and medical students and has historically led to progress in the math and science fields. To this day, you can find Supreme Court Justices using this technique to measure against our nation's standards and ideals.

The Socratic method is not about destroying an opponent's opinion or evidencing that you're cerebral. When executed correctly, it's a collaborative exercise. You never really know what answers you will be left with at the end of the conversation. It's a journey that two parties embark on together. It's not a judgment of what's right or wrong like the line of questioning we often experienced in our school systems. The goal is to foster ideas that are logically sound based on the assumptions that we are consciously making. This method requires trust and the ability to dissociate your identity from your ideas.

Wisdom-led Changemakers may not question everything to the depth that a career philosopher might, but they need to at least know how to use questions to identify and evaluate their principles and values.

Instead of hoping that the top students would ask questions, like the school system does in grade school, Lipman embedded it into his pedagogy. He knew how complex philosophy can seem, so he made it simple. He took notes from great minds like Plato and Charles M. Schulz (creator of the comic strip *Peanuts*) and created stories where the characters explore concepts that cause the reader to ask philosophical questions. His goal was to inspire discussion and inquiry in the students through storytelling. In addition to instilling the importance of a time of reflection by students after reading stories, he trained teachers to facilitate thoughtful dialogue. Children face more difficult questions than we give them credit for; Lipman wanted his students to be able to confront them and discuss them with their peers.

Dialogue is a potent tool. Speaking out loud, even to yourself, is a powerful act. Studies show that simply speaking out loud can motivate us, improve our focus and performance, and reduce our self-criticism.[41] For the philosopher, one of the main reasons discussion is effective is because it tests an idea. We are able to work through ideas and think critically about them when we discuss them out loud.

## Foolish Genius

*Test* is a word that comes with a strong negative connotation. I think back to not-so-fond memories of nervously filling in bubbles and looking at the classroom clock. That's not the kind of test I'm speaking to here, as it tends to solidify already held positions and ideas and is therefore generally less valuable to the philosopher. On the other hand, discussion can test—that is, evaluate and assess—your ideas, which is not the intent of a debate. Both discussion and debate involve conflict, but conflict doesn't automatically result in changed mindsets for those involved. All forms of growth involve a measure of pain or discomfort, but how much of those you endure cannot be used as a metric to measure growth; that is, all growth involves pain, but pain is not proof of growth. The conflict that comes from a discussion should be a shared conflict among those so engaged. While conflict in debate is often combative, it's individualistic and deals with one mind finding strategies to defend and attack the opponent's strategy—and mind—much like generals from warring nations. George J. Stigler said, "A war may ravage a continent or destroy a generation without imposing new theoretical questions."[42]

Opening your thoughts to others allows them to judge your opinions, evaluate them, and challenge your way of thinking. Like all collaborative exercises, this is helpful only when you are united under one goal, approach it with a humble posture, and embrace diversity of thought. Discussion with the sole goal of affirming and maintaining your own position will lead to the acceptance of only the thoughts that align with your worldview. And when you hear new thoughts that sound as if they align with what you believe, you won't assess them but will accept them blindly. Discussion within a thoughtfully diverse group acts as a safeguard against internal validation loops.

As touched on with Pitfall #5, in a room full of people who hold the same opinions, momentum will proceed only in the direction it was already moving. If progress is the goal, relying on the insight of a homogenous group will lead to blind and incomplete change. Movement will be achieved, but progress will be no closer than before the arrival of the room of people. This is the case for all singularly minded groups, whether they be liberal intellectuals, conservative practitioners, or your group of impassioned friends. Discussion without diversity of thought can be more destructive than no discussion at all. But when all three groups are metaphorically represented, ideas can be challenged and built upon. Perspectives can be shared and used to shape a final and holistic idea.

## A Philosopher's Revolution

Think back to the last time you had an epiphany or worked through a difficult question. You experienced this amazing feeling as soon as you had that revelation, but not long after, you were faced with a decision. You could either teach others what you learned, act on that revelation and test its validity, or simply do nothing. Yes, choosing to do nothing is as much a choice as choosing to act. It's not a choice that has any clout or esteem attached to it, but it is the easiest and most popular. If I implemented everything I have learned at any point, my list of regrets would be nonexistent. We don't like to admit that we choose inaction, but we often do. Inaction comes from following a Plan of Distraction.

Although philosophers are generally accepted as being a wise bunch, they aren't popular in today's society. I'd love to ask a kid "What do you want to be when you grow up?" and hear "A philosopher" in response, but I'd be hard-pressed to find a child with such ambitions. Of course, that's understandable. Outside of the exasperating thinkers of the past, philosophy has gained a reputation of being so lofty that it has limited application to daily life. Why would the average person concern themselves with unanswerable questions, impossible metaphors, and headache-inducing riddles?

Ignorance is a human trait. It's in our nature to educate ourselves only on things that are pertinent to our daily lives or make us feel better to know them. It's understandable why the Common Man would choose to focus on more tangible concepts: the modern philosopher has failed in educating the public on how relevant philosophy can be, and more importantly, how relevant philosophical thought is to daily life. Philosophical thought has regularly been disconnected from action; this was a big issue for John Dewey, an American philosopher influential during the mid-twentieth century.

Dewey believed that any type of thought was useless if not put into action. In fact, he went a step further, believing that the process of inquiry wasn't complete until the thought had been tested past the point of discussion and the results observed. This is especially important for the Changemakers who naturally identify strongly with the titles *philosopher* or *intellectual*. Among Changemakers, there is a spectrum of thinkers and doers, and although most of them execute a combination of both, some specialize in one area more than the other. For those who lean heavily on the thinker side, their influence often lies in the thoughts they have. People might "take their word for it" and put their thoughts into practice without testing to see if their thoughts are worthy of application. Without predetermined metrics, we often identify great-sounding bad advice with Wisdom. As Changemakers, we should actively look for ways to evaluate our ideas without fear of them failing. What could be more relevant in our lives than Wisdom, or more core than our principles? Philosophy matures informal logic (critical thought), one of the core requirements of Wisdom, in itself the tool by which we make decisions and live our lives. Wisdom is far too important a tool to confuse with anything else. It has to be part of the Changemakers' process if they are to act responsibly when sparking change.

Philosophers are known more for teaching than Changemakers are, but it's a responsibility that Changemakers share. A great teacher knows how to evoke questions out of their students; they know how to facilitate discussion. But above all, they inspire their students to do the same on their own. Think back to your favorite teacher. What did they do that the others didn't? I'm sure they covered the same material other teachers covered. I'm sure they weren't the only teachers you had who were taught how to facilitate dialogue. But if they were like my favorite teachers, they went above and beyond all these things and inspired you to take action outside of the classroom. Professor Lipman went to college to become an engineer. If he had never been inspired by his English professor, a true teacher, he may have never experienced a love of philosophy or created P4C. His philosophical doppelganger may not have arrived for another century. Bad teachers tell, good teachers facilitate, and great teachers inspire. They inspire you to be a leader and to take responsibility for your future, and they help you create a plan of action toward it. Philosophers—rather, *great* philosophers—have to be great teachers. Wisdom has to be teachable to the Common Man if they are to exercise their power as an equal participant in change: philosophers must explain their viewpoint in a way that inspires the Common Man to realize their power and start a revolution.

Lipman and P4C provide a great framework for how a Changemaker should interact with the Common Man. No, Changemakers shouldn't treat the Common Man like a child; I'm not a proponent of that degree of paternalism. Incorporating Lipman's thinking is not an excuse to belittle the people you are looking to lead; it's a way to empower them with the tools to properly vet the ideas you are promoting.

# Rules of Engagement

Even when two parties go through the same process of evaluating principles, they will often disagree on which are indeed foundational. In these cases, all one can do is hold them accountable to the principles they subscribe to, both personally and through group association. For example, if you identify as a proud member of a company founded on certain principles, it is your duty to hold the company accountable to the principles that they proclaim, not in the name of prideful cynicism but in the name of growth. If you disagree with the foundational principles, it is also your responsibility to leave or attempt to change the company. Both forms of responsibility require a love for yourself and the groups you identify with. Either you love it enough to see it improve, or you love yourself enough to leave it. This same love should be applied to other Changemakers. Changemakers often yield a certain respect to other Changemakers, all the while trying to best them. But this isn't necessarily a bad thing. If one Changemaker holds a set of principles and tactics that are openly contradictory to those of a Wise Society, they should absolutely be called out for that. However, the focus should quickly move from the person to the philosophies and principles involved rather than loitering nearby the people who failed to represent them well.

The first reason we should battle principles, not people, is that humans are complex and flawed. Even our most honorable leaders will fail to uphold their principles absolutely. Take Benjamin Lay for example. Despite being one of the most thoroughly principled men I've ever heard of, he once kidnapped a child. He gave up the child, who belonged to a slaveowner, only when the authorities arrived at his cave. Lay wanted to express to the Quaker parents how African parents felt when their children were taken and sold. His intentions were the same during his other bold and theatrical gestures, yet he crossed a line many career criminals wouldn't even cross. This action was enormously hypocritical, and in doing it, he betrayed his principles and, by extension, himself.

We think highly of Benjamin Lay today 1) because of his impact as an abolitionist and 2) because we don't focus on the times when he neglected his principles. In a similar light, many people look upon George Washington and Thomas Jefferson as uncompromising heroes. One signed the Declaration of Independence and the other fought to uphold it, yet neither extended the "all men are created equal" principle to the slaves whom they owned. This chapter is not a comment on moral relativity. (In fact, nothing in this book is meant to be a scale by which you measure the Wisdom of others.) I won't try to tell you how we should hold older generations accountable or that we should or shouldn't tear down statues they erected. I am much more interested in the accountability that we apply to ourselves. If, as a society, we are against slavery completely and that is one of our strongest principles, then why does our robust prison system still uphold it? As citizens, why do we support businesses that outsource work to forced labor? I have no issue criticizing the sins of the past if it is done without the pride of today's perceived morality.

A level of responsibility and accountability is conducive to progress, but that same scrutiny will be applied to yesterday's critic. Today's newborn will be criticized by the next century's youth, and next century youth will forget the Wisdom and perspective of today. As Common Sense ebbs and flows from one generation to the next, the standard of ethics will flow with it, and the only thing that will cut through the ever-changing stream of norms are principles. As a general practice, it is always best to check yourself for the same crime you accuse others of, and in that light, I encourage all of us to reflect on what principles (once we've identified them) we have let slide in our own lives.

> As Common Sense ebbs and flows from one generation to the next, the standard of ethics will flow with it, and the only thing that will cut through the ever-changing stream of norms are principles.

The second reason we should fight against philosophies and principles—not against the people who represent them—is because the philosophies we create and follow in one situation may not be the same ones we support in other situations. It would be nice if philosophers and Changemakers were resolute in their stances throughout their lifetimes: it would make judging them much easier. Unfortunately, people change, and with them, their views on life.

In 1921, Austrian-British philosopher Ludwig Wittgenstein released his only full-length book published while he was living. In *Tractatus Logico-Philosophicus* he argued that philosophy should provide clarity and that language should create images in the audience's mind. He believed that "impractical" philosophy serves no purpose and should be discarded. He summarized the book by saying, "What can be said at all can be said clearly; and what we cannot talk about we must pass over in silence."[43]

He was happy with the book, and it was received well. He is regarded as one of the most important philosophers in the twentieth century; some have even said he is the most important philosopher since Kant. But after his death in 1951, a second book was published in which he criticized his first. In his second book, he went as far as to say that "the author of the *Tractatus* was mistaken."[44] Many of his ideas later in life were contradictory to the ideas that built his reputation. Although they were not published during his lifetime, it is honorable that he wrote out those criticisms and questioned his own principles and viewpoints. Changing your mind is not a hypocritical act, but judging others by their words and not doing the same for yourself is.

Focusing on philosophies instead of the people behind them allows people to dissociate from their ideas. People are more likely to question their own thinking if they aren't demonized in the process. Regret at some point in your life is inevitable. Even Einstein, in 1945, wrote "The release of atomic power has changed everything except our way of thinking.... the solution to this problem lies in the heart of mankind. If only I had known, I should have become a watchmaker."[45] The trick is using that regret, and that's possible only when it causes a timely realization of values and a shift in principles. Giving people room to rethink and adjust their philosophy promotes growth over correctness.

The third and final reason principles should be the target of criticism and not the individual representing them is that philosophies don't bend to submission the same way people do. Oppression breeds activism. Keep in mind that any group who experiences a perceived injustice will use that oppression to justify their beliefs. No one gets hit and thinks, *Maybe they had a point.* In today's world, philosophies cannot be wiped out through violence. In the past, people may have gotten away with that through genocide or humiliation tactics, but today, philosophies spread like wildfire. They aren't segregated by people groups to the same extent that they used to be. Today, attacking a people group will either cause immediate uproar, if they are in favor with the Common Man, or if the Common Man views them as the oppressor, the philosophy will go underground, creating a grassroots following that will either die out or grow and take a new form once the tides change. The loving characteristic of Wisdom applies to people, not abstract concepts like principles. If you want to avoid getting lost in the opinions and diluted philosophies of the day, make sure you choose to fight your battles by a defined set of principles.

## Principles of a Wise Society

Every Wisdom-led Changemaker has a duty to uphold and protect the principles they subscribe to. Not only is it good leadership, but it also lowers your cognitive dissonance and keeps your mind at peace. That said, protecting your principles will be more about rejection than it will be about acceptance. The most common way to break down your principles is to adopt other philosophies as opposed to removing them. We live in a culture that will sharply criticize anyone who rejects principles that align with the current definition of Common Sense. If your goal is popularity, as it often is for the Common Man, principles should not be a concern. Once you've identified the foundational principles that you hold on to, you spend the rest of your life realizing the full extent of those principles.

Conversely, there are three principles that Wisdom protects and that every Changemaker should seek to implement:

1. All foundational principles are subject to the characteristics of Wisdom.

    Changemakers are principled people, but even the best criminals have a code. The worst people in history may have been principled, yet they neglected the loving nature of Wisdom. Keeping in mind the characteristics of Wisdom will preclude the repeated implementation of principles that have been used to cause immeasurable harm.

2. Everyone has a purpose in life.

    Every single person, Common Man and Changemaker alike, has an equally deserving and important role to play. Beyond that, without a strong sense of that purpose, it would be impossible to uphold the principles of a Wise Society over a lifetime.

3. Everyone is a leader.

    Everyone is not meant to be a Changemaker, but everyone is supposed to lead. Do you have to change the definition of Common Sense in a group to have influence over someone? Of course not. In relation to the previous principle, if our lives have a unique purpose, then our lives need to be self-led to some extent or else you'd be living in the purpose of whomever you were following. On a more social note, parents lead their children, older siblings lead younger siblings, and friends lead friends. This is why three out of the four I's of Change deal with personal leadership. Life is too social to neglect the role that we all play as leaders.

Just as the US Constitution serves as a standard by which we can improve as a nation, constantly working toward ensuring the principles cited in it are realized through policy, law, and practice, the Wise Society principles should be used as a basis by which we prove ourselves. How are we living out the characteristics of Wisdom? What principles do I hold that perhaps oppose them and therefore lead us away from a Wise Society? What does it mean to have a purpose, and how do we get a sense of one? What skills are needed to walk in it? What are the responsibilities of a leader, and what am I doing that undermines the leadership of my constituents? These are the types of questions that allow us to improve ourselves and our communities.

# 6

# Purpose

*Nothing is more creative…nor destructive…than a brilliant mind with a purpose.* – Dan Brown, *Inferno*

---

### Takeaways
- The motivating power of purpose is what fuels Changemakers to continuously uphold their principles.
- A sense of purpose is developed, not necessarily found.
- Developing a sense of purpose is a creative process.

---

So far we've been discussing the *what* of change. As great as *what* can be (and we'll go more into its value later), *why* is much more interesting. *What* is objective: it's productive, clear, and flat. But *why* is vibrant: motivations and stories emerge from the *why*.

When you meet a stranger, the question "What do you do?" is bound to come up within the first minute of conversation. Sometimes a person's answer is inherently interesting, but these conversations don't typically become memorable until someone asks, "*Why* do you do what you do?" The most common answers to this question start with some variation of "I knew I wanted to help people so…" or people give a roundabout answer explaining how their motives were to help themselves so they can later help others (this one is famous among entrepreneurs). But more often than not, a person's *why* comes around to using a skill to help others or to contribute to a larger cause.

The passion surrounding the *why* seems to be a powerful motivating force, so much so that people change their demeanor when they start to speak about it. I had heard quite a few people use Nietzsche's quote "He who has a *why* to live for can bear almost any *how*,"[46] but the people I had heard this from were often fairly well-off. Who needs a *why* to deal with the *how*, when, most of the time, money can do the trick?

In order to validate Nietzsche's claim, I searched for examples of people whose lives were shattered to the degree that their *why* was all they had left. It did not take me long until I stumbled upon the story of Viktor Frankl.

## The Story of Viktor Frankl

Frankl was a middle child born in Vienna, Austria, in March 1905. He quickly grew accustomed to a life of struggle as a preteen during World War I, when he and his siblings would on occasion beg local farmers for food. While facing these challenges he began to display his brilliance in academics. As early as junior high school, Frankl took a deep interest in psychiatry and started taking adult night classes. By the end of high school he was corresponding with one of the most famous psychologists of all time, Sigmund Freud. By fifteen, Frankl learned hypnosis and gave his first public lecture on a topic that would define his life's work. It was entitled "On the Meaning of Life."

As his career progressed, the young psychiatrist continued to dive into the intersection of psychology, therapy, and philosophy. His meaning-centered approach, logotherapy, gained him notoriety and would be the foundation for his initiatives moving forward. At twenty-three, he established counseling centers for adolescents, and two years later, his work was credited for the significant drop in youth suicides within the schools he worked. What was once called an "epidemic of teen suicides" became an almost nonexistent problem in Vienna.

After earning his medical degree, Frankl occupied the position of Chief Doctor over the "Suicidals Pavilion for Women," where he saw three thousand patients per year. His approach was effective, medically sound, and centered around the concept that life has meaning, and every human benefits from searching for it.

At this point, Frankl's life on the surface looked pretty good. He had challenged some of the greatest minds of his time, validated his theory, and was working as a chief doctor implementing his own ideas. In 1937, he decided to take this robust foundation and start a private practice. Unfortunately, his timing was less than stellar. Months after launching, Nazi restrictions forced him to close the doors to his business, although he stayed vocal about the misuse of German Nationalism in therapy and was allowed to serve as a director in a clinic.

The next few years would be tumultuous for Frankl and his family. Although being offered the opportunity to leave Austria, Viktor decided to remain in the country to be with his parents, who had not been given the same opportunity. Being Jewish in Austria, they were forced to submit to the numerous rules and restrictions placed upon them. Despite the danger, Frankl still used his position as a clinic director for good, ignoring Nazi procedures and protecting the mentally ill, who would have otherwise been killed.

In 1941, Viktor and his family were apprehended and taken to a concentration camp. During his three years of captivity in four different camps, he endured some of the worst horrors mankind has ever seen. He and his wife were forced to abort their child, he lost his mother to the gas chamber, he was with his father when he died of exhaustion, and he was separated from his wife and siblings, later finding out they died at Auschwitz. Despite all of this, Frankl still worked within the camp to meet with the new arrivals. He even organized a first response team to help the new arrivals adjust to their ghastly environment and deal with their psychological needs.

When I reflect on Frankl's story, I often think about the widowhood effect, the rather sad phenomena where someone's spouse dies and the remaining spouse, while being in good health, dies shortly after. In one particular study, those who witnessed the death of their spouse had a sixty-six percent increase in the probability that they would also die in the next three months.[47] It has been said that the pain and loss they experience quite literally breaks their heart, making them lose their will to continue on. With this in mind, stories like Frankl's are all the more extraordinary. This man went through suffering I could never imagine and still went above and beyond his own subsistence to assist in the survival and mental health of others.

In 1945, the camp where Frankl resided was captured by US troops, and Frankl walked free from one of the worst terrors in human history. Within the next year, over a span of nine days, he dictated the book *Ein Psycholog erlebt das Konzentrationslager (A Psychologist Experiences the Concentration Camp)*, which would later be translated into English and retitled as *Man's Search for Meaning*. Frankl then continued his work, eventually remarrying and living a long life, dying at the ripe age of ninety-two years old.

His book has sold over fifteen million copies and was listed by the Library of Congress as "one of the ten most influential books in the U.S."[48]

Given its reach, this might not have been the first time you heard his story, but every reader is impacted. Frankl was a living testimony to his own teachings, and he requoted Nietzsche in stating, "A man who becomes conscious of the responsibility he bears toward a human being who affectionately waits for him, or to an unfinished work, will never be able to throw away his life. He knows the 'why' for his existence, and will be able to bear almost any 'how.'"[49]

## What Is Purpose?

Viktor Frankl was a Changemaker who experienced things most people (Changemaker or otherwise) couldn't imagine going through, and he attributed his ability to endure to his sense of purpose. One of the key principles I mentioned in the section about the principles of a Wise Society is that everyone has a purpose. But what does that mean? The Dalai Lama said that "Our prime purpose in this life is to help others. And if you can't help them, at least don't hurt them."[50] But how do we know who to help and how to help them?

Can two people share the same purpose? If I were to work at a factory my entire life right next to someone else who worked at that same factory, would we share the same purpose? To answer these questions, look no further than the animal kingdom. Do wolves and coyotes have the same purpose? It seems like a silly question, but allow me.

Wolves and coyotes hang around the same crowd, look similar enough, and can both take down big prey. I don't know how many times I've been in the car with my family and heard: "Look it's a wolf!" "No, it's a coyote." "What's the difference?" Wolves are known for their strength and unity and have earned the title of apex, but the coyote might be the apex predator if wolves were not present. Why does the coyote exist when the wolf is present? And if the wolf were removed, would the coyote step into its place and leave the ecosystem reasonably unaffected?

Thankfully, these questions don't have to be left up to speculation. During the early 1900s in Yellowstone National Park, wolves were removed from the equation almost completely. Hunting laws were much looser, and lone wolves were seen only on occasion and never in pairs. This left the throne open, and who else would step in but the coyote? As the coyotes became the apex, things started to change.

## Foolish Genius

Although coyotes can bring down big prey, they usually play it safe and pick on someone their own size. With wolves gone, elk began to thrive. This doesn't sound too bad. Wolves, an animal seen as dangerous to humans, are gone, and elk, a majestic creature, are doing well. But as time went on, more changes began to take place, and the role wolves played in that ecosystem became more apparent. As elk grew in population, beavers seemed to vanish just as quickly. As it turns out, elk graze on the same plants beavers use for food and dam building. The diminishing beaver population led to a shift in the wetlands and many animals associated with the wetlands (birds, bugs, etc.) leaving the area. On top of that, animals that scavenge on dead wolves also suffered. With the increase in coyotes, the new apex predator, antelope and small animals decreased, leaving fewer to eat for foxes. All this disruption occurred because one species decreased.

This persisted until the late 1990s, when the gray wolf was reintroduced to the area and dethroned the coyote. Balance was returned to Yellowstone, and our original question was answered. Wolves and coyotes have overlapping niches, but their purposes are widely different.

Your purpose is the summation of the niches you are designed to fill, spanning from your birth to death. Purpose is the role you play in the world, while your niche is the role you play in a specific community. Think of your purpose as a puzzle and your niche as a puzzle piece. You figure it out as you go through life, and the further you walk in it, the more you understand it. Humans are dynamic; we have several characteristics and traits, and each one ties us to a community. My name is David Mahan, and I am a black male, a son, a brother, friend, mentor, mentee, and so on. The name "Mahan" ties me to my family, "black" ties me to a race, "male" ties me to a sex, and each part of my identity is tied to a relationship.

Each of our characteristics and titles have communities and subcommunities associated with them. The role you play in one community may not be the same role you play in another, and that's okay: one puzzle piece may look similar to another, but each one is unique.

We should be constantly growing, and in order for that to happen, we may not be able to remain in the environments and communities we are comfortable in. If you are true to your principles, it doesn't hurt to know how to express them in a number of ways. As you move from one community to the next, your niche may change, but each niche is crucial to complete the entire picture. Purpose, like Wisdom, can be difficult to understand conceptually, but also like Wisdom, it can be better understood by discussing its characteristics. Let's do that.

## **Process-Oriented**

As great as they are, social movements just don't hit like they used to. There's something about the old movements that made history even without the ease of today's communications. People gathered in the streets at the risk of death. These movements were harder to scale, but those that did had true impact. I know, I sound like a grandparent giving the "back in my day" spiel, but when it comes to social movements, there might be something to old-time thinking.

The combination of globalization and democratization has made it easier than ever for someone with no charisma or leadership ability to command the attention of millions. We call it going viral. We have influencers and thought leaders catching their time in the spotlight and doing everything they can to get their fifteen minutes of fame to last a lifetime. I don't blame them. They work hard and catch their big break, and the thought of going back to where they started from is enough to drive any ambitious person mad. It's human nature. That fight to maintain a sense of control takes place in everyone's life sooner or later, Changemaker or otherwise. And because of that, it's no surprise that we see it happening in social movements.

Have you ever watched a one-hit wonder crumble under the pressure of their newfound fame? The reason is the same that childhood stars often cannot survive their eventual fade from fame, sometimes even losing a portion of themselves. The one-hit wonder and childhood stars rose to a place of power without building up the muscles it takes to sustain their fame. You are only as strong as your character allows you to be, and the people who achieve fame and power too quickly soon realize that it's a process to build the character needed to survive success. We see the same thing happening in business, community organizations, and social movements. People can get the support of one million strangers within a month, but once their viral moment subsides, they have neither the team nor the strategy to be effective long-term.

Of course, viral moments can be extraordinarily helpful. Take Kony 2012 or the ALS Ice Bucket Challenge, for example. The Kony 2012 video ran thirty minutes and led to action against Joseph Kony, cult leader and war criminal. Although Kony was not captured, children's lives were saved, and the entire world became aware of his crimes against humanity. The ALS Ice Bucket Challenge generated more than one hundred million dollars, increasing the ALS annual research budget by almost two hundred percent. Even though these two viral trends were impactful, they didn't change the definition of Common Sense. The search for Kony officially ended a couple of years after it started, and most Americans wouldn't be able to tell you that ALS stands for amyotrophic lateral sclerosis. Viral moments can be extremely helpful, but they are more effective when put in the context of campaigns as opposed to social movements.

The difference between a movement and a campaign is the same as the difference between a purpose and a niche. A social movement is made up of campaigns, which are smaller, more focused initiatives that contribute to a larger vision. Viral moments and campaigns have short-term impact but are often ineffective when instilling lifestyle changes. Social movements can create lifestyle changes but fail if their work can be undone in a single generation. They have to create lasting change.

Social movements deal with purpose, while campaigns focus on smaller goals. In order for movements to succeed, they have to go through the same iterative process that Changemakers do to stay relevant and induce change toward their vision of a Wise Society. For example, say the goal of a social movement is to end prejudice against the Jewish community. Changemakers may create a successful campaign to build awareness of anti-Semitic hate crimes and another campaign to change legislation. With each passing success, the Changemakers will have to explain to their followers that their participation is just as necessary to the eighth campaign as it was on the first. At this point in the movement, the vision—a world without anti-Semitism—is as valid as ever, but if Changemakers fail to iterate their strategy, they will be deemed irrelevant (unless a tragedy occurs that sparks the people's motivation again). This iterative process will ensure that the viral moments that may bless your movement won't also destroy them.

Another reason why purpose, much like Wisdom, should be viewed as a process more than a set destination or accomplishment is because humans are nearsighted. When you are lost, you may know where you wish to end up, but you still need a process to find your path to get there. Changemakers have an idea of where they want to end up (the vision), but they may struggle to decide what steps lead to that end. As necessary as it is to have a vision of what you are working toward, understanding the process of purpose will allow you to work toward that vision intentionally and unceasingly. It gives you a sense of direction in a life filled with unending opportunities.

## Selfishly Altruistic

Purpose, just like Wisdom, is selfishly altruistic. It is inherently just as much about you, the individual, as it is about the world around you. A deserving purpose will extend past your lifetime. The world is filled with an infinite number of problems, and given our human nature, we will never achieve utopia, so there will never be a time when our mission as members of society is truly fulfilled. The issues of the world are reborn with every generation. Never will there be a time with too much justice, too little racism, too few murders, and so on. To say you have completed your purpose would mean that the remainder of your life is no longer useful to the rest of the world. Society is much too interdependent, social, and flawed to say that you can no longer contribute to the world in any way. A purpose can be accurately evaluated only at the point of death, and for those who truly live in purpose, their death progresses the same purpose in which they lived. Anything less than a loving purpose that supersedes a single individual is either an unrealistic goal or an unloving mission. Regardless, it does not lead to true progress.

> Purpose, just like Wisdom, is selfishly altruistic. It is inherently just as much about you, the individual, as it is about the world around you.

Walking in purpose is a win-win. The first win is altruistic: it's a win for the community. Purpose deals with providing value; it's the combination of niches that you fill. The size or number of those niches does not matter as long as you are filling the niches you are meant to fill. By doing so, you are providing value. The gray wolf plays its part and, unknowingly, keeps the entire ecosystem intact. The wolves provide value and have an impact, even though they may not be appreciated (like many leaders) by those in the community they are impacting.

The second win is a win for you. Altruism gets a bad rap because those who focus on human-centered jobs are often stereotyped as also being financially dependent. This perception is spurred by scores of poorly run nonprofits. But in the same way that nonprofits can be well-run and, in some cases, fairly sustainable, altruism can benefit the individual providing value. If you recall from Chapter 3, the goal of a Wise Society is a high quality of life, which can be broken down into widespread wealth, health, and meaning. Purpose, more than any other concept in this book, touches on all three.

The meaning and wealth aspects come from the value you provide for other people. Your niche gives meaning to your day-to-day activities, and a sense of purpose gives meaning to your life as a whole. Walking in purpose increases your odds of being successful because it is motivational in nature and can't be fulfilled without adding value to others. Studies have shown that older individuals live longer if they have a sense of purpose.[51]

Beyond that, Changemakers need the motivation that comes from walking in purpose because creating change is not easy. Most entrepreneurs fail to succeed within the first few years of business, and the majority of business owners can't afford to pay themselves a living wage for those early years. Those who do make it often say two things: "provide value" and some variation of "do what you love." Creating lasting change is much harder than starting a successful business. Without a sense of purpose, there is no chance of navigating all the struggles Changemakers face. Without a cause and convincing principles, it's not worth the trouble.

Beyond the benefits, purpose has an immense impact on your life. The John Templeton Foundation summed it up beautifully with their statement:

> Purpose is a central component of most leading conceptions of optimal human development and psychological well-being (Bronk, 2013). Psychological well-being refers to not just the absence of negative states (e.g. depression and anxiety) but also the presence of positive ones (e.g. optimism, hope, life satisfaction), and discovering a purpose in life is associated with a wide range of positive states, including feeling good about oneself (self-esteem) and one's abilities (self-efficacy; Boyle, Buchman, Wilson, & Bennett, 2009; Kass et al., 1991; Lyubomirsky, Tkach, & DiMatteo, 2005; Steger & Frazier, 2005).[52]

Having a sense of purpose does wonders for your health on several levels, as the last fifty years of research on the topic indicates.[53] Walking in purpose can be just as selfishly motivated as exercising daily. This is another reason why Changemakers should not only walk in purpose themselves but also keep the purpose of those they work with in mind. No one purpose should be viewed as more important, and the lack of purpose in today's society should no longer be discussed only by those with a spiritual inclination or an entrepreneurial bent. A purposeless life needs to be recognized as the health crisis that it is. Living life without the one concept that ties together all three components of a high-quality life can lead to true suffering.

## Conceptual Components of Purpose

Purpose can be a polarizing topic, and when I think about what America's Common Sense says about purpose, my brain is left going in circles. On one hand, we live in a society where positive psychologists and Simon Sinek quotes run rampant. They are thrown around by every business podcast, self-help Instagram page, and mindset coach on the Internet with statements like "Find your why" and blog posts on "How to find your path." These are all centered around the concept that you have a purpose, and you just have to go out there and find it.

On the other hand, purpose discussions that I hear most often adopt a more humanist view. Someone hearing the phrase "purpose in life" thinks, *Nah I'm just gonna do me. Why live my life in obligation to others if I can't control what happens to them?* The positive psychologist may think of this as lazy, but to be fair, we can influence but not control our outcomes. In one way, this is a humble approach: why would we have the hubris to think that our lives, if walked a certain way, would have an impact on the world, when after all the Changemakers of the past have come and gone and we are still left with the same struggles we've had since Mesopotamia? This view suggests all humans have done is innovate to make our struggling more efficient.

The difference between these two ways of thinking is exposed with an understanding of the three qualities everyone needs in order to experience a sense of purpose.

## *1. Hope*

You have to hope that what you are working toward will benefit mankind. Without hope you are left with either apathy or despair, and neither are effective long-term motivators to creating positive change. Why work toward a better future if the work you do has no impact, or worse, a negative one? Hope provides you with the directional aspect of purpose.

## Foolish Genius

Pulitzer Prize nominee and decorated author Barbara Kingsolver put it beautifully when she said, "The very least you can do in your life is figure out what you hope for. And the most you can do is live inside that hope. Not admire it from a distance but live right in it, under its roof."[54]

As a Changemaker, hope is something you will have to guard with your life, and it better be undergirded by more than good intentions. Your hope will be what others will follow, and this snowball effect will motivate others to fight for Wisdom-led change even after you are gone.

## *2. Faith*

Every successful form of change requires faith in order to make a true impact. Without faith, you would be left with the fear and uncertainty that comes from the unknown or an ego so large that it thinks change isn't necessary. With faith, you can overcome the doubt and fear that will encompass you during the difficult portions of your journey. Without faith, change of any kind would not be difficult: it would be impossible.

You need to have faith in your principles/belief system, your worldview, and your decisions. If you don't believe that what you are doing on a day-to-day basis has a positive impact, then you will not be motivated long-term to see your efforts come to fruition. But more important than the faith you have in yourself, you need faith that your principles are in fact the truth. You need faith that, despite your limited knowledge, the principles and belief system you have built a life and movement on will guide you and anyone who follows. Now, implementing this faith should come only after evaluation and testing of your principles as discussed earlier, but then the data should be extrapolated beyond what you have experienced.

This type of faith isn't blind. It's built in the second "I" of change, Intimacy. What would you do if a stranger walked up to you and asked, "May I borrow your car for an hour? I need it to drive to the grocery store." If you're like me, it's an easy no. I consider myself to be a giving person, but I would not let a total stranger take my car. But if one of my close friends or family asked, my answer is an almost immediate yes. That's because my faith in the people I have gone through life with is much greater than someone whose character I have no basis for judging. Faith is built up through intimacy—the intimacy that comes with work, sacrifice, and earned trust. That earned trust comes from the process of questioning, testing, and evaluating your principles and relationships.

## *3. Personal Responsibility*

Last, the third component everyone needs in order to experience a sense of purpose is personal responsibility. If you remember, personal responsibility is in the list of requirements for Wisdom. Personal responsibility is the glue that keeps every other component of Wisdom together, and it has the same function when it comes to purpose. Hoping that a particular future will arrive would be pointless if no one were ever working toward it. Then, and only then, should hope be abandoned. Hope and faith are useless without personal responsibility and the work that comes from it.

Work and responsibility go hand in hand. When you interview for a job, the company informs you of the responsibilities you will take on, and as you work hard and demonstrate you are reliable, you will be given more responsibilities (if the company is managed well). You cannot work without absorbing some duties or responsibilities. Changemakers carry an immense amount of responsibility because change as a process is very hard work. For any form of personal development, you must take overt responsibility for your actions in order to grow. When leading a fight for social change or accepting the authority given to you by someone, you are also responsible (in part) for your followers' actions. Responsibility, when paired with hope and faith, pushes you to continue forward, no matter what obstacles arise. Responsibility gives you the drive to endure. As Viktor Frankl says,

> Ultimately, man should not ask what the meaning of his life is, but rather must recognize that it is he who is asked. In a word, each man is questioned by life; and he can only answer to life by answering for his own life; to life he can only respond by being responsible.[55]

Responsibility is a key component, one you can't ignore when attempting to develop a sense of purpose or share it with someone else. A beautiful example of all three components (hope, faith, and personal responsibility) in action is parenthood. Every good parent loves their child and wants the best for them. They hope that their child lives a fulfilling and happy life, they have enough faith that they can prepare them for that future, and they take responsibility for taking care of that child until they are able to handle that responsibility on their own. Take away any one of the three components and parenting becomes more of a burden than an honor.

# Foolish Genius

Your purpose is an honor. Having the ability to change the world in a way that only you can is an honor. But as soon as you lose hope in your mission, faith in your strategy and worldview, or responsibility in your role, your purpose will seem much more like a burden or controlled narrative. With all three working in tandem, you will have the motivation and determination to fight unceasingly alongside your team.

## A Sense of Purpose

Since your purpose is essentially the culmination of all the gaps you fill in the world, pursuing it can be broken down into a continual process of identifying, understanding, and filling those gaps. Social movements that do not face a challenge or a "bad guy" fail. Similarly, if participants within a social movement don't feel challenged or needed, the movement will die. People, just like social movements, cannot reap the fulfilling and replenishing benefits of walking in purpose without adhering to the gap-filling process.

A sense of purpose lets you know that you are filling a gap. It may or not be the gap you are supposed to fill or a gap that should be filled, but when a sense of purpose is paired with information from the previous five chapters, you can be confident that the purpose you are pursuing is a deserving one. An effective process to develop a sense of purpose has four steps.

### *1. Internal Self-Awareness*

A month or two after COVID-19 hit America, there was an interesting gap when no one knew what to do. Scientists were working, politicians were at a loss and didn't know whom to believe, citizens were in a confused panic, and all people were isolated and forced to be with themselves. Isolation and silence are powerful because they facilitate you noticing yourself. I love focusing on these moments because they're so rare nowadays. Quiet moments without distractions are hard to come by, but they are nonetheless necessary.

In the same way that love is found in the perfect balance of two mediums (e.g., independence and dependence, logic and emotion, or commitment and intimacy), purpose requires an examination of both social interaction and self-reflection. How much someone should prioritize one aspect should be determined by how much their personality or circumstances tend toward the opposite side. In America, there is no shortage of distractions, as attention is the most valuable form of currency. So when I ask someone about purpose, they tend to focus on extrinsic motivations but not much on intrinsic motivations. This makes discovering one's purpose almost impossible. How can someone hope to begin to understand something as powerful as purpose without ever examining themselves: their motivations, desires, inhibitions, biases, and everything else that forms how they see the world? Absent a self-examination process, one cannot form or be conscious of their own perspective, and will, in turn, seek to fulfill a purpose that would better suit whoever's perspective they adopted.

Everyone thinks, but whether you beneficially think for yourself is determined by how well you know and understand your principles and your perspectives in relation to the world around you. As a leader, the consequences of avoiding your responsibilities or neglecting your principles are similar to those of not pursuing purpose: you unknowingly follow someone else's. It's in our nature to follow, but what sets leaders apart is their awareness of what they are following. The first step to intentionally walking in purpose is becoming self-aware. Self-awareness doesn't create anything, it only pushes things to the surface and allows us to act with a more accurate perspective.

For Changemakers, self-awareness is not always incentivized. But if you incentivize a fool with a following, they won't reconsider their stance; they'll double down on it. An audience is validation that other people relate to what you represent—your definition of Common Sense. All too often, enjoying an audience is used as a metric for something else like intelligence, truth, or even Wisdom. Those who have grown accustomed to that validation are more likely to ignore their own ignorance and dive deeper into whatever appeals to their audience, whether true or ridiculous.

Dr. Tasha Eurich specializes in self-awareness, self-insight, and their relationship to leadership. As much as we'd like to believe otherwise, humans are not very self-aware, and before you consider that a problem experienced more by the Common Man, slow your roll. In a *Harvard Business Review* article discussing her research, Dr. Eurich writes:

> Relative to lower-level leaders, higher-level leaders more significantly overvalued their skills (compared with others' perceptions). In fact, this pattern existed for 19 out of the 20 competencies the researchers measured, including emotional self-awareness, accurate self-assessment, empathy, trustworthiness, and leadership performance.[56]

Foolish Genius

Her research estimates that less than fifteen percent of leaders are truly self-aware (although ninety-five percent believe they are), so of that fifteen percent, high-level leaders are in the minority.[57] This is just another example of how ego can creep in and keep Changemakers from walking in purpose and Wisdom, and why inspiring trust and soliciting feedback as a servant-leader is more effective in the long run than traditional leadership methods.

Dr. Eurich and her team split self-awareness into two categories: internal and external. She states that internal self-awareness consists of "how clearly we see our own values, passions, aspirations, fit with our environment, reactions (including thoughts, feelings, behaviors, strengths, and weaknesses), and impact on others."[58] You can build this form of self-awareness through self-reflection, but the mind is not always a pleasant place. If you are like me, getting stuck in your own head can mess with you for days, if not longer. Introspection is a dangerous game and should be respected as such. When successful, it can lead to a clearer sense of purpose, a stronger sense of control in life, more contentment, and stronger relationships. When unsuccessful, it can lead to depression, anxiety, a lower self-esteem, and a worse social life. The mind is the most powerful tool at your disposal, so be cautious, but it is still a tool, and you can learn to use it to your advantage.

Since introspection remains the most popular path to self-insight, let's break down the one simple word that can turn a positive intent to know yourself into a self-destructive habit: *why*. When we take time to analyze ourselves, we tend to ask *why* questions: Why did this happen? Why am I like this? Why is my leftover sandwich not in the fridge? Dr. Eurich and her team found that asking *why* often misleads your brain into picking an answer that seems to make sense but is not reality. We tend to reject criticism when answering *why*, so we place blame where convenient. It gives the illusion of self-awareness with none of the benefits.

When Dr. Eurich and her team returned to their participants, they found a group of "self-awareness unicorns" (those who went from scoring low in self-awareness to scoring high). These unicorns rarely asked *why*. Instead their introspection was filled with questions that began with the word *what*: what dialogue is inside my head, what are my interests, what can I do to respond better? Asking *what* allows us to manage and process our emotions without placing blame. Although *why* questions are great for motivating change and are necessary for any Changemaker, *what* questions keep us sane enough to get there. *Why* should be for looking toward the future and *what* for looking to, and learning from, the past.

Understanding yourself will help you build faith in yourself and in the strategy you choose to follow. It's important to reiterate that walking in purpose is filling gaps in the world that you are uniquely designed to fill. These gaps are not just physical. If you have a sweet spirit that can reach people who are guarded, many of the gaps you will fill could be emotional ones. Of course, this doesn't preclude you from doubling as a phenomenal project manager or businessperson, deriving practical and physical solutions for a different target audience. Learning to look at yourself as a dynamic individual will allow you to engage the creative strategies discussed in the next chapter, and it will open you up to make changes in innovative ways.

Changemakers should be asking questions like the following examples for internal self-awareness:

What thoughts give me hope?

What are my personality traits?

What are my skills?

What are my values? (Based on my current actions and demonstrated priorities)

What are my principles? (Refer back to chapters 4 and 5)

What places and experiences in my life have shaped my perspective?

What have I overcome in my life?

What issues and injustices move me to action?

What inspires and excites me?

Whom do I admire, and what did they do to earn that admiration?

If a documentary was to be made about my life, what would I want the takeaway to be?

## *2. External Self-Awareness*

The second form of self-awareness is external, which focuses more on our understanding of how others see us. Dr. Eurich notes that "people who know how others see them are more skilled at showing empathy and taking others' perspectives."[59] Empathy, a characteristic of Wisdom itself, is also tied to pursuing purpose and effective leadership. Unfortunately, having a high internal self-awareness does not mean that you also have a high external self-awareness; in fact, Dr. Eurich's team found no relationship between the two. Growing in external self-awareness takes a dedication to trust and accepting feedback, two things that leaders must continuously and intentionally seek.

Changemakers should be asking questions like these to understand how others see them:

What do people around me say my value proposition is?

What do people believe my values and principles are?

According to my team, what strengths and weaknesses do I have?

What can I do to build more trust?

What can I do to realize my principles more fully?

When my team hears my name, what words come to mind?

## *3. Strategy*

Steps 3 and 4 move on to the creative process. During the first two steps, you are developing as a human and a Changemaker, yes, but you are also creating the components for your strategy. If you have answered the example questions in Step 1, assume you've discovered that injustices, issues, and inspirations move you to action. Now write down your top three and choose what you want to change. Many people are inspired to create change after an incident or a "spark." If this is the case and you are certain of the area you want to impact, there is no need to note other topics. For each one you record, provide three to five high-level strategies for how you can make an impact in that space.

For example, if you are certain that police brutality is a problem (one that spurs you to action), and you know you are not connected to any policymakers, but you are an excellent educator, maybe your strategy could be creating a program that teaches people about the intricacies of police brutality. Or you could create an alternative training program to be used by police stations that are looking to avoid mistakes and the bad PR that comes with harming minorities.

Once you have your nine to fifteen strategies (three to five for each of the three topics you recorded), list the barriers that would keep you from accomplishing each strategy. For the police training example, a barrier may be not having much time, as you are working two jobs. Another may be that you don't know how to build a training program, a third that you lack knowledge about how police train their cadets, and a fourth the negative relationship your local police station has with police brutality protesters. Your ability to overcome these barriers will inform your decision on what strategy you choose to implement.

Your issues may not address something as controversial as police brutality, and your strategy may not be as bold as changing how cadets are trained. As long as the topic moves you to action, the change can create a higher quality of life for the Common Man, and if your tactics and principles follow those that are defined in this book, you are good to go. Nobody's purpose should be seen as more or less important than that of someone else. If all you can afford to do is babysit the children of the person creating the training program, the role you play is no less valid or important. Do you recall who has more impact: the person who starts a movement, or the first follower who validates their conviction?

Once you have a list of strategies to choose from, select your top three. These three should be challenging but still achievable. All that is left is making a plan that works for you.

## *4. Bridge the Gap*

Bridging the gap is about going from an idea to a realistic plan. You may need to develop other skills to achieve the goals and to walk out the strategies you listed above. Do you have the knowledge necessary to enact these strategies? If not, how could you learn or who could you network with to fill that gap? What groups are already involved in this area, and how could you join them? We all have limited time and resources, so it's important to be intentional with our activities. Start assigning yourself small tasks that will help you fill the gaps that are preventing you from engaging one of the strategies you listed in step three. Keep in mind that the barriers you listed should not be insurmountable, but they shouldn't be so easy that you can accomplish them without creativity.

"Complete these steps, and you will know everything about your lifelong purpose"—wouldn't that be nice! These four steps outline a process that can lead you to better understand your niches and realize your purpose over time. They will help you with direction, but not necessarily execution. A few pages on purpose will not do the topic justice, and what your purpose is, I have no way of knowing. What that process looks like will be different for every individual. It could be as time-consuming as starting a business or as simple as cutting out a bad habit that's inhibiting your growth.

No matter what your path is, keep in mind that purpose is developed more than it is discovered. Keep moving and stay intentional, and your understanding of your purpose will grow over time.

These steps are iterative. The more you return to them, the better you will understand your current niches and the niches you may expand into. They are a way that you can start identifying how you have already been working toward your purpose and how you can continue, no matter where you are in life. As you dive deeper into purpose, you'll find that the process of purpose is very much a creative one.

> Creativity can exist outside of purpose, but walking in purpose requires creativity.

## Creative Process of Shared Purpose

Creativity can exist outside of purpose, but walking in purpose requires creativity. Every person should seek to develop a sense of purpose, but organizations and Changemakers are faced with the additional task of inspiring a sense of purpose in their membership. Creative teams are successful only when they are aligned under one goal or a shared purpose.

We'll explore the concept of creativity in the next couple of chapters, and most of the examples in those chapters look at creativity from an individualistic point of view. This is partly due to the importance personal creativity has in our everyday lives and partly because of the limited research done on distributed creativity (creativity that is produced through collaboration or the social interactions of many). But as a Changemaker, group or distributed creativity should be just as important to you as personal creativity. If you get a group of people together, the outcomes need to be far greater than any one team member could have produced on their own, and for this, you'll need a shared purpose.

Purpose is something that you will never fully understand in its entirety, until (maybe) the moment you leave this earth. But until then, you may understand pieces of it, and the more pieces you have, the more accurate your vision will become. Purpose and creativity have very different meanings, but when broken down into their components, they overlap a lot. Both require an understanding of yourself as an individual, an understanding of the holes you are uniquely designed to fill, and an idea about how you will fill them. Again, creativity can be applied to anything and can exist without a sense of purpose, but a sense of purpose cannot be achieved without creativity. When paired together, they complement each other nicely.

In a group setting, distributed creativity occurs when the individuals come together to create, and the closer they are as a unit, the more creative they can be as a group. A shared purpose ensures that unity. It is something that will not be determined solely by the leader, and it won't be fully understood by any one member of the group. But as the team collaborates with a shared purpose, over time, each member will start to strengthen their personal sense of purpose, and the group will be able to create something even the leader could not have imagined. Distributed creativity under a shared purpose has a number of benefits.

## *Collaboration over Cooperation*

For a sense of purpose of any kind, people need to feel as if they are contributing to a larger cause and that their individual skill sets and qualities are important to that mission. Cooperation occurs when the individuals in the group experience the latter, but not the former, and collaboration occurs when they experience both. For a shared purpose to truly be taken on, an individual needs to believe it's a part of their identity and aligns with their personal purpose. If I'm at a job that doesn't align with what I'm supposed to be doing with my life, I won't contribute all that I can because all that I am doesn't seem to be relevant to the work. But if everyone's personal purpose aligns with the group's shared purpose, and that shared purpose isn't reliant on the founder's or current leader's vision, the members will be more motivated to add their individual talents and commit to the project fully. Cooperation requires more traditional forms of incentive (money, brand awareness, social capital, etc.) but the only requirement for collaboration is a shared purpose. Even if the individual members are similar in skill set, they will eventually specialize in the niche that sets them apart from the rest of the team and will be valued accordingly.

Teams with a shared purpose enjoy the benefits of effective collaboration, as pointed out in a study done by the Institute for Corporate Productivity (i4cp) and Dr. Rob Cross: "high-performance organizations are up to 5.5x more likely than lower-performers to incentivize individual, team, and leader effectiveness in collaboration."[60] When they looked at over one thousand companies, they discovered that "the difference between productive and unproductive collaboration can be summed up in one word: purpose."[61]

Of course, cooperation still has its place. Say you want to build a new house for you and your spouse. You have worked out the kinks, put everything on paper, and have the vision for exactly what you want and how you want it to look. When you start to hire contractors, looking for someone to collaborate with may not be the best idea. Instead, you want someone who will provide a service and get the job done exactly how you and your partner desire. The contractor will receive their payment and maybe a recommendation, and you'll get the house you desire. The contractor's end goal and your end goal are not the same, nor should they be.

It's okay to work with people who don't want to see the same change that you do. More than that, it's inevitable. At the end of the project, both parties can leave their partnership satisfied. With that in mind, collaborating or partnering with another person or party requires intentional effort. The first thing to determine is if your purpose, not your goals, align. Here are two signs that you are successfully working under a shared purpose.

## *1. There Is Room for Improv*

When I first got started in business, I took a lot of pride in my ability to strategize. I felt that I could identify the players, map out a game plan, and put together the right team to execute. In college I worked with my partner to create a three-business brand that would fulfill our personal needs and wants while being streamlined enough that we could operate all three while still being full-time engineering students.

Given how ambitious the task was, I told my business partner that we should delay launching the business for about eight months while all the pieces were being aligned. After the eight months passed, we had compiled all the legal documents necessary, learned about the software we needed, started talking to some potential interns, and even began to put together our onboarding and training processes. I was satisfied with our positioning and thought the strategy was a thing of beauty. Everything seemed ready to go, and the next month, we launched.

The first client to put us on retainer paid us fifty dollars a month for a service that was not meant to be our main offering, but it was a start. Our

# Purpose

next client paid us for that same service. I started to get worried. For the strategy to work, we needed to be making more money from our main offering. It was the most scalable and the least expensive to produce, and it would help us get the other businesses off the ground. But another month went by, and the only clients we could close wanted our secondary service.

Finally, much to the pleasure of my partner, I went back to the drawing board and made a new strategy that would benefit all three businesses with the secondary service as the central offering. I had the niche selected, pricing completed, and sales pitch decks at the ready. About a month after our launch, we had switched niches, still hadn't made a conversion off the pitch deck, and were deciding prices on the fly.

My ego took a huge blow. I would go back to the beautifully organized Google Docs with our three-business master plan strategy and mull over it for hours, only to get started on implementation, hit a roadblock a week later, and start from scratch all over again. At the time, I didn't understand two things:

1. This was my first B2B business and first time working with a team. My expectations and confidence in my own ability to strategize were much too high.

2. Every strategy and team need to leave room to improvise. At first, every pivot seemed like a failure that exposed my lack of experience and foresight, and to some extent that was true. But those pivots were not at all failures. In fact, the core business ended up creating products that were better and more creative than I had imagined they would be during the original planning. In the end, the strategies improved and were helpful to the team, but what was essential in our decision-making throughout it all was the shared purpose that we established when we started.

That first business challenged me with what all good startups pride themselves on: the ability to adapt and improvise. The plan and preparation were still helpful in hitting our goals, but whenever we arrived at a fork in the road, we glanced at the strategy but based our decision more on what we believed our purpose was. Based on that, we would adapt our strategy as needed.

In his book Getting to "Yes And": The Art of Business Improv, Bob Kulhan states, "Improvisation thrives at the pivotal intersection where planning and strategy meet execution."[62] In order to allow for creativity in our execution, I had to learn how to let go of what I had predicted and leave room for decisions to be made in the moment. Of course, those decisions still need to be based on something. That was the shared purpose.

As mentioned earlier, purpose is one of those concepts that you may not fully understand, but the more you piece it together, the more complete a picture you obtain, and the clearer the picture, the more direction you have. In an improv troupe, you have to be accepting of whatever direction you are given and try to make the best of it. In a group setting, no one member has all the answers and understands what the end result will be, but everyone should have the same sense of direction. This leaves room for creativity to flourish.

## *2. There Is Collaborative Emergence*

The second sign can be seen when collaboration and improvisation collide under a shared purpose, producing what is known as *collaborative emergence*. This is a rather dramatic term that means that whatever is produced is more than the sum of its parts. It's a term used by psychologists who study distributed creativity and how certain groups create things that are truly spectacular, while others remain at a nominal level of creativity.

In a paper titled "Distributed Creativity: How Collective Creations Emerge from Collaboration" leading psychologists in this field Dr. R. Keith Sawyer and Stacy DeZutter found,

> Collaborative emergence is more likely to be found as a group becomes more aligned with the following four characteristics:
>
> The activity has an unpredictable outcome, rather than a scripted, known endpoint;
>
> There is moment-to-moment contingency: each person's action depends on the one just before;
>
> The interactional effect of any given action can be changed by the subsequent actions of other participants; and
>
> The process is collaborative, with each participant contributing equally.[63]

When discovering purpose, you need a combination of both internal and external mechanisms, just like creativity. Fulfilling your purpose is just as much about you as it is about the people around you. We aren't very good at uncovering individual purpose because the process we use to determine purpose is itself rarely understood. Creativity works the same way. True creativity is not possible without an intimate understanding of who you are as well as the environment around you.

In the Wise Society, teaching creativity as a general and necessary skill is almost as important as the pursuit of purpose because creativity is the process by which one finds purpose. The process that a creative person uses to input their own experiences and perspective into their craft is the same trail that Wisdom-led Changemakers take when exploring how they will approach change. Creatives look to solve a problem or gap within a given field. Purpose does the same thing: fills a (larger) gap. Creativity is the mechanism that drives purpose and is a reason why following your purpose inherently creates change.

Innovation does not exist inside the realm of Common Sense, and innovation would not be possible without creativity, yet we need innovation to create lasting change.

# 7
# Creativity

*There is no doubt that creativity is the most important human resource of all. Without creativity, there would be no progress, and we would be forever repeating the same patterns.* – Edward De Bono

---

### Takeaways
- Creativity can be studied and should be taught.
- Creativity is problem-finding and problem-solving.
- Creativity is one of the most powerful tools available to man.

---

## A Picture Worth a Thousand Warriors

"[He] did more than all the armies in Europe to bring me down." This quote from Napoleon Bonaparte was not aimed at a politician or general, the likes of whom Napoleon often opposed. It was not aimed at a beneficiary of generational wealth or someone with a powerful family. The man he described was an artist.

James Gillray was the son of a soldier and sexton (someone who takes care of the grounds and equipment of a church building). Gillray was born in London in 1756, went to boarding school five years later, and received an education for about four years. His father, and the boarding school he attended, were strict and no doubt stifling to young James. Like many people who grow up in no-nonsense environments, Gillray was attracted to the arts, so much so that he became an apprentice to an engraver at the age of fourteen. At twenty-one, he furthered his education and continued honing his craft. After college, he did what most young people do: discern how to make the most money with the skills that they've acquired. Just like today, the arts were not

# Creativity

where the highest paying jobs could be found, but James discovered that he could make a more-than-decent living as an engraver.

He would later become famous for his political caricatures, but at the time, that niche was seen as a low form of art, and although it was growing in popularity, the money was not there yet. He had admired certain caricaturists growing up, but since engraving and other art forms were more respected and higher-paying, Gillray decided to tiptoe in that space for a few years before diving into political caricatures.

I can just imagine a young James finding his style, wondering if he was wasting his time as an artist, and worrying if he was unqualified to make political commentary through his work. At first, most of his work dealt with social topics, which were safer to address. But as time went on and his skill improved, he took more risks, and those risks are why some refer to him as the father of the political cartoon.

In the 1780s, Gillray's name was becoming more well-known. In the late 90s, he turned his attention toward Napoleon. Napoleon had just fled an active campaign, abandoning his command when the outcome looked bleak. He was seen as a coward in the eyes of many British and French citizens. Gillray jumped on it with a caricature entitled "Buonaparté leaving Egypt," which marked the early stages of a series of attacks on Napoleon that would span the remainder of Gillray's career as a caricaturist.

The hype built around his work was similar to that of a Walmart Black Friday sale before the internet. Gillray would post his artwork in the window of a print shop, and the townspeople would fight just for the chance to look at it. One individual stated:

> The enthusiasm is indescribable, when the next drawing appears.... It is a veritable madness. You have to make your way through the crowd with your fists.[64]

With such popularity his biting satire and skillful paintings had mass appeal and swayed the opinions of his fellow countrymen; indeed, they still influence how we imagine Napoleon to this day. Take a moment and think of him--try to form a mental picture. What do you see? Do you imagine him to be a tall, commanding figure, or do you see a short, pudgy Frenchman yelling up at his soldiers? I see the latter, and I'm guessing you do too. But what we imagine is unlikely how he was viewed while building his empire. For instance, Napoleon was of average height—some say he was, in fact, a little above average. Our mental image of Napoleon today is strongly influenced

Foolish Genius

by the caricatures and artwork created by James Gillray. Gillray, never seeing him in person, often portrayed him as a short and angry little man. For an example, look up "The Plumb-Pudding in Danger;–or–State Epicures Taking un Petit Souper" or "Maniac-Raving's;–or–Little Boney in a strong Fit."

For someone to be overseas yet still feel your impact you have to truly be a Changemaker. Mind you, this is in a time when images couldn't be sent over the ocean in a matter of seconds. And remember, Gillray could have left caricatures and political commentary alone altogether, and to a young James in the 1700s, that may have seemed like the more logical decision. But he went through the creative process diligently, applied the four *I*'s of Change, and (negatively) impacted an infamous military leader from the comfort of a small print shop.

## Social Change with Creativity

Napoleon wasn't the only leader to understand the impact art and entertainment could have on their regime. It must be straight out of a dictator's playbook: Hitler, being a failed artist himself, went to great lengths to control the flow of creative expression. In 1933, Joseph Goebbels (the Nazi Propaganda Minister at the time) founded the Reich Chamber of Culture. In order for creatives to do their work, they were required to be members of this group and adhere to their policies. According to the manual of the Reich Chamber of Culture, this organization supervised art produced in the fields of music, literature, architecture, film, theater, press, fine arts, and radio.[65] In 1937, Goebbels set his eyes specifically on artists and their artwork, and sought to criminalize art he deemed dangerous to his authority or that failed to portray the ideology of a "pure German." He travelled Germany collecting pieces that did not fit his criteria and put them on display as "Degenerate Art." After collecting over six hundred works of art and haphazardly scattering them around in an exhibition, the public walked through the exhibition and were meant to react in a disgusted manner. In 1937 alone, Goebbels and his team confiscated twenty thousand pieces of modern art, only to pass a law approving the sale of said art and throwing an international art auction two years later to sell the pricier and rare items.

Stalin also recognized the power of creative expression. He christened certain writers and artists as "engineers of the soul."[66] He perpetuated Socialist Realism using the artists of his country to skillfully develop effective propaganda.

You'll note that in these examples the authoritarians didn't seek to end creative expression; they sought rather to control and monitor it. Certain art forms, like jazz, would not die, and for each resistant art form, a growing number of resistant citizens defied the authority of the regime. For anyone who wishes to hold on to power, whether it be an employer, government, or other authority, creativity will always be their greatest threat—but it can also be their greatest asset.

The Nazi regime had a challenging time restricting every form of art they deemed unfit for their culture, and an even harder time making culturally sticky art. Similarly, Stalin's push for Socialist Realism had some temporal impact, but died almost as soon as he did. For these leaders, creative expression was evidenced more through political strategy and military cunning than through art. To be clear, this chapter is about creativity, not arts and entertainment.

For the purposes of this book, I'll use Oxford's broad definition of art as "the expression or application of human creative skill and imagination."[67] With this definition, art requires creativity. However, I don't want to confine art to the experience of visual or emotionally striking pieces that you enjoy in a museum or play through your headphones: I mean to include any product of creativity. For Gillray, it was his caricatures. For a musician, it could be a freestyle. But art can also take the form of an architect's innovative design for a new stadium or a lawyer's sound argument.

Creativity is an essential skill for anyone looking to make an impact with their work; it shouldn't be thought of as having utility only in the fields of arts and entertainment. I'm using these two related field as an introduction for two reasons: 1) With the definition above, art requires creativity, and 2) the authoritative examples I used reveals the impact creativity can have on the Common Sense of a culture. In reality, creativity is so broadly applied that it would be impossible to measure its impact. As we dive into the components and characteristics of creativity, think about what you can be creative in and what forms your art can take.

# What Is Creativity?

Some people believe the term "creativity" should be used only to describe the works of the greatest creatives of all time (the likes of da Vinci, Bach, Kanye, etc.). Although studying creativity through the lens of the all-time greats has its place, it would not be as relevant if it applied only to a distinguished few. Other people, and I am one of them, use creativity in a broader sense to describe the creative process, which is something that anyone can grasp and employ in their day-to-day lives.

The formal and scientific definitions for creativity are widely debated, and although it would be nice to have a single definition that all psychologists and educators agreed on, this is not the case. But to be honest, I couldn't care less. I don't want to get lost in the semantics of the word or do a deep dive into the language behind it. Like every other concept mentioned in this book, I'm much more concerned with the application of creativity. Thus I will not provide a definition or opine on those of others, but I will go over a few key characteristics that are widely accepted in the field. The goal of this chapter, and more broadly this book, is not to strike up debates or offer controversial opinions for naysayers to pick at but to express the need for a Wisdom-based approach to social change. That being said, I won't spend too much time stating or defending each characteristic, but I will provide an overview of them.

## *Characteristic #1: Creativity Is a Process/Work*

There's almost nothing more romanticized in the field of creativity than the eureka moment. This is the fateful moment that changes the life of every successful tech entrepreneur and esteemed artist when the *momentous* idea (that later defines their life's work) hits them like a ton of bricks. This was the basis for many of my favorite shows and movies growing up. Who didn't get excited when Jimmy Neutron had a brain blast or when Batman found a way to save Gotham at the last second? As great as these epiphanies are for entertainment, sometimes they can spin a false narrative.

Maybe the most infamous of all epiphanies is the story of Isaac Newton and the apple tree. If you are not familiar, imagine a disrespectful young Newton, still in his early twenties, spending a secluded summer at his family farm. Newton, a young bookworm and recognized genius, had already invented a sundial that was accurate to the minute, a water-drop powered clock, and a windmill that ground wheat. This would have been impressive today, but it was completely unheard of in the 1600s. There is Newton doing what he always did in summertime: sitting alone and thinking. One fateful day, he chose to sit outside under the shade of an apple tree, and an apple fell, hit his head, and changed the course of history. Most people would become annoyed or laugh it off and never give it a second thought, but not Newton. As the story goes, moments after the apple fell, he was struck with a eureka moment that would ultimately lead to his theories on gravity and fixed space.

This is genuinely an incredible story, especially since it is highly likely to be true, and you can still view the same apple tree today. After hearing a story like that, I want to sit under any fruit tree I can find, start thinking of life's mysteries, and hope something other than bird droppings fall on my head. I might even watch a YouTube video on unsolved physics mysteries just to prepare. But even if I spent all week under some fruit tree, I would never experience such a life-altering "aha moment." In reality, eureka moments are not as whimsical as they seem. Before the apple fell, Newton was an applied genius, the operative word being *applied*. Newton had consumed himself in his studies since he was a young boy, giving him years of uninterrupted focus in the field of physics by the age of twenty-three.

As easy as it would be to write off someone as creative or uncreative from birth, we shouldn't do so. Creativity is a process: something that can be built upon and applied to a skill. You think Newton could have had the impact he had on science if he had run the farm like his mother initially wanted him to? Of course not, even with his naturally high IQ. Renowned neurologist BD Burrell said it well, "Given the choice between the myth of the natural genius and the sobering reality of hard work, popular culture usually opts for the myth."[68] A lazy genius is simply untapped potential. As you would expect, the writers who write the most tend to create the most creative and recognized works. The same applies to artists. The rule of thumb is that the creative process requires work in order to produce excellent products. Of course, there are some exceptions, but they are rare. To be a truly creative individual you need to work—and work hard.

## *Characteristic #2: Creativity Is Problem-Finding and Problem-Solving*

Entrepreneurs find problems in the world and create solutions they believe consumers will appreciate. Content creators find new and interesting topics on which to opine. Artists search for new ways to stir up emotions in their audience. For all these examples, finding the problem is just as important as finding the solution. For the content creator, finding new ways to entertain may be more difficult than actually making the content, but if they do not execute, they will lose their audience. For the startup owner, finding the problem may be simple, while the execution, getting the business off the ground and running, may be much more difficult. But if an entrepreneur builds a business just to learn that potential consumers don't care about the problem as much as they do, business acumen won't matter much. The problem has to be adequately recognized so that people can identify with it. According to CB Insights, the biggest reason for startup failure is a lack of market need.[69] Every serial entrepreneur, every established content creator, and every successful musician knows there is an art in finding a problem. Likewise, the solution can't be so novel that it is too far ahead of its time or not novel enough to convince consumers to switch from the status quo. There is an art in finding the right solution to an appropriate problem at the appropriate time.

Creativity is the process of looking at the world, seeing how things are operating, finding a problem or a gap in knowledge, and creating a solution that is original and relatable enough to bring value to that space. Once that value is presented and the gap in knowledge is filled, the time to search for a new problem begins.

The leader and community developer inside you should cause you to dig deep to understand the skills and potential of the people you're leading. The creative in you should look for problems your community is experiencing and find ways you and your team are uniquely able to solve them. Businesses hire people to fill a particular need. People go to college in an attempt to achieve a higher income; the problem they're hoping to solve in this case would be avoiding a low-income lifestyle or missing out on the job of their choice. The world runs off problems and solutions; it is the process of finding a gap and creating an excellent product that fills that gap. A work is not seen as creative if it has been accomplished repeatedly at that level or provides no new value.

The process of creativity can be applied to any field. Agriculture is not popular for its innovation, yet the ag-tech sector is ever-growing. Therapists are not known for their creativity, yet they seek solutions to new problems every day. No matter who you are, what job you hold, or what type of life you live, problems arise on a daily basis. Would you say that a student is prepared for life if he or she lacks training in how to properly find and solve a problem? Of course not—but we say it every day, and especially so at college commencements.

## *Characteristic #3: Creativity Is Combination*

The word *creativity* is a fairly modern word dating back to the late 1800s, although it was not commonly seen in dictionaries until after World War II. It derives from the English word *create* and the Latin word *creatio*, which means "to make or grow," usually in the context of biology. Despite the word's biological roots, humans are incapable of true creation. Everything we create or invent is a combination of other components that already exist. When Steve Jobs created the iPhone, he created something new in the eyes of the world, and it changed the game forever. But why? It was not the first smartphone. It was not the first phone with email capability. He didn't create the first phone with a calculator or built-in apps. All of that came over a decade before the first iPhone was introduced. What Jobs did was take the inventions of others and compile them in a way that was new, fresh, and exceedingly user-friendly. When it came to specifications, the iPhone was not groundbreaking, but the way in which the apps and design were delivered made for an experience that other smartphones couldn't touch. Jobs once said:

> Creativity is just connecting things. When you ask creative people how they did something, they feel a little guilty because they didn't really do it, they just saw something. It seemed obvious to them after a while. That's because they were able to connect experiences they've had and synthesize new things.[70]

Let's try a quick exercise. Think of an alien. That should be fairly simple, given that we've grown up watching sci-fi movies and cartoons. Now think of an alien trying not to base its image off of any television show or movie. This gets more difficult but should still be doable. Now think of an alien, trying not to include any parts from any human or animal that you've ever seen. This is an impossible task. You cannot think of an alien without including something you've seen in your lifetime. Creating new ideas from scratch is simply not in the human toolbox. We like to think that what we do is completely new and novel, but when boiled down, it is always building off ideas and concepts we have experienced at some point in our lives.

We all do it. To reference Newton again, he once said, "If I have seen further, it is by standing on the shoulders of giants."[71] T. S. Eliot stated it poetically when he said, "Immature poets imitate; mature poets steal; bad poets deface what they take, and good poets make it into something better, or at least something different. The good poet welds his theft into a whole of feeling which is unique, utterly different from that from which it was torn."[72] Realizing we are limited by what we experience takes the pressure off us. We don't need to create something out of nothing, we can simply focus on taking in new experiences. True creativity is an act of God, combination is what we do to compensate.

> True creativity is an act of God, combination is what we do to compensate.

## *Characteristic #4: Creativity Is Learning*

"School is not for me; I'm much more of a visual learner." Every time I hear this statement, I cringe a little. It gets worse when everyone else nods in agreement and starts throwing jabs at the school system with no real discussion of workable solutions. A part of me always wants to join in and get in a quick one-two (and that part wins out more than I'd like to admit), but the school system weaknesses aren't why I cringe. I don't cringe because of the nonconsequential complaining either; that's just human nature. I cringe because of the last two words: visual learning. The meshing hypothesis states that learning takes place when the students' learning style preferences match the delivery methods.[73] For example, students who prefer to learn visually will learn more when they watch someone perform a task or when kinesthetic learners get to touch and interact with the object they are studying.

This hypothesis has been circulated throughout the education system and has gained immense popularity, particularly with the critics of the school system. It does seem to make intuitive sense, but, unfortunately, the majority of the research on this topic appears to contradict it. In fact, one could easily argue that learning styles don't exist. A more fundamental idea is that learning takes effort. The meshing hypothesis has much to do with the preference of learning style, but if learning takes effort, the preference doesn't make much of a difference. Students are merely saying "learning is easier when taught *this* way."

When teachers use a variety of teaching styles, everyone benefits. The focus shouldn't be on matching styles with students as much as it is on consistently providing a diverse array of delivery methods. When students are put in situations that cause them to think and actively apply their cognitive abilities, they remember more of what they learn during their experience. This can be demonstrated through the disfluency effect.[74]

True learning is proven with demonstration: teachers assess students' true learning with tests that allow them to demonstrate their knowledge. They give students problems similar to but not exactly like the ones covered in lectures, in hopes that they can apply what they have learned to the test, and, if successful on the test, in their life. Based on the first characteristic listed above, we know that creativity is problem-solving. True learning takes place when students can take what they learn and use it as a foundation for more learning. Any form of learning outside of this is memorization. Creativity is interdependent with true learning. You can't have creativity without true learning, and you can't have true learning without creativity. As Dr. Keith Sawyer has written,

> A non-creative learner is one who's able to solve problems just like the ones presented during instruction (retention problems), but not able to solve problems that weren't explicitly taught (transfer problems). Creative learners are the students who do well on both types.[75]

The goal for a Wisdom-led Changemaker is to use their power to enable the Common Man to lead a high-quality life. With the onset of the internet, memorization is not as important a skill, but problem-solving and problem-finding are as important as ever. If students cannot apply what they are learning because they don't know how to think and solve problems, then education is a waste of time for both the teacher and the student. Knowledge is useful only with application, and one cannot apply information when the creative process is neglected.

## A Creative Deficit

You may look at the fourth characteristic and think, *If creativity is learning, then why doesn't everyone know how to express their creativity?* It's a fair question. The majority of us spend our entire childhood going to school, only to get a diploma or degree and work at a desk doing a monotonous job as prescribed in a manual. To understand the state of creativity in our nation, one factor worthy of examination is how our culture views and develops creativity, specifically in our school systems.

A school system is put through the wringer every time a new exception steps into the limelight. By exception, I mean the billionaire college dropouts, the rappers who made it out, and the ADHD student turned impassioned serial entrepreneur. Everyone has heard a rap lyric bashing the teacher who said they'd never make it or seen a social media post with a quote from Musk or Zuckerberg trashing the school system, paired with some random photo of Leonardo DiCaprio from a scene in *The Wolf of Wall Street*. We've all heard the success stories, we know the names of the exceptions, and we can easily point fingers, but we still can't create a solution without defining the problem.

Of all the concepts discussed in this book so far, creativity is likely the most misunderstood. On the surface, everyone seems to be on the same page. But are we? Creativity is a mystical force that one can harness if you break down boundaries and stay open to any and all ideas. It's like a spirit that flows through the open-minded and naturally right brained, but it also seems to come at a cost. Creatives most likely hate school, will be an underdog for years, occasionally lash out against authority, see Kanye West as a creative genius, watch *Rick and Morty*, and may be seen as a little crazy. Some of this is true: creatives are often misunderstood, it does help to be open-minded, and Kanye West is, in fact, a creative genius. But much of what people think of as creativity is based on urban legend, outdated theories, and observational bias. So: how can we instill creativity when we don't know what it is?

The study of creativity is a relatively new one. It arguably started in 1937, but there wasn't much empirical data on the topic until the middle of the twentieth century when it started to gain traction. Not long after research began did people start to understand how much of a gap there was between the perception of creativity and what creativity looks like in real life, especially the classroom.

A hundred-odd years ago, Ellis Paul Torrance, who would later be known as Dr. Torrance or the "Father of Modern Creativity," was born in 1915 on a farm in Georgia. Like other boys in his town, he went to a military college, but unlike others, he graduated with highest honors. Dr. Torrance began his career in 1937 as a high school teacher in a Minnesota vocational school. His early years as a high school educator gave him an experience similar to many educators today: he did his due diligence, taught ninth graders the typical classes, and, intentionally or unintentionally, studied the behavior of his students. The next year he began teaching courses at Georgia Military College, where he had received his education, and became the principal of the high school department, where he would start on his first set of creativity tests.

Torrance was inspired by the children whom teachers often want to avoid the most: the loud, constantly active, and seemingly rebellious group. He watched as some of those children grew up and went on to become successful. How did they end up so? What did they have that was making them seemingly fit well with the world but not the classroom? Not all rambunctious students graduated and became successful, of course, but there was something in this group that the school system wasn't accounting for. The group's distinctive attribute, Torrance recognized, was creativity.

In his quest to incorporate creativity into education, Torrance surveyed 142 studies from five countries to see how the teachers felt about the behavior of creative students. Importantly, these studies did not consider opinions on the students themselves but rather opinions on the characteristics or behaviors that these students shared. He compiled the "Ideal People Checklist" with sixty-six characteristics, including items asking if the child completed work on time, was energetic/vigorous, haughty or prideful, obedient or submissive to authority, had a sense of humor, demonstrated initiative, etc. Torrance's analysis indicated teachers not only held negative opinions of characteristics commonly found in creative individuals but they also approved of behaviors that are often considered detrimental to creative thinking.

Dr. Ellis Paul Torrance was a giant in the field of creativity and an early pioneer of attempting to understand it through scientific means. Much of the research we have today is either straight from one of his teams or from individuals inspired by his work. In 1995, researchers Erik L. Westby and V. L. Dawson took Torrance's research and went a step further. Instead of testing how teachers rated the behaviors of students, Westby and Dawson investigated how the teachers viewed the students.[76] Most teachers will agree that creativity is generally a positive thing, but not every teacher (fewer than you may expect) know what creativity looks like.

Westby and Dawson were a sneaky pair. Their goal was to record the teachers' opinions on creativity, assuming they would be positive, then juxtapose them alongside their negative opinions on creative students. They set up two studies: one similar to the 142 studies mentioned above and the second exploring the contradiction. The results, as you can probably guess by now, implied that teachers do not value the creative individual nearly as much as the conformist, and they saw creativity more as a burden than an asset.

According to the National Center for Education Statistics, in the US, students spend on average a little over six and a half hours in school for about 180 days a year.[77] This adds up to over one thousand hours a year for twelve years that our students are subjected to the opinions and biases of our teachers. It is no secret in education that the opinions, blind spots, biases, and beliefs of the educator can heavily influence the student. Training in this area has increased over the years, and I truly believe the majority of our educators work diligently to impart the best to their students, but the area of creativity has been such a blind spot in the eye of the education system that our teachers are left correcting and condemning behavior that could be contained for the benefit of the student. Since training on the science and meaning of creativity has been neglected, our teachers do not have the proper tools to encourage creative thought, and no one suffers as much as the student.

Decades of studies and consistent research have exposed a lack of understanding of what creativity is and what it looks like. Even now we're facing many of the same misconceptions, and they are showing up in our classrooms, curricula, teacher trainings, and school procedures. These misconceptions must end. In the 1950s, fallacies about creativity were understandable, given how new the field of study was, but our inability to implement what we have known for years shows how ill-suited our current system is for today's student, and progressively, how inappropriate it would be to usher these outdated mindsets into the next phase of our development: the Age of Wisdom. If we continue to entertain error about creativity, we will not only be alienating a large percentage of naturally creative individuals, but we will also be depriving all of our students, especially the high achievers, of tools and processes helpful to both individuals and society.

Creative thinking is essential to progress of any kind. Accountants and security guards can be just as creative as artists, and artists can lack creativity on the same level as the stereotypical accountant or security guard. Educating our students on the science of creativity and coaching them in creative processes should no longer be considered optional for the eccentric teacher to indulge in, but rather a necessity for all educators and a pillar of the education system itself.

For Changemakers who likely grew up in this system, the creative process is one that must essentially be self-taught. But also as a Changemaker, your personal creativity is not what is most important. Your creativity alone will not accomplish lasting change, but the creativity of a large team might. Learning the science of creativity may help you harness your creative ability, but more importantly, it will help you coach those around you to express their creative ability in ways that are unique to them and not dependent on your limited personal experience.

The responsibility to inspire creativity with an understanding of its characteristics and components falls on you. Not only will you benefit from your team becoming more innovative, but you will also empower the people around you to be more self-sufficient and thus able to meet life's challenges.

# 8
# Overcoming the Deficit

*Art is realistic when it strives to express an ethical ideal. Realism is striving for truth, and truth is always beautiful. Here the aesthetic coincides with the ethical.* – Andrei Tarkovsky

---

### Takeaways
- Creativity requires individuality, perspective, boundaries, and excellence.
- Creativity without ethical leadership promotes unethical behavior.
- Ethical leadership is built on principles.

---

Creativity is the art of finding inspiration in the world, adding it to your unique perspective, executing your idea, and publishing your work to inspire someone else. As all large concepts, creativity should be broken down into its components to be palatable. Creativity requires four things: individuality, perspective, boundaries, and excellence. Individuality requires a deep and conscious understanding of yourself, perspective requires the openness and humility to learn from whatever is outside your typical comfort zone, excellence requires specialization, and boundaries force you to work with critical thought and intent.

## Individuality

Individuality is the most intuitive part of creativity and the portion students complain about the most. All things considered, the complaints are warranted.

## *In Education*

When you zoom out and take the time to look at it, the uniformity in schools is almost militaristic. Dr. Beghetto, an expert in creativity and education, summed it up well:

> Students of the same age tend to be grouped in the same classroom, so they can be taught the same topic, in the same way, and at the same time (Glaveanu & Beghetto, 2016). Students are expected to complete the same learning assignments, using the same procedures, and arriving at the same answer.[78]

The lack of individuality in K–12 schooling is easily recognizable and widely agreed upon, so there's no need for further emphasis: it's a self-evident issue. What *are* highly debated are the reasons and solutions to this problem.

Have you ever seen *Peter Pan*? If you haven't, do me a favor: dog ear this page, break out the old VHS player in the attic, and watch the original 1953 version. If you have seen the movie, you understand the premise: no one wants to grow up, but eventually you must, and, as you do, your imagination dies and, with it, everything that is fun and novel. Although the burdens of bills, family, and the other responsibilities of adulthood can be enough to crush the spirit of any grown-up, I believe the spirit-crushing starts the moment the school bell rings.

## *It's Personal*

I love a great villain. They are relatable, typically have better origin stories, they don't act like they have a responsibility in the world, and they uncover the humanity that is in all of us. If a movie has great ratings and a villain or anti-hero with conviction, I'll probably be first in line to watch it. Based on these qualifications, I knew I had to watch *Kill Bill*. I'm not one to watch gory movies, but the allure of the villain and the complexity of the story pulled me in. While I was watching it, I was thinking, *This is good, but I would hate to live in the mind of whoever directed this.*

A few years later, I started dabbling in directing, making commercials for small businesses and sports companies. During that time I studied the creative process and style of many of the top directors and writers, including Quentin Tarantino. He once said,

## Foolish Genius

> I mean Kill Bill was insanely personal. I don't necessarily want you to know why it's so damn personal and why it was, like, ripped from my heart.... I bury it inside a bunch of other stuff, but it's all very real, and it's coming from me. I really like taking my story, what I have to say, my tale, my little autobiographies, but sticking them in a crazy genre world.[79]

The best creatives take things personally, and Tarantino is no exception. Tarantino has been named the most influential director of this generation, and every movie he makes seems to be bloody, violent gold. His writing style, the cinematography, and most of all, his ability to shock and invoke visceral emotion from his audiences puts Tarantino alongside the greatest directors his industry has ever seen. But where does this emotion come from? He said that *Kill Bill* was "insanely personal." Ripped from his heart. How could that be? *Kill Bill* is about an assassin who is seeking revenge on everyone who contributed to the plot to kill her on her wedding day and for the loss of her unborn child. Tarantino was born in reasonably peaceful Knoxville, Tennessee. In many ways, he was similar to the average student growing up. He lived a semi-normal life: hated school, loved watching movies, etc. He wasn't in a gang, wasn't a murderer, and didn't have a target on his back. He wasn't married and didn't have a child until over a decade after *Kill Bill* was released. Where was he getting these emotions, and why did he use such vivid and painful imagery like "ripped from my heart"?

At the core of every human is the need for connection. We love stories because we can relate to them, and they speak to us in diverse ways. The storyteller has the power to invoke from the story whatever emotions they choose, and how much effort the storyteller puts into it often determines how good the story is. The better the story, the more emotion and effort it requires from the storyteller. That's why it is common to see some of the best actors in Hollywood become consumed by their roles; actors play an essential part in the storytelling process, and when they can't identify with the part, the audience can feel it. So the best actors obsess over their part: they live it. They do whatever they need to do to identify with it. The role of the writer or director is similar. They have to make sure the story is coming from a place within them, and if they find that difficult, they simply need to dig deeper within themselves.

A delightful story isn't determined by the actual storyline; it's determined by how it makes the audience feel. That's almost a universal truth.

## Overcoming the Deficit

Every marketer knows that the core of a good marketing campaign isn't the product; it is what the product does for customers, the state of mind it puts them in, and the emotions they feel when they use it. Emotion and connection are at the core of everything we do because they are the essence of human existence. Creativity is just as much an inward-focused process as it is an outward one.

In an analogous way that an excellent marketer can create engaging ads for a product they didn't create or don't own, directors can put emotion to stories that aren't their own. Tarantino's task as an A-list director is to learn so much about himself that he can identify with every moment in a movie. This isn't an easy process. Every great and truly creative work takes a measure of introspection and self-searching that is not intuitive and is extraordinarily uncomfortable; they must be "ripped from your heart."

We go through our day-to-day lives with an idea of who we are, but that idea and who we truly are often are two different people. It takes humility and a willingness to step out of your comfort zone in order to truly evaluate yourself. It seems crazy to say, but a lot of people go twenty, forty, even sixty-plus years without really knowing themselves. Introspection is an uncomfortable process but one that yields remarkable results. George Orwell, one of the greatest writers in modern history (and a personal favorite of mine) described his process for writing:

> Writing a book is a horrible, exhausting struggle, like a long bout of some painful illness. One would never undertake such a thing if one were not driven on by some demon whom one can neither resist nor understand.[80]

The first step in building individuality is introspection or self-therapy, learning who you are. What makes you similar to other people and what makes you unique? What drives you? Why are you the individual you are today? The combination of answers to these questions creates a style that can be applied to however you choose to express your creativity. It's a cycle of learning more about yourself and weaving that new discovery into your work. That's why, for example, good musicians evolve over time yet keep their distinct style.

This introspective and creative process really is therapy. It's common to hear great artists or creative individuals say, "I do this as a form of therapy." Half of a therapist's job is to help you search deeper into yourself—into areas that you would likely otherwise ignore. Creativity forces you to go through

## Foolish Genius

the same process; creative breakthroughs do not come without a deeper than average level of individuality. Pulitzer Prize winner Aaron Copland said it best:

> Each added work brings with it an element of self-discovery. I must create in order to know myself, and since self-knowledge is a never-ending search, each new work is only a part-answer to the question "who am I?"[81]

By working toward something intentionally and intimately, you learn more about yourself as the object of that study. The more you work and the deeper that intimacy gets, the sooner you graduate from a mindset of "what I am doing" to a mindset of "where I am going."

## *And What If*

> And when this happens, and when we allow freedom ring, when we let it ring from every village and every hamlet, from every state and every city, we will be able to speed up that day when all of God's children, black men and white men, Jews and Gentiles, Protestants and Catholics, will be able to join hands and sing in the words of the old Negro spiritual, "Free at last! Free at last! Thank God Almighty, we are free at last!"[82]

The crowd erupts. Martin Luther King Jr. waves and accepts the applause, not knowing the impact his words would have on our nation. King moved the crowd and the country in a way that was unheard of. His words ring out to this day, and the "I Have a Dream" speech is still repeated in the mouths of children across the nation. It is one of the most well-known speeches in our nation's history, and he is easily the most well-remembered black man in American history. His words not only gave inspiration to his supporters but also swayed the indecisive middle to support what would become known as one of the most impactful human rights movements in the world.

I'm not commenting on his politics, beliefs, lifestyle, or any of that. That is for another book. What I'm interested in is the title of his speech: "I have a dream." King did not chase a logical appeal. His speech was not littered with hard-hitting statistics that proved the blatant racism and biases in play. He did not end his speech after he expressed the horrific state the nation was in. His speech was not known for how eloquently he spoke on what was happening that day, nor for his knowledge of current events. Martin Luther King Jr. was best known for having a vision of the future and dedicating his life to it, knowing full-well that the future he imagined was not going to be realized in his lifetime, if at all. King was not the best orator of his time, or even in the black community. Yet he swayed the country to believe in a dream—a dream that was unrealistic for the time (arguably any time) yet still had to convince comfortable people of the importance of uncomfortable topics and ugly truths. No easy feat. But one thing was clear: he created a strategy and implemented it.

As kindergarten teachers read picture books to their students, the stories develop lives of their own in the imaginations of their students. The students exercise their imaginations, just as Martin Luther King Jr. did, but needless to say, all realized imagination does not have the same impact. The imagination of Martin Luther King Jr. led to one of the greatest speeches of all time and undeniably changed the course of history. The imagination of young students is entertaining but most likely not particularly impactful. Why? First, the obvious reason: it's usually fantasy (although I'm sure much of the black community in 1963 would have agreed that the level of equality MLK was referring to was a fairytale). But there's more to it than that: second, King turned his dream into an actionable strategy and worked toward it with a conviction you cannot fake.

Everything we imagine is not worth pursuing, and every story is not worth telling. Our imaginations are responsible for our greatest ideas but also some of our greatest disappointments; reality rarely matches what we picture in our mind. Using our imagination is not something we can discontinue at will. Turning an imagined future into reality, or a budding leader's vision into an actionable plan, can be stopped, and the school system does just that with extreme prejudice.

The death of imagination is not treated as a catastrophic loss because its importance is not understood or respected on the level it deserves. Creativity relies on imagination, and there is ample data that indicates poor creativity stems from poor imagination. But even without diving into studies, creativity's dependence on imagination is fairly intuitive. Rarely does lasting progress occur by accident. Every invention, life-saving initiative, tear-jerking song, semi-original thought, or solution of any kind comes from an individual willing to imagine it. On one hand we praise the visionaries of our society, while on the other, we snuff out the visions of children. "What if" becomes

"It is what it is," and the desire to seek a better future diminishes. We demand to see problems solved, but we reprimand anyone willing to undergo the creative and imaginative processes that lead to solutions. Our focus turns from imagining a path of freedom to dealing with the shackles of the present day. As E. D. E. N. Southworth writes in her novel *Capitola's Peril*,

> There is some advantage in having imagination, since that visionary faculty opens the mental eyes to facts that more practical and duller intellects could never see.[83]

The pressures of adulthood will force the perspective of a harsh reality without the help of any external forces. Changemakers have to view their lives realistically, become familiar with the appropriate tools and practices to cope with that reality, allow themselves to imagine a reality better than the one they are currently in, and finally (and equally important), learn the processes and mindsets it takes to make what they imagine a part of their reality. This can be considered the prep work to the four *P*'s of Change. One of the main goals of this book is to help with these mindsets and processes. Without application, this book would contribute to a path to knowledge, not a path to progress. But that path to progress can't begin if we feel so stiffened by the reality we live in that we cannot, for a moment, consider a future beyond it. You must become a dreamer before you can become a visionary, and a visionary before you can become a Changemaker.

# Perspective

## *Specialization Catch-22*

If you talk to someone who studies mold (a mycologist), they will tell you the study of mold is essential to every human being, and they are likely right. The same conversation would happen with experts in any field. Everyone wants to believe what they do is an essential piece of life's ecosystem, and who knows—perhaps everyone would be right. But if you ask a fitness guru or a priest to create a list of items that are essential in our day-to-day lives, you'd be hard pressed to find one that mentions mold. Why is that? Is it because the mycologist is wrong?

If you ask an engineering student if physics is as important as art, they will likely look at you as if you are wearing your underwear on your head. No doubt, the next five minutes of your life will be spent hearing about all the things we do every day that couldn't be possible without our current understanding of physics. Now if you ask an art student the same question, they may disagree, saying something to the effect that while life may be extended through physics, life is only worth living because of art. Who's to say which is more important? Should you listen to whoever has a higher degree? Remembering that perspective isn't binary, no one can truly see the full mosaic or measure the impact a single field of study has had over everyone on this earth. But if you ask someone with tunnel vision for directions, they will undoubtedly point to whatever direction is right in front of them.

Changemakers are extraordinary in that they typically leverage skills or aptitudes to set themselves apart. These could be their networking or public speaking abilities, the gift of identifying and highlighting the skills of others, or a personal humility others find inspiring. No matter what the skills are, Changemakers learn these strengths and how to use them to accomplish their goals. This is part of the individuality aspect of creativity and the second "I" of change (Intimacy). As Changemakers learn more about themselves and dive deeper into their strengths, they naturally become more specialized in what they do.

In society, generally speaking, the more specialized you become, the more respect and compensation you earn in your field. I have no problem with this reward system. Once you are an expert in a field, it is easier to identify gaps in knowledge, explore fresh solutions, and be the authority on a topic. Experts have earned their credibility and, thus, should be compensated for the value they bring. It makes sense because specialization helps to strengthen the intimacy side of creativity. But specialization can inhibit a different aspect of creativity.

As Abraham Maslow once said, "If the only tool you have is a hammer, it is tempting to treat everything as if it were a nail."[84] Your perspective limits your toolbox and, therefore, limits the number of solutions you can provide. We know that by the time James Gillray was thirty, he had worked for twenty print sellers, each having taught him about different techniques, topics, and people in that field. If he had stayed with one style his entire life, the growth of his art would have been capped. If you become so engrossed with seeing the world only one way, you miss out on the opportunities available through divergent thinking.

Foolish Genius

## *Divergent Thinking*

Out of all the horrific and irritating first world problems, losing your car keys is top tier. If you are older than sixteen, I'm sure you know what I'm talking about. You never look for your keys unless you need to be somewhere, so there is never an appropriate time to lose them. Once you realize you've lost your keys, your first instinct is to tap all your pockets, as if bulky keys could have slipped past your grasp the first time. Then you check the place where you're supposed to leave your keys every time you come in the house (the key rack in the front room, miscellaneous basket by the mail, top of your drawer, etc.). Then you ask a person you live with if they have seen them; they say no and then ask the worst question of all time: "Where did you see them last?" The next step is the most important and is what makes losing your keys relevant to creativity: you take a second, gather yourself, and think of all the places you could have left them. At this point, you should congratulate yourself for practicing divergent thinking.

Divergent thinking is the process of looking for all viable solutions to a problem. Examples: finding the perfect caption for an Instagram post, considering your next move in Scrabble, creating a business name, etc. Divergent thinking is the first step for any problem-solving or problem-finding exercise, and since creativity is problem-solving, you can imagine its importance to the creative process.

A study was done in 2020 comparing the differences in creativity across 2,277 art and STEM students.[85] Divergent thought, being recognized as "the core cognitive process associated with creativity," was assessed by asking the participants to undergo several idea-generation tasks. The researchers concluded,

> Whether industrial engineer, electrical engineer, mathematician, natural scientist or artist, divergent thinking – a defining element of creativity – appears to be present to a statistically similar degree. The implications for elementary, secondary, and tertiary education are therefore similar to those discussed for openness and CSE [Creative Self-Efficacy]. Divergent thinking is a key domain-general creativity skill.[86]

Divergent thinking naturally widens perspective. It forces you to approach a problem from several different viewpoints and include options you would not normally consider. It's a skill the most intelligent inventors, esteemed artists, and everyday individuals benefit from.

I began my undergrad as an engineering student, and like most STEM students, I had the joy of taking some of the most painstaking math classes my school could throw at me. Every exam brought its own combination of stress, nerves, and anxiety, but one was extra special. It was my second midterm in the course, and the first hadn't gone so hot, so the pressure was on. I did the preliminary scroll-through that I did every time I took an exam: I scan the entire test to determine where the easier questions are so I can tackle them first and increase my confidence. Normally, this method is rather pointless since my college exams were equally difficult, but this time was different. The second free response question was worth a substantial number of points and involved a lot of steps, and I knew how to do every single one. I went to work.

Fast forward to the TA passing back our exams, and, as it turns out, my second midterm results weren't great, either. I opened the test packet, started to flip through the pages, and stopped at the second free response. Out of the eight points available, I had received only one: the point given for answering the question correctly.

In school, when there was a method taught that I personally didn't like, I would try to find other methods. Every now and then I would create my own method, but most of the time I would just research other ways of doing something to avoid reinventing the wheel. For this particular math exam, I had used an alternative process I found to arrive at the correct answer. Since the question didn't specify which method I was supposed to use, I saw no problem with my change in methodology.

After receiving the graded exam, I brought the question to my TA to ask what was wrong with my work. He stated that the method the rubric graded for was different than the one I used. Now, I understand the importance of practicing a certain methodology, but the principle remains. In school we are typically taught a specific topic in a specific way in a lecture-esque setting. There is no room for divergent thought, and there is nothing that forces you to widen your perspective. If you are made aware of something new, it is because it is included in the curriculum, which all the students in your grade receive. As a result, everyone is exposed to the same, limited information with an equally limited ability to find out information on their own. A shift in the times requires a shift in education—one that will best serve today's students—and teaching them how to widen their perspective on their own should be included.

After starting my first business, I was peppered with questions about the process I walked through. My answer to the most popular, "How did you know where to start?" was always the same: I Googled it. In an age where information is readily available, the hardest part about figuring out what to do is choosing what questions to ask. Learning how to think about all the things you don't know is more valuable than being able to recite facts. The first step in widening your perspective is discovering the areas you want to pursue further. In order to do so, you have to think divergently.

The importance of an ever-widening perspective has surfaced several times in this book. By now, I hope the message is clear: the ability to continually broaden your perspective is essential to personal growth, creativity, and Wisdom.

## *Diversity*

Diversity and perspective are closely related but are not the same. Perspective is the lens through which you see the world, and the wider your perspective is, the more holistic your worldview. If perspective is the goal; diversity is the plan. Diversity inherently leads to perspective. It is a means to an end. Perspective is an invaluable attribute but is not easily acquired. It requires constant upkeep and an open mind, and it will greatly challenge your preconceived notions.

Since diversity has turned into a buzzword as of late, it can be easy to lose sight of its functional value. Everyone uses the word *diversity* in a way that leaves a string of unanswered questions: Why is it important? How can it be applied realistically? What are the different types of diversity? Is there one form that has proven better than the rest in respect to creativity and performance? And so on.

As we begin this discussion of diversity, I would be remiss if I didn't mention at least one of its misconceptions. Randomly hiring people of different ethnicities, even if they hold the same academic qualifications, does not guarantee that your team will become more effective or innovative. In relation to creativity, not all forms of diversity are created equal. In a comparable way that diversity is a means to gain perspective, ethnic, racial, and gender diversity should be used simply as tools to reach cognitive diversity. If your main goal is not cognitive diversity but rather diversity for diversity's sake, you can actually damage a group's creative ability by randomly throwing in lesser forms of diversity.

Organizational diversity often refers to the level of ethnic diversity (or the lack thereof) in the organization's leadership or staff. Since public schools usually cannot specify the ethnic backgrounds of admitted students, the first way schools can improve diversity focuses on what they have complete control over: whom they hire.

Consider two social movement organizations: one where much of the top management and leadership looked the same but had different cognitive backgrounds (education, professional focus, regional roots, etc.), and a second where everyone is of a different race and ethnicity but grew up in the same region. Given the two options, I would bet that nine times out of ten the first would be more creative and innovative in their approach.

Throwing people of color onto a team doesn't guarantee cognitive diversity, nor does it guarantee the ethnic diversity will benefit the team. There is somewhat of a sweet spot in how much diversity is beneficial to creativity, and it comes with a couple of qualifiers: all group members need to 1) have a shared level of devotion to achieving the group's goals and 2) be united under the same purpose. Adding diversity of any kind without vetting for a shared purpose will decrease the level of creativity of the group. Purpose needs to be at the center of everything we do, even in creativity, and especially in diversity.

That said, it is fairly rare to see a large group of K–12 teachers who look the same and enjoy significant differences in perspective, experience, and opinion. As a rule of thumb, hiring individuals of different nationalities and ethnicities does improve the level of divergent thought, perspective, and all-around creativity, but it is just important to remember that hiring for race should not be the *main* goal but rather a strategy to achieve divergent thinking. The *main* goal is uniting the group members, who have diverse backgrounds and mindsets that will add value to the group's pool of perspectives, under one purpose. Adding members with diverse ethnicities is simply one of the easiest ways to achieve that.

It is important to note that hiring staff who look different from each other can help break down unhealthy schemas and biases in the minds of the students, who may be negatively influenced in this regard outside the classroom. For example, a student who is told at home that one race is less intelligent would have a harder time accepting this bias if their favorite teacher was of that race.

Chapters 9 and 10 note how Changemakers who consider themselves the heroes of their movement or organization will not want to forfeit their perceived importance to members of their team, thereby stunting its creativity. But Changemakers who think like a community developer will lead with humility. Not all leaders love the concept of diversity because conflict will inevitably arise, and everyone may not agree with the way the leader does things. A unified team is necessary for success, and some leaders have a tough time marrying the concepts of unity and diversity. But as I see it, the need for unity is present only when diversity of thought is achieved. Under certain leadership styles or differing goals, unity and diversity can be incompatible. For example, in any oppressive state, the oppressor protects their authority by enforcing as much singularity in thought as possible. Singularity keeps things simple, but it is also unrealistic (and egotistic) in nature. To believe that your way of thinking should be duplicated in the minds of others is a flawed perspective, hubris even, and will create a less sustainable team.

Diverse teams are bolder, more strategic, and more innovative, but they are more adaptable when they are unified under a single goal or shared purpose. The team you choose to champion the idea that you want to become Common Sense will need to be all of those things in order to overcome the conflict that will inevitably arise.

## Boundaries

> Just as kites cannot fly without strings, and Wisdom cannot exist without critical thought, society cannot exist without rules, and creativity cannot exist without boundaries.

It's not uncommon to see young creatives rejecting rules and having trouble submitting to authority. Boundaries are never fun to talk about, and they get a terrible rap. They are often viewed as the opposite of freedom, but can anything exist without boundaries? Societal freedom requires rules or else anarchy would ensue and personal freedoms would be impinged. Just as kites cannot fly without strings, and Wisdom cannot exist without critical thought, society cannot exist without rules, and creativity cannot exist without boundaries.

Imagine I want to flex my creative muscles and create an innovative company. Thinking outside the box is fine for most of the company decisions, but what about when it comes to the packaging we'll use to send our products? The US Postal Service has rules about the sizes and shapes of parcels they will mail. The balance between practicality and boundaries is defined in this case by the person mailing packages. Visionaries aren't supposed to push boundaries as much as simply selecting which boundaries to operate within.

For the Changemaker, their boundaries are the principles they hold to.

## *Convergent Thought*

Lorne Michaels once said, "There's no creativity without boundaries. If you're gonna write a sonnet, it's 14 lines, so it's solving the problem within the container."[87]

Divergent thought is a popular topic in the realm of creativity; it's the most attractive portion, and it's what people are naturally drawn to. But every time divergent thought is employed, convergent thought closely follows. Divergent thought is concerned with providing the right ingredients, while convergent thought is concerned with combining them in the right way.

Once you think of all the places you could have left your keys, you need to choose a place to look (convergent thinking). If they are not at that spot, you will repeat the process of divergent to convergent thought until you find the keys. The same process applies to the making of every creative work. As this loop repeats, the ideas are refined and the product's quality improves.

Convergent thought introduces some of the most unpopular sides of Wisdom. Making decisions requires a level of critical thought and personal responsibility—things no one intuitively enjoys. With personal responsibility comes criticism, both positive and negative. Since hindsight is twenty-twenty, the "right decision" will always seem much more intuitive for the onlooker, who helps populate the "I could've made that" and "Why didn't you make it this way?" crowds. And if you have ever been to Subway, you understand that divergent thinking is not as easy as it seems. It is difficult to make decisions when there's a large number of options, so sometimes convergent thinking is simply easier.

## Foolish Genius

Given convergent thinking's unpopularity, it's not surprising that this is a component of creativity that our sometimes backwards school systems fully comprehend. Throughout the school day you can find examples of students using convergent thinking: responding to teachers' narrow questions, taking multiple-choice exams, and going through the lunch line. Schools use a fairly appropriate amount of convergent thought given how many decisions children have to make and how many they will have to make as adults. The issue lies in the balance between convergent and divergent thought. Even if they don't know the term, students are familiar with convergent thought, but since it is disconnected from its counterpart, students don't associate creativity with convergent thought—thus they see it as a burden, much like any other boundary-using practice.

But their distaste for convergent thought is unfounded. The difference between a free man and an imprisoned one is not in their use of convergent thought but in the balance between divergent and convergent thought. Prisoners in jail still make decisions. They can choose who to interact with, what they say, and, to some extent, what they do. They do not think any less than anyone else does, but they have fewer options to choose from. Their divergent thought is limited, and that's the real difference. Your room may be the same size as a jail cell, but you are afforded the freedom to think divergently about how to decorate it, when you'd like to leave, and so on. You enjoy your room, and it is comforting even though its four walls are technically boundaries. Boundaries bring comfort, protection, and sanity. We all accept the need for boundaries in our lives, and we even grow to like them, as long as we are afforded an opportunity for divergent thought.

The Common Man stays within the boundaries of their time, not stepping outside of Common Sense. Both the Foolish Genius and Wisdom-led Changemakers push boundaries, but the former does so much more flippantly. Both are visionaries and both are creatives, but the Foolish Genius does not understand the principles that influence their work. They may feel that art is meant to push boundaries (and I would agree), but movement is not necessarily progress, and certain boundaries should not be crossed. In our culture, any artwork that glorifies pedophilia would be considered boundary-breaking, but it would be an illegal and immoral boundary that shouldn't be crossed. Behaving as if creativity has no boundaries is not only inaccurate; it's also dangerous.

# Excellence

*Creativity is a distinctive trait of human excellence in all domains of behavior.* – E. Paul Torrance

Think back to when you were young, back when life was simple. Imagine you had just turned five and three-quarters, and today has been a wonderful day for you. You learned how to tie the strings on your light-up Sketchers, and you just finished the greatest masterpiece you've ever seen. Your teacher even called you a "young Pick Castle." (She actually said "Picasso," and you don't know who that is, but she was smiling when she said it, so it had to be a compliment.) The macaroni on your masterpiece just dried, so you slip your work into your bookbag. You have it all planned out. You'll wait for dinner when your parents will inevitably ask how your day went, you'll smile and have them guess what you made, and then, when the buildup is just right, you'll whip it out from behind your back and *BAM*. They'll respond with the same awe and satisfaction that you had when you first looked at your finished Macaroni Masterpiece.

Fast forward to that evening. The dinner table is set, and the time comes to unveil your masterpiece. You pull it out, and there it is, in all its glory. Well, almost all its glory. A few macaroni pieces fell off, but you think it's still pretty good. You look up, and your parents are glowing. They shower you with compliments, and Pick Castle comes up again! You are satisfied, and they even more so. Your artwork is placed on the fridge to be displayed for weeks, next to the piece you finished last week. You stare and admire your mini art gallery on the fridge and smile. It was a job well done.

Excellence, or a job well done, is the proof of true creativity. The level of execution and originality make the difference between a creative work and simply a clever idea. Execution and originality silence the "I could've made that" crew mentioned earlier. As Abraham Maslow said,

> A first-rate soup is more creative than a second-rate painting. . . . From another man I learned that constructing a business organization could be a creative activity. From a young athlete, I learned that a perfect tackle could be as aesthetic a product as a sonnet and could be approached with the same creative spirit.[88]

In order for true excellence to be achieved, you have to work an undue amount over an extended period of time. As a trend, the best writers are the ones who write the most. The best basketball players practically live on the court. In order for someone to become a true creative, they need to have the intrinsic motivation to put in the time and effort to reach excellence.

In a similar way that the topics of boundaries and perspective intersect when discussing creativity, excellence and individuality do as well. Pushing for excellence without individuality preaches a false narrative of perfection without purpose. This can lead to one or two possible outcomes: 1) pushing themselves to succeed for reasons that fade over time, which, in the Age of Wisdom, is a setup for failure, and 2) abandoning the pursuit of excellence, instead accepting the emotional burden of mediocrity. As a Wisdom-led Changemaker, you want your team to succeed, and in order to foster an environment of intrinsically motivated excellence, you must encourage individuality by fostering genuine relationships and learning about your team beyond what is on their resume.

Ricardo Semler, the man to whom I attribute the Age of Wisdom concept, was originally a Brazilian businessman. During his time as a CEO, he increased his company profits from the low tens of millions every year to hundreds of millions, but the impact he had on the income sheet was not what gave him his reputation. He did that while extending a radical amount of freedom and decision-making power to every individual in his company. His pervasive corporate democracy, nicknamed the "Semco Style," brought a newfound Wisdom to the business world, but he did not stop there. After conquering the business world, he took his concepts of radical Wisdom and applied them to education. In 1993, he opened the first Lumiar School.[89]

The Lumiar School is designed around the development of the student, and in order to properly guide each student, the teacher's role was split in two: the Tutor and the Master. The Master has the more traditional role of a teacher, giving the academic guidance needed to complete the assigned projects. The Tutor walks alongside the students and makes sure they are developing as humans, not just students. Tutors invite impassioned senior citizens to impart knowledge and Wisdom to the students. Let's focus on the Tutor and Master concept for the moment.

In order for a spirit of intrinsically motivated excellence to take root in a student, they need to be able to trust the people whose job it is to guide them. Students need to be able to follow the instruction of those more knowledgeable about their shared interests, and they need to be able to open up enough so individuality can shine through their work. The traditional teacher does their best, but even the greatest teacher has a demanding time caring for the personal and academic needs of each student. Semler understands the importance of education and mentorship and divides these responsibilities while instilling Wisdom from individuals who have not spent their career in the classroom. As much respect I have for the traditional teacher and the service they provide, it can be difficult for a student with specific passions to relate to a teacher who gained knowledge only to pass it on. Bringing in the retired and seasoned, when they are properly trained, adds a level of application that the traditional teacher cannot offer their students.

As adults, Changemakers should learn just as much from the Common Man as they learn from fellow Changemakers, but in order for excellence to become the norm, trust needs to be built—so much so that the Common Man can be vulnerable to explore themselves while still being pushed to study their craft and develop their skills.

# Ethical Creativity

I've discussed creativity in the way most people do: positively. Creativity is great! It's the most powerful tool in the Changemaker's toolbox. And just like any powerful tool, it cares only about how it's used, not what it's used for. Your car doesn't care where you take it as long as you maintain it well. Creativity is the same way. We talk about creativity in a positive light because it is used in the creation of all our favorite things: music, culture, tech. We like to be around it, we like people who seem to know how to leverage it, and we love it when we see our children learn to use it early. I'm sure Abraham and Esther were the same way.

### *'The Brain'*[90]

Abraham and Esther were a picture of the American Dream. Growing up in the Bronx in the 1860s, Abe made a name for himself as a proper businessman, providing value, devising solutions, and eventually earning himself the name "Abe the Just." He settled down with his wife Esther, and the two of them raised five children backed with the honorable Rothstein name.

You may be familiar with this story, and if you are, you know that Abe and Esther aren't the main characters. No, the main character is one of their children, the one who took after his father as a creative and a businessman. Unfortunately, his creativity was not as justly applied as his father's.

## Foolish Genius

By his early teens, it was assumed that Arnold, would lead a life of crime. He became a loan shark before he reached his twenties and was deep into gambling. Yet despite his knack for trouble, all agreed his brilliance never waned. Throughout his entire career, he was known for seeing gaps and finding creative solutions to fill them. While his brother was preparing to become a rabbi, Arnold was becoming a "fixer." He would make sure his associates would be protected from the law by bribing officials and finding ways to make interested parties look the other way.

As organized crime was on the rise, neighboring gangs fought over territories. Arnold used the skills he had gained as a fixer to mediate between gangs to maintain a certain level of peace. He demonstrated the rare talent of attracting and leading individuals who were by most accounts immoral to build on their inherent skills. Among these people was Lucky Luciano, the "Father of Modern Organized Crime."[91] Lucky was able to do what he did largely because he stood on the shoulders of Arnold, who took organized crime and made it into a true business. He was "the J. P. Morgan of the underworld; its banker and master of strategy."[92]

A lot has changed in America since 1920, but if there's one thing that has stayed consistent, it's our infatuation with alcohol. Despite alcohol being linked to a higher risk of cancer and impaired brain communication pathways (along with it being the third highest preventable cause of death in the US[93]), if a society removes it from the shelves, there will be hell to pay. During the Prohibition era, Arnold was quick to pick up on this revelation and found a way to import smuggled alcohol from overseas and distribute it to his clientele, all while avoiding the law and maintaining a high-class persona. By all accounts, the man was truly gifted, and while his father earned the nickname "Abe the Just," Arnold became known as "the Brain." It is widely believed he rigged the 1919 World Series by bribing eight members of the Chicago White Sox. If he set his sights on it, there wasn't much that anyone could do to stop him, short of ending his life.

What he did for organized crime required a level of creativity, leadership, and drive that only Changemakers achieve. He did all of this while deterring police and competitors from stepping on his business. His eventual downfall did not come at the hands of the law; in fact, he successfully evaded all charges ever brought against him. He died at forty-six years old, less than a decade from the average lifespan for men in 1928[94], from a gunshot wound incurred for refusing to pay a debt. He stuck to his principles (in his own

## Overcoming the Deficit

criminal way) even to the end, refusing to snitch on his own killer. When the cops asked about the shooter, Arnold, lying on his deathbed, replied, "You stick to your trade. I'll stick to mine."

Now to be clear, in no way do I want to glorify crime. I think we can all agree that Arnold did not create change toward a Wise Society, his principles didn't align with the three outlined in Chapter 5, and his actions certainly don't follow the characteristics of Wisdom outlined in Chapter 3. But what his story does show is that, although we speak about creativity in a positive light, it can just as easily be used to produce negative outcomes. Some people would argue that creativity inspires negative behavior more than it does the opposite.

Several studies have highlighted the "dark side" of creativity, but one in particular conducted five experiments that highlighted the negative behavior associated with a higher level of creativity. This has been a study-heavy chapter, so I'll spare you the details. But in their abstract, the researchers summarized their results, stating,

> In [five] studies, we show that participants with creative personalities tended to cheat more than less creative individuals and that dispositional creativity is a better predictor of unethical behavior than intelligence (Experiment 1). In addition, we find that participants who were primed to think creatively were more likely to behave dishonestly than those in a control condition (Experiment 2) and that greater ability to justify their dishonest behavior explained the link between creativity and increased dishonesty (Experiments 3 and 4). Finally, we demonstrate that dispositional creativity moderates the influence of temporarily priming creativity on dishonest behavior (Experiment 5). The results provide evidence for an association between creativity and dishonesty.[95]

Studies with similar results have been published repeatedly. We would all like to see ourselves as the hero driven by a righteous mission, but what would you do if you knew you would have to compromise that self-righteousness in order to be more creative than the villains of your story? This is the plight that most fictional heroes encounter: will they cross their boundaries (ignore their principles) and open themselves up to more apparent ways to defeat their enemy? In fictional stories, the principled protagonist always wins out, but what if playing fair wasn't all that it's cracked up to be? If you knew that those without boundaries would always be more creative,

Foolish Genius

wouldn't Wisdom suggest to ignore your principles and do what you need to do to accomplish your goal? Would that mean that Wisdom isn't as process-oriented or holistically and compassionately empathetic? Should Changemakers simply proclaim the loving nature of Wisdom to keep up appearances but let go of their principles to get the job done better than their competitors?

You should test every principle, value, and belief you hold to see if they endure in real life. What I believe about the characteristics and process of Wisdom should be able to withstand questions like these. If it doesn't, then my definition shouldn't be portrayed as Wisdom but rather the hopeful thoughts of a kid in his early twenties. Creativity equips Changemakers to solve the complex issues that plague our world, but there would be no point in pursuing Wisdom if the Foolish Genius were already able to do this. Principled and ethical creativity must win out over unethical creativity, or else all would be pointless. Fortunately for you, the reader who is eight chapters in, principled creativity can do just that. All it takes are ethical leaders.

## *Leveling the Scales*

Leadership, much like creativity, is often spoken of in a positive light, and unethical leadership doesn't get nearly as much attention as positive leadership does. But leadership can have a strong impact on the type of creativity being promoted. In 2021, two teams of researchers took some time to explore these concepts and their relationship.[96] The researchers studied the mountain of research about the advantage that unethical creatives have over their do-good counterparts, and they wanted to know how to level the scales. They designed four studies to take place in China and the US.

For the first study the researchers tested whether individuals who felt a duty to uphold their moral convictions, also called a moral responsibility, were creative. So they hired a team in the US to survey supervisors (supers) and their subordinates (subs). The subs self-reported on their moral responsibility and their supers' level of ethicality, and the supers were asked to rate the creativity of their subs. The second study took place in China and took on the same form, but this time, sixty-three bank branch leaders were surveyed as well as their 574 employees.

The third study returned to the US and took place at a big East Coast college. A pre-survey was given to 131 students, where they rated their moral responsibility. A week later, they were asked to come to the actual study where they were given a scenario. The students were told to pretend they had been a member of their school's Marketing and Communications department for three years running. As members of that department, it was their job to boost the school's reputation by generating new slogans. The students were then assigned to different environments, some having leadership with high moral standards, defined principles, and values, and others being explicitly told that compromising on ethics was the norm. After their time to write slogans concluded, they were asked to evaluate how ethical their department supervisor was.

The fourth and final study started out much like the third, with college students in the US taking a pre-survey on their level of moral responsibility, moral identity, and moral attentiveness. But after this, the students were set up to play a game and split into two groups. The goal of the game was to identify as many uses for the paper clip as they could. One group was told they were playing on teams of four where one person would be randomly assigned as team leader. The second group rotated leadership roles with each turn, and during each turn, the assigned leader could give only one answer to the use of a paper clip. If the leader was able to give an answer, the team received a point, and the leader would end the turn and assign the responsibility of providing an answer in the next round to someone else. If the leader could not give an answer, they were allowed to skip their turn and move on. This second group was also told that the game couldn't determine if their answers were legitimate, so they could write in nonsense and receive points.

After the four studies were complete, the two teams of researchers compiled their data and concluded two things. The first was that moral responsibility negatively impacted creativity. This was no surprise due to the past work done in this field, but the second finding was much more interesting: the researchers found that the negative relationship between an employee's moral responsibility and their creativity could be mediated by ethical leadership.

# Ethical Leadership

Leadership is a very broad topic, and we will address it in the more in the next chapter, but here are three actions ethical leaders pursue to actively promote ethical creativity.

## *1. Ethical Leaders Create Environments Embedded with Principles*

The mountain of research done on the "dark side" of creativity has been piling up for a while, and the narratives are similar across the board. The general consensus is that while unethical people may not be born with a creative gene, they are willing to cross some lines and take some risks that their do-good counterparts shy away from. In short, they aren't afraid to cross boundaries.

Boundaries are what keep ethical and principled individuals in line, but they can also be the very thing that gives unethical creativity an advantage. On one hand, boundaries are essential. After all, they are one of the four components of creativity. But it's important to balance boundaries with two things: focus and perspective. Boundaries that stifle perspective stifle creativity. If you neglect perspective and keep boundaries at the forefront of your mind, you will have a tough time innovating and staying focused on the creative process. As a creative, your initial set of boundaries (your principles) need to be established early as lines you will not cross. Then they should be placed in the back of your mind, not so out of sight that you completely forget them, but far enough that you aren't dwelling on them when you should be widening your perspective. That is, don't abandon intellectual flexibility.

No group environment is devoid of behavioral expectations. Even crime organizations have their own codes of ethics. (Remember, Arnold Rothstein had lines that he wouldn't cross.) Think back to a past employer or new social group. When you joined, you got a sense of how everyone acts. You may have felt you were in a crowd of "yes men," where everyone kissed up to the leader and was afraid to suggest anything that he or she wouldn't approve. You may have been in a group you viewed as being overly masculine or one that was distrusting and divisive. You may have even been in an environment that stated they are "like family," but once you were there, it felt intrusive and cliquey. Once you discern what a group's culture is like, you can choose to either stay, leave, or try to change it.

Leaders, like everyone else, are partly products of their environment. To some extent, they will begin to conform to the mold of the environment they are in. So what sets excellent leaders apart? Critically, what leaders have that not everyone else has is a self-appointed opportunity to shape the very same environment they are shaped by. Some of the negative aspects of group dynamics are based more on personality differences than principles, and in that case, transformative action may not be necessary. But in other cases, where foundational principles are being overlooked and unethical behavior is the norm, then leaders should either leave that environment or seek to change it.

In Chapter 5, we discussed how every Changemaker has a duty to uphold and protect the principles that they subscribe to. This protects not only you, since you will eventually be affected by your environment, but also those around you who share the moral responsibility.

In the study's conclusion, the authors wrote, "Ethical leadership can help employees higher on moral ownership maintain their core self of morality while also regaining their creativity."[97] Ethical leaders create environments embedded with the group's principles. This group structure leads to a shift in perspectives on boundaries: the do-good workers break only the boundaries they are comfortable breaking, which forces unethical leaders to think twice and take fewer risks since the culture around them promotes creativity by ethical means.

For this change to happen, the leader must also ensure that the group sees unethical behavior as a risk. The researchers emphasized that ethical leadership not only rewards ethical behavior, but it also punishes unethical practices. If we have environments where ethics are neglected or not enforced, then unethical creativity will remain the most prominent form of creativity. As Changemakers, we have the ability to exemplify ethical standards in our own lives, integrate those underlying principles with the environments we are in, and promote creativity that pushes the right boundaries.

## *2. Ethical Leaders Are Process-Obsessed*

There's a lot of talk about the unethical practices of large, multinational companies. Some of the topics include the negative cultural effects of globalization and "McDonaldization," some focus on the forced labor or labor exploitation that is common with large organizations, while others criticize the unfathomable wealth bestowed on the company CEOs, and the list goes on. But if you look at the branding of these companies, you would never think they could be capable of negatively impacting, or even harming, people. Yet, it happens all the time. For example, the company whose mission statement is "to become the world's most valued company to patients, customers, colleagues, investors, business partners, and the communities where we work and live" is the same company that paid the largest health

Foolish Genius

care fraud settlement for fraudulent marketing and has been labeled a "habitual offender" for their history of illegal practices.[98] This isn't to say that all the work they do is bad or that their employees are evil. The same year the company paid the $2.3 billion settlement they were pronounced one of the "Best Employers for Women" and received several other accolades recognizing their culture of diversity.[99] This company has helped millions, if not billions, with their products. To those women and the patients who have been helped, I'm sure the fraud didn't seem so bad. But others, like the United States Department of Justice, could not let the company's fraudulent practices slide, regardless of the company's other good deeds.

Ethical leaders understand that the end very rarely justifies the means: that no matter how much good is done, it cannot be cited to justify unethical practices. Focusing only on good results can blind you, pushing you to be more lenient in areas you know should be investigated; that which is left unexplored is the breeding ground for unethical creativity. In fact, if you are not in an environment where unethical creativity is explicitly checked, then it will be present. As the study above supported, the default behavior for creative environments is unethical due to the nature of creativity, and this can be mitigated only if ethical leaders are bold in etching out environments where principles are esteemed and enforced.

## 3. *Ethical Leaders Promote a High-Quality Life*

On a basic level, leadership should push toward progress and the standard of a high quality of life; ethical leadership does that:

> In extant studies, scholars have found that ethical leadership can facilitate employee positive attitudes such as affective commitment and job satisfaction (Brown et al., 2005; Neubert et al., 2009), promote employee positive behaviors such as citizenship behaviors and job performance (Avey et al., 2012; Chen & Hou, 2016), and reduce deviant and unethical behaviors (Mayer et al., 2012; Mayer et al., 2009). Our findings show that ethical leadership can also help relieve employees with high morality from being preoccupied by moral role responsibilities and enable them to regain creativity. This finding expands our knowledge of ethical leadership and also offers a possible solution for 38 practitioners to solve the morality—creativity conundrum.[100]

If you as a team leader are overburdened by the weight of paying your bills or taking care of your health, your mind will have a hard time forgetting your problems long enough to find anything more than a Band-Aid solution to unethical practices. However, ethical leadership allows for better performance, better morale, and positive creativity. If progress toward ethical leadership is not the focus, then what are we left with? A standard of mid to low performance, low workplace morale, and a culture that continues to reward unethical innovation.

Many of the issues in corporate America align with what can be expected when ethical leaders are not put in place. As Changemakers, the weight of your responsibility to drive toward a Wise Society should motivate you to be an ethical leader at all times; should you do so, the innovations powered by ethical creativity will always follow. No doubt you are already a leader in some facet of your life; the first step in fulfilling that responsibility as a Changemaker is to understand the ways our society has confused ethical and principled leadership with the opposite within traditional and competitive management.

# 9
# Servants and Supers

*Change your opinions, keep to your principles; change your leaves, keep intact your roots.* – Victor Hugo

---

### Takeaways
- Principled leadership differs from traditional leadership.
- An uneven distribution of leadership is inevitable.
- Whether the Common Man or a Changemaker, everyone is a leader.

---

"I'm just not the hero type, clearly. With this, uh, laundry list of character defects, all the mistakes I've made, largely public. Truth is…I am Iron Man." —Tony Stark, *Iron Man*

Cameras flash, the room erupts, a Black Sabbath song blasts, and the Marvel Cinematic Universe is born. After watching *Endgame*, those words, "I am Iron Man," mean so much more. The first *Iron Man* movie was a game changer. He was the first superhero in phase one of the Marvel Universe, with many more to follow.

Iron Man had a strong box office debut, and now it seems like every two years Marvel puts out a film that places in the top ten grossing movies of all time. Comic books and superhero movies were big in 2008 but not nearly to the extent that they are today. You can get away with skipping the *Justice League*, but, at this point, you're out of touch with culture if you haven't watched the major Marvel movies. Thanos dominated meme culture for a time, and when the first *Black Panther* was released, any critic with negative comments was deemed racist and executed on Twitter's chopping blocks. We have grown up with superheroes, and (much to the delight of Marvel Studios) we can't get enough of them!

## Servants and Supers

Although every comic universe starts with the story of a single hero facing a single villain, they never end that way. After the initial battle, the next villain creates an even worse situation, and this cycle continues until the heroes are no longer fighting just local villains; they're battling villains from around the world, or even across the galaxy! It seems that the more a hero fights, the more adversity he faces, creating a never-ending and ever-enlarging snowball of conflict. This trend seems to suggest that, when confined to a single event, heroism is fantastic! But when heroes maintain a degree of influence over time, the responsibility that they happily received early on will be their downfall if not willingly passed to the next hero in line.

Eventually, heroes must join forces with other heroes to fight the most powerful villains, but no matter how sizable and faithful their allegiance, the heroes are still dwarfed by the enemy. As the battles escalate, despite their intentions to save the world from certain doom, the heroes' actions may be driving the world closer to it. Just like in the movies, when a plan of action goes awry, the Common Man must deal with the collateral damage.

Changemakers, both Wisdom-led and foolish, are dangerous. Even a hero who pursues Wisdom and stays true to their principles can do more harm than good if their idea of leadership is inspired by the characters they've spent their lives watching. Those in power should never remain stagnant: leadership, for those of us who don't have superpowers, should flow cyclically. The cycle starts with the masses, the Common Man, then power is transferred to a Changemaker of their choosing. Issues arise when the Changemaker decides to impede the cycle of power instead of searching for ways power can be returned to the Common Man.

As Changemakers, we like to see ourselves as the heroes of our time, and the parallels are real. When you carry a passion with you so strongly, you are bound to receive some following or admiration. We know what it means to be go-getters, to walk the path untraveled, and we like to be appreciated for our courage and sacrifice. Without us, the Common Man would still be living with their inconveniences and injustice. We take pride in our titles, whether it be thought leader, entrepreneur, visionary, or CEO. We decide the direction our teams go and who is part of them.

It's hard for us to imagine a world without heroes—a world where the cycle of leadership stops at the Common Man. But does that mean a world without heroes shouldn't exist? In today's world, heroes haven't lived up to the hype. The Me Too movement[101] exposed a lot of them: leaders who had become demigods in the minds of the Common Man turned out to be more like demons, and people were forced to weigh the Me Too sins of their icons against the positive impact of their careers. The loss of respect for authority has not only impacted our immediate influencers: US presidents on both sides of the political spectrum have dealt with a widespread loss of admiration and audience decorum. And in the workplace, employees don't trust their bosses to treat them fairly; they'll quit their job if the boss's actions confirm their suspicions. Even parents are minimalized: parents of children who consume hours of media daily wield far less worldview influence than parents did one hundred years ago. Many people who set out to be heroes have seen their impact analyzed by the Common Man and instead been branded more like well-intentioned villains. Overall trust in our heroes has fallen.

In the wake of this loss of faith in today's heroes, a term that has progressively increased in popularity is *leaderless protest* or *leaderless revolution*. Essentially, this is a movement without a hero. We are used to seeing a face for every organization and a hero for every revolution, but the internet has changed how we organize. Today we can do things much more democratically. In the summer of 2020, protests were sprouting up all over the nation, and although many of them were shouting "Black Lives Matter," which is a nonprofit organization with set leadership and direction, numerous protests were being organized without a designated representative. A few of the protest organizers I talked to don't even like Black Lives Matter (BLM) as an organization, but they believe the phrase and hashtag has a life and meaning beyond the nonprofit.

The downsides of a leaderless protest are apparent. As with the Boston Tea Party, the protesters could feed on mob mentality and opt for civil disorder over civil disobedience. The Boston Tea Party may be recalled fondly, but, more often than not, a mob mentality has a negative narrative attached. On occasion, a BLM protest would devolve into a riot, resulting in the destruction of several city blocks, but it was difficult to assign responsibility due to how democratic the entire affair was. It seemed more that the nation was angry, leveraging protests and a hashtag to express their anger, than an organization was recruiting and organizing. No matter what your opinion is about these examples, leaderless protests are becoming more common and, thus, worthy of conversation. What would the world look like if the cycle of leadership ended with the Common Man?

## Servants and Supers

One recent leaderless protest attracted worldwide attention when one million protestors congregated in a single location over a single cause. As beautiful a sight it may have been, it all began from a story that is as ugly as they come. In February 2018, a young couple left their home in Hong Kong to vacation in Taiwan. Although the man and his girlfriend both arrived at their destination, the man was the only one to return home. A month after touching down, he confessed to strangling his pregnant girlfriend, stuffing her in a suitcase, and then seeking refuge back in Hong Kong. Despite his confession, Hong Kong authorities could not punish him because he did not commit a crime on their soil. Normally, when a crime like this occurs, the home nation agrees to send the fugitive back to the country where the crime was committed in accordance with the extradition agreement between the relevant nations. Unfortunately, Hong Kong did not have an extradition agreement with Taiwan, meaning that the murderer would go unpunished. Unsatisfied with this outcome, the Hong Kong government proposed a retroactive extradition agreement with Taiwan but also with their neighbor/parent, China, in February 2019. This is when the real conflict began.

Although Hong Kong is a part of China, it operates with a high degree of autonomy under a democratic system. China and Hong Kong have a complicated relationship, and citizens of Hong Kong are often suspicious when China tries to exercise power over their region. In 2017 and 2018, articles had been published claiming that China was silencing pro-democracy activists and booksellers within Hong Kong's borders. Hong Kongers were outraged and hostile to the idea of more Chinese involvement in Hong Kong affairs and legislation. So the locals, disagreeing with their government's agreement, saw the extradition law mentioned above as an indefensible intrusion into their region that would result in the disintegration of their current political status.

They wouldn't stand for it. Fights broke out among members of Hong Kong's legislative council. The business sector staged their largest protest in Hong Kong history, even though many of the corporations were incentivized to work with China. On June 9, one million protesters gathered with a set of five demands. A week later, two million gathered, and, eventually, the extradition bill was dropped completely. This was a feat in and of itself, but the young protesters boasted about how their movement came to be: they saw it as a real people's movement. We all share great pride when the people rise up, more so than when a hero decides on their behalf. This movement speaks to the understated potential of the Common Man, a positive attribute often overlooked by Changemakers.

In October 2021, Francis L. F. Lee and Hai Liang, professors at The Chinese University of Hong Kong, published an article discussing how this miracle of a movement formed with no central leadership. It focused on the forum used for communication: the LIHKG Web Forum. After analyzing millions of comments shared on the platform, they concluded that although the movement had no formal leadership, the power among all participants was not evenly distributed. Despite how democratic this movement was, "leaderless" is an inaccurate description. Opinion leaders, basically topic-specific influencers, were the informal and dispersed leaders. In Lee and Liang's discussion of their analysis, they state,

> Online discussions, or at least those on LIHKG, do share certain basic characteristics regardless of the topic involved. They can also illustrate the point that even an apparently structureless and leaderless movement is not completely structureless and leaderless, when one understands "leaders" in the broad sense of individuals having significant influence over others.[102]

Although the participants did not look to organizational leaders, they did look to a handful of opinion leaders for their information, whether intentionally or otherwise. Similarly, in the Black Lives Matter protests, there was always an organizer or a person with a bullhorn leading the charge. Power and influence never distribute equally if no structure exists to foster something more organized. It seems leadership is both inevitable and necessary; heroism is not.

The Common Man isn't looking to be saved: they are looking to be empowered. They don't want to forfeit their seat at the table; they just want someone to guide them to it.

Leadership is still alive and well, but Changemakers will not be good leaders if we are still looking to be the Superman of the Common Man's world. The world doesn't need any more heroes. It needs leaders who are examples,

> The world doesn't need any more heroes. It needs leaders who are examples, not legends. It needs leaders without the ego and with a strong sense of and dedication to ethics.

not legends. It needs leaders without the ego and with a strong sense of and dedication to ethics. The world needs principled leaders.

# Principled Versus Traditional Leadership

We covered principles and traditions in Chapter 3, but if you're ever wondering if you are executing principled or traditional leadership, assess your mindset. The intent of this self-assessment is to discern the beliefs influencing your actions and how you respond in light of them. Analyze whether you deem the following ten traditional misconceptions true or false; for each you believe is true, your erroneous perspective will prevent you from leading as well as a Changemaker should.

## 1. If I don't do it, it won't be done right.

This is an idea I used to perpetuate and can still find myself endorsing it if I'm not careful.

You are not a god, and the way you do things will likely be improved upon sometime in the future, as it should be. Those improvements won't happen through your team if you try to control everything. A team is collaborative in nature. Without creative freedom, your team won't grow: it will be limited by your personal shortcomings and perspective. If you believe this misconception, you may get things done quickly, but ultimately unsustainably, and you will build no one up but yourself. If an individual is built up apart from the team, you are looking at traditional hero-minded leadership.

## 2. I can't find good workers these days.

Now, hear me out, employers. What we identify as laziness and a lack of discipline is often a lack of purpose or investment. Are your systems human-centered? No one wants to work if they aren't valued by the system they are working in. Both ethical leadership and leadership guided by Wisdom are about taking undervalued communities with underappreciated people and giving those people the tools necessary to build the community up. Learning how to develop natural assets found within people, then reap the benefits of developing other leaders, is a much more valuable trait than simply knowing how to place people who have already experienced that process.

Foolish Genius

### *3. If I'm the leader, I need to be the greatest.*

If you see your followers as competitors, you are not seeking to make them the greatest they can be. You are capping the potential of your group at your (lesser) individual potential.

### *4. Vulnerability will be seen as weakness.*

Don't confuse meekness with weakness. You should cultivate an authority that encourages openness and communication instead of fear and submission. Deep, not merely surface, respect is harder to earn via this leadership style, but anything worth earning is difficult to achieve. Leadership based on heroism builds quickly, but leadership based on servanthood endures. Wisdom hates shortcuts; build trust for long-lasting change and appreciate how vulnerability helps do that.

### *5. You need to be given a platform.*

As humans we cannot thrive without other human interaction. The worst punishment in the world isn't mass hatred or criticism: it's isolation. Social interaction is what drives our society on every level, so much so that we forget we have a platform simply by living our day-to-day lives. Our family, friends, workplaces, social media accounts, and contact lists all contribute to our platform; if you wait until someone magically bestows on you a highly influential position, and even if it appears, you likely won't have the discipline and character needed to retain it. Use your gifts and your stories to influence the platform you have now. Word of mouth remains the best form of marketing. When you are intentional with the platform you have now, it will blossom.

### *6. Everyone can't be a leader.*

Behind every great Changemaker is a friend, spouse, mentor, or community of some sort that supports them and keeps them accountable. The impact those people have cannot be understated. There is no Barack without a Michelle, and vice versa. When it comes to Changemakers, there are no right-hand men or women without the moniker of leadership.

In the first chapter, I mentioned that everyone is not meant to be a Changemaker and that Changemakers shouldn't look down on anyone who chooses not to become one. Creating change comes with responsibility but also privilege, both earned and unearned. Forgive the double negative, but this does not mean that everyone is not supposed to be a leader. Everybody is not meant to spearhead change, but every single person is meant to be a leader. That's an important distinction.

This sixth misconception is closely tied to the fallacy of the fifth: you need to be given a platform. We wield so much power in our realm of influence that we don't appreciate how much we impact the world around us. Children look to their parents every day and night for protection, food, guidance, and love. All the parent has to do is accept the responsibility of parenting and be intentional about providing for their child's needs. How can we say that every parent who does so is not a leader? The same principle applies to older siblings, spouses, and true friends. We lead each other every day. The only ones who don't become leaders are those who deny the responsibilities associated with the roles they already have.

Leadership is more about realizing the responsibilities you hold now and living them out than it is about pursuing or accepting new ones. It's not enough to say we are all supposed to be leaders; in some circles, all members already are. The real question is whether you are a good one, but if you view leadership as having influence, you are already a leader in others' lives as well as your own. Whether or not you are a good leader lies in your acceptance of your position's accompanying responsibilities, as well as your ability to realize and pursue a vision.

## *7. All leaders are adults.*

Children are often overlooked as leaders, and unfortunately that is one of the reasons why leadership is not a trait of the Common Man. Leadership involves conviction and accepting responsibility, and even children make decisions that carry some weight. Obviously, children should not feel the same weight as responsible adults, but they should be allowed to make decisions about their convictions and be taught responsibility for their decisions. Every now and then, extraordinary children do just that and show adults what leadership really looks like.

Malala Yousafzai was eleven years old when her school was shut down by the Taliban. They took control of her town and banned girls from going to school. This sparked her journey as a world-renowned Changemaker. Four years later she was shot in the head for telling her story and speaking out for other girls like her. She survived and, at seventeen years old, became the youngest person to receive a Nobel Peace Prize. Greta Thunberg was fifteen when she stood on the steps of the Swedish Parliament and protested. She not only garnered the support of more than twenty thousand students, she also received a nomination for the Nobel Peace Prize for climate activism and is the youngest person to be named *TIME*'s Person of the Year. Kelvin Doe is a Sierra Leone inventor who started fixing issues in his community at eleven years old. He made batteries in a tin cup with acid, soda, and metal, and by thirteen years old, he was providing the power for houses in his area.

Children are looking to find their passion and their voice, and if we don't give them the opportunity to be bold, then we miss the opportunity for training them into ethical and Wisdom-led leaders, but they will be leaders regardless.

## *8. Leaders are loud.*

Every so often, the Presidential Historians Survey sets out to survey which US president was the best. They ask the top historians and biographers around the nation to opine. Their most recent survey was in 2021, and over the last twenty years, one president has ranked at the top of list, and he so happens to be one of the most introverted leaders this nation has ever appointed.[103] Abe Lincoln was not the commanding manly man you would think could guide our nation through its greatest divide. Instead of being strong and brawny, he was described as being "tender and warm. His whole nature was simple and sincere."[104] Instead of speaking every chance he could, like the stereotypical politician, he is quoted as saying it is "better to remain silent and be thought a fool than to speak and to remove all doubt."[105] This is not what I imagine the personality of a political wartime hero in the 1800s would be, yet he is regarded as the best president this nation has ever had.

This misconception is one I bought into when I first started to consider myself a leader. I saw the quieter students on my leadership team and noticed that they would take a backseat when the more vocal students took initiative. I assumed because of this that they simply weren't cut out for leadership, at least not like the extroverted students were. But when we started to go on mission trips and volunteer in the community, I had a change of heart. The introverts knew how to truly connect with the people we were working with. They may not have been the most popular, but they knew their strengths, showed exemplary empathy, and demonstrated an aptitude for leadership I never noticed in our strategy meetings.

## Servants and Supers

Extroverted leaders will always get more press. Their presence and voice carries, their boldness implies innovation, and their confidence implies accuracy. Everyone looks up to the Steve Jobs of our time, but Apple wouldn't exist without Woz, and it probably would have gone under without Tim Cook. Yes, change is social in nature and to make a difference you need to find your voice, but it may benefit you to use a gentle one.

The research on extroverted and introverted leaders has stayed fairly consistent over the years. Although there aren't as many out there, introverted leaders tend to be better listeners, and they better represent their team's voice. Extroverted leaders work better when the team they lead is passive. But in a group of extroverted and participatory members, introverted leaders bring home the bacon. When each individual on a team contributes and openly discusses ideas, introverted leaders deliver better results.[106]

Both introverted and extroverted leaders are needed, and both serve a purpose, but in order to excel as a community developer, the ability to listen to and understand your troupe is essential. For extroverted leaders, the urge to become the hero will likely be stronger than for the introvert who appreciates working behind the scenes. The temptation of control may be the bigger challenge for the extrovert, but for the introvert, the temptation will be not seeking out the people you should in order to grow. Introverts may be better listeners, but they are also less likely to strike up conversations with the people they should be talking to. Winston Churchill once said, "Courage is what it takes to stand up and speak; courage is also what it takes to sit down and listen." Extroverts excel at the first part of this quote, and introverts excel at the latter. The best leaders can discern their surroundings and implement both when needed.

*Loud* also doesn't have to mean vocal. Some leaders don't talk that much but are aggressive and abrasive in their demeanor. Although they aren't heard often, their presence alone is enough to demand attention and instigate fear. As negative as this method sounds, it can be rather useful to a leader taking a problem-based approach to change. If you don't need to truly communicate with the people you are leading, all you need is submission and respect, such as in battle. The principled leader can command the same respect, if not more, but their presence may have a softer undertone, one that is approachable and understanding. Their demeanor is still strong, eliciting respect from their followers, but that expectation is neither threatening nor vengeful.

# Foolish Genius

Some leaders don't share the same presence as others, but their influence is felt if they are removed.

Principled leadership is not about your personality traits. As an ethical leader, you have a range of ways to communicate to and influence your community. Principled leadership is about your dedication to the cycle of accepting power the Common Man has bestowed upon you and working, immediately, on how and when you can best return that power to those who trusted you with it in the first place.

## *9. Leaders aren't followers.*

I remember sitting in a high school biology class as the girl sitting next to me was talking about how she is the rebel in her friend group. She kept repeating the phrase "I'm a leader, not a follower." Now that I'm older, I seem to hear that notion everywhere I go. In marketing it might be communicated as "be a creator, not a consumer." In an academic setting it might sound more like "be a free thinker" or "encourage original thought." I understand the sentiment behind these phrases, and we absolutely should encourage novel and even dramatic ideas, but this does not mean we should abandon the advantages of intentional followership.

The cycle of leadership is as follows:
1. The leader makes the conscious choice to be a leader.
2. They accept the responsibilities of a leader.
3. They then fixate on an area where they will become a leader.
4. They submit under a leader or ideal already in that area.
5. They practice diligence and proactivity as a follower.
6. They influence those who are also looking to become leaders.

The cycle repeats: at the beginning, you may be a mere student, but once you have completed the cycle once, you will always be both a student and a teacher. I'm sure you have heard the expression, "Monkey see, monkey do" or heard the metaphor that humans are like sheep. No one wants to be described as an animal, especially not a monkey or a sheep, but as it turns out, we may not be as different from our furry (or wooly) friends as much as we'd like to think.

## Servants and Supers

We are followers. We'd like to think that we grow out of this state as we grow and mature, but I disagree. The same reason children pick up behavioral tendencies from their parents is why influencers get paid in the hundreds of thousands of dollars just to wear clothes with a certain logo; it's also why the Common Man follows in the paths set out for them by Changemakers. We never grow out of following, but that's okay—we're not supposed to. Instead of denying our nature and trying to avoid following something for the rest of our lives, we should be more intentional about choosing who or what we are following.

> What separates a leader from others is not that they don't follow anything, it's that they are aware and proactive about who or what they are following.

The leading misconception surrounding leadership is that leaders aren't also followers. Aristotle said it accurately when he stated, "He who has never learned to obey cannot be a good commander." What separates a leader from others is not that they don't follow anything, it's that they are aware and proactive about who or what they are following.

For change to occur, The Common Man and the Changemaker need to team up. The Salt March wouldn't have made the impact it did if Mahatma Gandhi were the only one marching. Gandhi led it, but even he started with only about eighty people, seventy-nine of which played an essential part in growing the march to its eventual fifty thousand people. Every movement needs a leader to get things moving and followers to push it forward. Following something is not a negative trait; in fact, it's a necessary one. We are born followers, and that never changes. The difference lies in what we are following and how intentional we are about it. Even Changemakers follow something. The Common Man unintentionally follows people, the Foolish Genius intentionally follows Common Sense, and Wisdom-led Changemakers follow purpose.

The Common Man is playing a risky game by following people: he has no control over the motivations or convictions of the person he is following. Moreover, it's likely that the person the Common Man is following is in turn following others: the blind leading the blind. This makes the Common Man much more susceptible to fads and trends. If the people they follow support it, the Common Man will support it. As soon as a person they follow is "canceled," their loyalties will simply shift to the next person up their perceived chain of leaders.

But just as Common Sense agrees with Wisdom at times, following other people doesn't always end badly. There is a chance that the people the Common Man is following are Wisdom-led Changemakers. In this case, the support that the Common Man gives their leaders will be put to good use: the Common Man will be a part of a social contract that results in true progress. However, even in these cases, the Common Man is not a leader because what they are following is decided largely by the opinion and storytelling abilities of others.

Changemakers of all kinds also follow other people of course, usually in the form of mentors or teachers who speak into their lives and share solid guidance. What makes this relationship different from the Common Man's affiliation with his leaders is his motivation for following others. For the average Changemaker, or Foolish Genius, their north star is typically a deep-seated desire they've broken down into goals, such as becoming so wealthy that they never have to worry about paying a bill again. Goals vary, but what Foolish Geniuses are pursuing usually revolves around the concepts of wealth, freedom, and/or happiness. None of these are bad things, and in a perfect world, everyone would have all these things, but a life-long pursuit should always be one that extends past your own, a desire the Foolish Genius lacks. For the Wisdom-led Changemaker, their motivation is always their purpose. Since Changemakers decide what they are following and are intentional about their pursuit of it, all Changemakers are leaders. They undergo all four I's of Change, especially the third I, Influence. The quality of the leader they are is defined by their ability to adhere to their principles and serve their community.

## *10. Leaders control their environment.*

In traditional leadership, the head honcho calls all the shots. Stereotypically, they get what they want when they want it, and they fire whomever isn't on board. The Foolish Genius views leadership as a means to control, but Wisdom views it as a means to serve. The difference lies in the distinction between influence and control. If you were to ask the average leader if they want influence or control, they would likely say influence. Control has a harsh connotation, and nobody wants to be seen as a dictator, especially in today's climate. A simple question such as this, when it prompts an immediate, first-blush answer, is great for exposing areas where we lack self-awareness. Our lack of self-awareness often stems from assuming things about ourselves in order to avoid facing a critical question. We don't want to see ourselves in a negative light, and God forbid that anyone else would, so we usually skirt the question, answering as we know we are "supposed to," and go along with our day. But what if we could control everything that happened in our lives? If we were honest, most of us would want that.

Before leading anyone else, you are first and foremost a leader of your own life. There are a lot of things we cannot control, and frankly, that can be annoying. It would be nice if we could control what happened in our lives and whom it happened with, but we can't rule everything. Statements like "you are in control of your life" sound nice, but if true, why do our hearts go out to those who lost their job, or experienced loss, or took ill? Platitudes such as these are simply not true: we do not control every aspect of our lives. We can control our actions, but life happens and outcomes often surprise.

If you believe a leader's role is to control, then true leadership would require totalitarian domination of everything in your life. Imagine the growing anxiety and frustration that would cause as you tried to manipulate all of your life's details. What we *can* do is heavily influence our lives through our choices, and we, as leaders, should be affording our community members the same opportunity.

When it comes to leading others, the best we can hope for is to inspire them to lead a high-quality life. Anything more aggressive than that is dangerous, approaching the realm of exploitation and unaccountable power. The role of the president of the United States is to steer the country, make decisions, and positively influence behavior. Influence leaves room for independent choice among the followers, while control tactics are one sided and extreme: Party A makes decisions and Party B submits. If Party B decides not to submit, they will be excommunicated from Party A.

Control is the easier of the two routes. Since trust is not a prerequisite to control, many people start businesses without a partner, for instance, and collective impact is ignored as a means to motivate collaboration. Fewer hands in the pot mean easier and faster decision-making and application. Control is most easily executed with as small a group as possible. Control in larger groups leads to micromanagement and an inefficient use of time and energy. This is part of the reason why control is short-lived: as soon as Party

## Foolish Genius

B chooses not to submit to Party A, their relationship will end and each party will exist independent of the other.

Influence is about facilitation, delegation, and trust. It is an exchange. If Party A suggests an option, Party B can accept or deny. Party B accepts responsibility for their actions since they were given an explicit choice. Either way, Party A will support Party B, even if Party A doesn't support Party B's decision. The influence Party A has on Party B will continue much longer since trust is present and Party B was open to hearing the advice of Party A.

The wish to be the hero of a community can likewise stem from an unhealthy focus on control. As well-intentioned as it may be, saving someone or something can wrongly involve acting on their behalf and keeping them out of the solution to their problem. If concepts like ethical leadership that integrates all players on a path to success stresses you out, you may be used to having greater control of how things are done, and that's okay. Remember that leadership is inevitable in a large community: people will learn to trust a voice whether it is yours *or not*. Learning to delegate responsibility and build trust with others mitigates the here propensity; increasing responsibility and trust are not only healthy practices but also more conducive to sustainable solutions—absent the hero.

Another problem with the hero's fascination with control and seeming leadership is a basic one: humans get tired, even aspiring heroes. Solopreneurs fail every day because they have goals and dreams that are outside of their own capabilities. As difficult as it may be, yielding control and optimizing for influence is the best approach for the community.

# 10
# The Heart of Wisdom

*Change is a threat when done to me, but an opportunity when done by me.* – Rosabeth Moss Kanter

---

**Takeaways**
- Community development is the essence of Wisdom.

---

## Community

*Community* is a word everyone uses but can mean something different to every person who does. For example, to the entrepreneur, *community* means security. Its importance is stressed in the language of niching down and building an audience. To the business manager, *community* means cohesion, high employee morale, and dedication to the company. All of this, of course, results in higher output and more revenue for the company. To the life coach or mentor, *community* means camaraderie and accountability. The more people take an interest in one another, the more invested they will be in their mutual growth and success. To the evolutionist, *community* means collaborative success, which may be communicated in terms of prosocial behavior and collective survival. In Douglass Rushkoff's impassioned book *Team Human*, he wrote that

> survival of the fittest is a convenient way to justify the cutthroat ethos of a competitive marketplace, political landscape, and culture. But this perspective misconstrues the theories of Darwin as well as his successors. By viewing evolution through a strictly competitive lens, we miss the bigger story of our own social

development and have trouble understanding humanity as one big, interconnected team.[107]

He spends the next few pages explaining how humans, as well as other organisms, have found success through their ability to communicate and ideate as a group. Community is not only beneficial; it's essential to our survival.

To the Changemaker, *community* might mean any and all of these, but it's also inherently tied to purpose and social impact. Greg Satell, the author of *Cascades*, wrote that "the strength of a movement is not large crowds, but small groups,"[108] and he's right. If principles are the building blocks of truth, communities are the building blocks of change. Sharing your purpose typically starts with word of mouth and sparks conversation: "What do you think of this?" "Don't you think this is wrong?" "It doesn't make any sense why we…." After speaking with enough like-minded individuals, you'll find yourself with a small group, all passionate about the same cause and willing to act. Today, Mothers Against Drunk Driving is one of the most impactful single-issue lobbying groups around with over three million supporters, and you'll recall it was started by a single woman and her group of mothers meeting around a kitchen table.

Community, in its relation to social change, has several main benefits, and the first is that the individual has a larger role in the group than if acting alone. To establish a secure sense of purpose, we need to feel that our role is having an impact. Small groups establish that first connection. Since your influence is appreciated by others, you're encouraged to be creative and explore how you as an individual can make a difference.

The second benefit is that communities inspire engagement. It can be difficult to build sympathy for your cause, but building engagement is a whole different beast. For some, talking the talk will always be preferred to walking the walk. For others, they may be fighting for their own cause and won't have the ability to engage with yours without sacrificing theirs. Either way, more people will sympathize with you than will join as an ally. In 2018, published research explored what incentives cause people to take action that aligns with their sympathies. Their biggest finding reported,

> Students are most likely to behave in line with their personal sympathies when they know that they have friends attending the protest. Interviewed participants support this notion; students and activists acknowledge that they feel the strongest pull to at-

tend events that they have friends at, and an organizer suggests students who want to attend a protest often only will if they can find people they know personally going.[109]

Small groups are intimate: you learn about the people you are working with as you go through life together. It's a lot harder to shift responsibility to a friend than it is to a nameless employee you have no connection to and share no obvious interests with. The small group is the bond that keeps movements going, not the flashy events or news-making protests. These activities play a part, but they would not be possible without the teams of small groups that organize and keep a movement going, even when it's not in the press.

The third benefit, as the entrepreneur knows, is that communities tackle niches. In the beginning of a movement, all you have is a single niche and a small team. After you achieve your first set of victories, the time will come to redefine your objectives and begin working on a new set of goals. When this happens, the hype will die down and many of the short-term supporters will fall off the wagon. Nonetheless, building pockets of grassroot communities will ensure these transitions are successfully absorbed and even leveraged. There is no way around it: if you want to create a movement and change the definition of Common Sense, you need to be able to build and develop communities.

Wisdom cares about how a community is built; in fact, it's obsessed with it. Although the ability to identify principles and think critically have been mentioned time and time again throughout this book, you cannot understand Wisdom as a Changemaker until you have a heart for the people around you. The essence of Wisdom is found in community development. I don't know of any other concept that incorporates the characteristics of Wisdom so well. In order to create change, community has to be the focus. In order to create positive change—movement toward a Wise Society—community development must be a *passion*. I believe that, as in Rosa's case, the desire for community development should be what drives the change you want to see.

> The essence of Wisdom is found in community development.

Foolish Genius

# Rosa Guamán

Mrs. Guamán's story[110] takes place in Licto, a small town in the mountainous Chimborazo region of Ecuador. Ecuador fell under Spanish rule during the Spanish Conquest of the 1500s and remained under Spain's dominion for about two hundred years. During that time, the indigenous peasantry were placed under new restrictions, creating a relationship between the upper and lower classes similar to a master-slave agreement. Even after their independence in 1822, the semi-feudal system persisted for at least another 120 years. By 1970, the government attempted to put an end to the service tenure system and redistribute the land to the indigenous people. However, despite their best intentions, those efforts were largely unhelpful to the rural lower class, and even less so to the indigenous women of Licto. Although they were once a proud people, boasting an extensive knowledge of their land and natural resources, they were now impoverished, humiliated, struggling to provide for their own families, and reliant on NGO resources.

Rosa Guamán, a woman with very little formal education, decided it was time to speak out against the injustices she was experiencing in her community. She knew that her culture was once formidable with communities thriving exclusive of outside assistance. She was ashamed that the land under their feet was fertile but they had lost the knowledge required to take advantage of it—to sow and reap for the benefit of all. So she set out to improve things, but her path was riddled with roadblocks. As bad as it was for the indigenous lower class, it was particularly bad for their women. They were forced to sit in the back of the bus when traveling, they were not allowed a voice in the presence of a man, but worst of all, most of the indigenous women in Licto were illiterate. Rosa's first step was to seek out other women in her community who were willing to pursue change. They had all the passion and drive necessary, but they were mothers who needed to ensure their families had food on the table. Initiating an uprising would have resulted in a loss of consistent income—something they could not risk. So Rosa and these women networked and waited.

During the mid-1970s, a parish priest named Estuardo Gallegos came to Licto. Soon he greatly impacted Rosa and her group, inspiring them to execute a process of personal change while working toward communal independence. He trained them as pastoral workers, which was no easy process, as Rosa and her friends had associated the church with discrimination and

## The Heart of Wisdom

prejudice. In church, before Estuardo arrived, the lower class had been forced to kneel on the floor instead of sitting on benches with the rest of the members. Estuardo ended this practice, building rapport in the process, and ensuring that everyone would be treated as equals while inside the church building. Still armed with passion and now with the support of the church, Rosa and her band started to look for ways they could lift their community out of its dependent state.

In the late 1990s, Rosa heard of a failed project to sell medicinal plants. It was dropped because it was deemed unprofitable, but Rosa saw the untapped potential of the land, the women in the community, and that idea. Rosa's team tested the idea by growing the plants in the wild and observing how the community responded when displayed at the local market. The response was convincing, and in 1997, Rosa and her team leveraged this knowledge to persuade other local women to grow traditional medicinal plants. Rosa would purchase them, store them in an old church attic, then find dependable buyers for the supply. By 2000, Rosa and her team had attracted attention from organizations outside of Ecuador, and in 2001, their company, Jambi Kiwa, had its own factory, legal status, and first major contract with a national tea company.

Not only did Rosa and her team give over five hundred families an opportunity to create a consistent income, but they also reconnected their village to its roots. The women growing the plants would share their mothers' and grandmothers' stories of how they would concoct different medicines and ingeniously administer them. Jambi Kiwa was built on the collective work and family histories of their village. The team also began to teach literacy classes to local women, as well as classes focused on making clothes, learning craftwork, and entrepreneurship. Rosa impacted her village in almost every way possible because she decided to include the village—the people in community—in her solution. She knew what the village had to offer, and she worked to build upon that. In an interview translated into English, Rosa summed up her philosophy by explaining,

> We always think that the farmer, the native people, cannot do it. In my country, a businessperson is considered to be someone with money, a profession, or a qualification. We have broken this barrier; we have taken on the management of the company. I am not an educated woman. I'm like most women in our industry: a mother, farmer, producer—but with a different vision. All the

workers are partners. The partners have gardens, large or small, but with a variety of plants. The farming is organic; we work under the influence of the moon. We are in the national and international markets, exporting to France, Spain, Belgium, Germany. We have products in Italy, Canada, and the United States. That's our work. It is a new business model: farmers and indigenous entrepreneurs, because indigenous people have never been seen as entrepreneurs. Our self-esteem changes. We don't generate pity; we generate employment![111]

Rosa's story is an inspiring one but without any particularly extraordinary people, at least not at first sight. The characters were an uneducated group of indigenous women, a passionate group of mothers, and a priest, all of whom were considered poor. Yet they were all pivotal to the success of Jambi Kiwa.

Although Rosa is portrayed here as the "main character," she is hardly the only leader in the story. If Estuardo Gallegos and other members of the local church had not done their part as community leaders, then Rosa's group would not have been organized or trained. Their faith in the church would not have been restored, and Rosa may not have developed the foundation she gained as a pastoral worker.

The mothers in the community were all leaders. Each one faced the choice of investing time to plant and tend a garden while they also reared children and pursued other jobs. Each one owned their vision to provide a better life for their family and community. They could have killed Rosa's idea in utero when she presented the goods at the local market, but they didn't. A servant leader cannot be the only leader in this or almost any successful story. All participants were built up by leaders, and they in turn identified their leaders in a cycle of mutual growth and empowerment.

With no education, startup funds, or an ability to use written communication to spread their vision, Rosa and her team built a social enterprise sourced by villagers, eventually enjoying international success. Rosa was a servant first, but, more than that, she was a community developer. Robert Greenleaf wrote that the test of a servant-first leader was that they

> make sure that other people's highest priority needs are being served. The best test, and difficult to administer, is: Do those served grow as persons? Do they, while being served, become healthier, wiser, freer, more autonomous, more likely themselves

to become servants? And, what is the effect on the least privileged in society; will they benefit, or, at least, not be further deprived?[112]

Rosa tied her success to the development of her village. Every party involved in the creation of Jambi Kiwa went through financial, cultural, and personal growth. The village's overall quality of life improved; today's average business doesn't approach that level of impact. If Rosa did not address her neighbors' needs and in return receive assistance from them, her business would have failed. She saw not only the issues in her community but also its strengths, incorporating the proud, strong history the village once enjoyed. She pulled from the techniques of the mothers and grandmothers who had once lived more autonomously and shaped an organization that honored their past as well as their future. Once you're in a space where you are uplifting those around you in such a holistic way, you take on an entirely new role. You are no longer just an entrepreneur or leader—you are a community developer.

Community developers tackle the unique assignment of changing the culture of entire cities. While economic developers bring new businesses into their region, community developers are the soldiers on the ground working with the people in their city. They see individual lives affected by the work they do, whether positively or otherwise. Traditionally, community developers have taken a problem-based approach. The basic premise of this approach is that you enter a community, hear their problems and views, and then those with capital and capabilities inject resources, programs, and initiatives to solve that community's problems. Seems intuitive enough. But surprisingly, although this method can work, many times it does more harm to the community than good.

The issues this approach introduces can drag the majority of the community down instead of lift a portion of it up. Moreover, these are the same concerns that show up when you combine a hero mindset with the More Mindset; typically, these are quick fixes offered as solutions for complex problems with a well-meaning hero spearheading the mission. The hero may be understanding and kind, and may even have the talents to solve a few issues in the community, but as soon as they leave, the community finds itself even more dependent and mentally shackled than before.

This phenomenon can be seen throughout our society. Many investors don't invest in a company unless they know the founder will be there 24/7, even after an exit. They know that, with our current view of leadership, the founder is the hero. Founders will take control and get done what needs to get done, but as soon as they get sick, experience a perspective-changing event, or move to the next challenge, the company tanks. The same principle applies in community development, but instead of a start-up failing, an entire community collapses. Instead of a few wealthy people taking a loss on a high-risk investment, an entire city grinds to a halt with the shared mindset that they cannot help their situation.

Two professors who had been entrenched in urban affairs and saw the firsthand the dangers of problem-based community development sought to find a different way.

## Learning Our ABCDs

John Kretzmann, John McKnight, and their team of researchers went to twenty low-income cities that presented a high level of citizenship to study how those cities could thrive as a community despite the countless challenges they faced. After analyzing over three hundred neighborhoods, Kretzmann and McKnight wrote the book *Building Communities from the Inside Out* on their findings. They concluded that "all the historic evidence indicates that significant community development takes place only when local community people are committed to investing themselves and their resources in the effort. This observation explains why communities are never built from the top down or from the outside in."[113] This "inside-out" approach is called Asset Based Community Development, or ABCD.

This is not to say that the problem-based approach doesn't have a place in the world. It does. It's appropriate when you need to patch up a problem while you work on a longer-term solution. In February 2018, a study by Hanna Nel was published comparing ABCD to the problem-based approach.[114] They dissected the two methods and the conditions of their successes and failures and found that problem-based approaches were more successful in the short-term, but ABCD approaches were more sustainable. Patches are great if they aren't viewed as permanent.

This is not a criticism of NGOs or people who donate resources to other communities. NGOs are typically groups with a social mission, many of which are run by volunteers. Think of a nonprofit on steroids. And like nonprofits, they are run by some of the most kind-hearted people on earth, people who see disenfranchised groups and devote their life to helping them. These have a role to play. You play a similar role when you give money to someone living on the street. It would be silly to think that the money alone would be the solution to the biggest challenges they are facing, but it may alleviate their most immediate needs. However, if you pair this role with a hero mentality, or one that overestimates the impact that helping hand will have, the community will likely suffer some consequences.

ABCD is based on the idea that a community is best served when it is directly involved in the solution. It focuses on what the community has to offer, as opposed to what the community needs. The ABCD approach absolutely offers solutions to problems in the community, but it looks to solve them from within the community itself instead of relying on outside influence. It goes beyond figuring out what is wrong with a community to finding solutions from within the people in the community. The key: relying on members of the community instead of outsiders.

Rosa Guamán and her team used this approach when they built Jambi Kiwa. When others had tried to help the indigenous people of Licto, they employed the needs-based approach. Rosa mentioned in her writings how they would receive help from NGOs sending food and resources. Yet, when Rosa saw it, she became embarrassed and ashamed. It wasn't that she was angry at the NGOs for extending a helping hand; it was what problem-based assistance was doing to her people—prescribing a Band-Aid for an internal bleed.

No ABCD project is the same, but the general process (as I understand it) happens as follows. First, a struggling community is identified. I don't have to go in-depth to define a struggling community; we all know one when we see one. An ABCD-trained individual is then dispatched to that area and immediately gets to work. Their first job is to identify community connectors. These connectors are people who have reached the third "I" of change. They may be a nonprofit founder, politician, or a regular citizen, but they must be well-respected and well-known in their community. These are people who have a proven track record of good intentions, even if their results have not proven fruitful.

After connectors have been identified, joined the project, and gone through training, the next step is asset mapping. Asset mapping is one of the mechanisms that sets the ABCD apart from other forms of community development. In this stage, called a capacity inventory, leaders assess local institutions, organizations, and people to determine what skills, passions, and opportunities are lying dormant in the community. The inventory looks at the community members' skill sets, community interests, enterprising interests and experiences, and the personal information needed to follow up with them. The paid staff of the organization sponsoring the ABCD campaign and the connectors are trained to guide the community members through a process to help them see the potential impact they could have, even if never before experienced. In addition to following this process with the locals, the connectors and staff do the same with local organizations and institutions, reaching out to all the stakeholders involved.

After hundreds of conversations, the connectors and staff break down the information and search for themes that can be used to shape the solution. These "building themes" are extracted to form a strategy the community can eventually come to own. At this stage, much of the process is similar to other community projects: forming necessary relationships, fundraising, and building hype around the newly formed idea.

What does this process mean for Changemakers? If you are the leader of a team, organization, or even your friend group, you may have a sense of how to develop your own community. This may not seem necessary if your community seems to be alive and well. If so, that assessment may reflect the thinking of someone who has reached the third "I," Influence, and has positively impacted their community, but is now comfortable with remaining there. Creating and sustaining a single community is a difficult task in and of itself, so if you are content with that level of impact, more power to you. But if you are aspiring to become a Changemaker, to dip into the fourth "I" and extend your influence to other communities, you must pursue that expanded mission in ways that are tailored to and accepted by them.

Whether you see yourself as a community developer, servant leader, Wisdom-led Changemaker, or all of the above, the concepts you internalize will seem simple at first but will appear radical in application. This is always the case when pursuing Wisdom. It may seem simple enough to use the community to fix the community, but what if you go there and the people are convinced that they are incapable of helping themselves? What if they are perfectly fine with Band-Aids?

Setting out to create tangible and lasting improvement is a difficult and painstaking process, one that will take more out of you than any other process I'm aware of. Becoming a Changemaker in general is not an easy task;

the Foolish Genius, on the other hand, has the liberty to accept or deny any responsibility that they see fit because they are not pursuing progress. The Wisdom-led Changemaker, since they are pursuing true progress, has a much tougher job. Personal change occurs when you break down your own mental barriers and preconceptions and walk intentionally and consistently toward a single vision. Societal change, redefining Common Sense, happens when you convince an entire community to do the same. That will always be an arduous battle.

The ABCD approach assumes that the members of your community will eventually attain the confidence and self-worth to create the change they want to see. That takes time, investment, and conviction, but it's the best strategy we have. Working alone is easy but limiting. Working collaboratively is harder but possesses a greater potential for impact. Working collectively with a community that has been trained to be saved by heroes is perhaps the most difficult thing anyone can set out to do, but it is the only solution that will lead to lasting change and a Wise Society.

The opening sentence to this book reads "given the choice between liberty and bondage, Common Sense chooses the latter, inevitably mistaking the two." The Foolish Genius tries to create change by imposing their definition of Common Sense onto others who do not share the same cultural background. This is a sterile, top-down approach to change, and it can work with the right messaging, mental strong-arming, and manipulation. Common Sense is not something that is consciously formed. By imposing it on others, it may feel like you are liberating them, but, in reality, you are forcing them to abide by what you believe simply because you believe it. Change that is inspired by Common Sense and introduced to other communities will always feel forced. As Rosabeth Moss Kanter stated, "Change is a threat when done to me, but an opportunity when done by me."[115]

Wisdom is a process that cannot begin without intentional pursuit. A Wise Society can be created only if those affected by it are directly involved in making it happen. It can happen only if the underlying principles are accepted by the individual communities, and those individual communities are allowed to create unique solutions based on that same foundation. ABCD applies the same principles every time, yet every solution is different because it is created by the people who are most affected by the change. This is the path to a Wise Society: a path that needs Wisdom-led Changemakers, motivated by their passions and a sense of purpose, to discover and birth

Foolish Genius

the innovative solutions lying dormant in those who have not had the privilege or skills to do so themselves. That describes, even defines, true Changemakers: those who empower the Common Man to the same extent that they themselves have been empowered. This is the path of equitable change, the path that has Wisdom as its sole guide and is always inviting another Foolish Genius to follow.

# Afterword

I love stories. I can't get enough of them. There is no better way to make a principle come to life, to relate with a complete stranger, or to ensure that the values of your culture are passed from generation to generation. Every powerful story executes on the three *C*'s: character, conflict, and conclusion. When I'm told to think of my life as a story, my mind jumps to the conflict and the conclusion. *This is what crazy thing happened and this is how it ended.* I don't focus on the other participants because, in my story, the focus is on what happens to me. But each life tells a different story, and people will remember your character in relation to the other players. "He was always kind to me." "She always knew how to compose herself in a difficult situation." "They were always so forgiving." Characteristics like these will epitomize your life as others observe how you impact the people around you. We can't produce something that isn't in some way already in us, but we can craft a story easily embedded with those same characteristics. Storytelling works.

Some of the concepts in this book are described alongside their characteristics, like Wisdom and purpose. In some chapters I cite pitfalls or misconceptions in addition to or in place of characteristics. I share this so that we can check *ourselves*—not others who haven't subscribed to the Wise Society concept. As you gain experience and move through the four *P*'s of Change, ask yourself how closely your characteristics align with those of Wisdom. How are they reflected in your story? Would someone think that you were a friend of Wisdom? Or is that a goal you are still working toward? Do you find it difficult to let go of some of the pitfalls or misconceptions identified?

Each characteristic of Wisdom should become your own, and if they are not, I hope you're inspired to become intentional about improving in those areas. This is how Wisdom becomes your guide: by taking time to outline your story thus far, then working toward the character development you want to see both in yourself and reflected in those around you.

No matter how intimate we are with Wisdom, there will always be a little bit of a Foolish Genius in us, and that's okay. The intent of this book is to help you along the path to Wisdom and eventually, a Wise Society—and certainly to focus on the ways you can change and grow along the way. While we are all born with Common Sense as our basis for decision-making, by reading this book, you've hopefully learned the value of Wis-

Foolish Genius

dom and come to realize that, with it, you can be the kind of Changemaker who leads us to a Wise Society.

# Endnotes

[1] *The Scientific American*, quoted by Edward L. Bernays, *Propaganda* (1928; repr., Brooklyn, NY: Ig Publishing, 2004), 49–50.

[2] Edward L. Bernays, *Propaganda* (1928; repr., Brooklyn, NY: Ig Publishing, 2004), 74.

[3] Erica Chenoweth and Maria J. Stephan, *Why Civil Resistance Works: The Strategic Logic of Nonviolent Conflict* (New York: Columbia University Press, 2011).

[4] Arthur C. Clarke, Profiles of the Future (New York: Harper and Row, 1962), 2, quoted in the Ron Nessen Papers at the Gerald R. Ford Presidential Library, online at https://www.fordlibrarymuseum.gov/library/document/0204/1511924.pdf.

[5] Zoe Leviston, Murni Greenhill, and Iain Walker, "Australian Attitudes to Climate Change and Adaptation: 2010–2014" CSIRO, Australia, 2015, https://doi.org/10.13140/RG.2.1.2149.0001/1.

[6] Leviston, Greenhill, and Walker, "Australian Attitudes to Climate Change and Adaptation," 6.

[7] Leviston, Greenhill, and Walker, "Australian Attitudes to Climate Change and Adaptation," viii.

[8] Melissa G. Hunt et al., "No more FOMO: Limiting social media decreases loneliness and depression," *Journal of Social and Clinical Psychology* 37, no. 10, https://doi.org/10.1521/jscp.2018.37.10.751, 751–768.

[9] Melissa G. Hunt, "Too much of a good thing: Who we follow, what we do, and how much time we spend on social media affects well-being," *Journal of Social and Clinical Psychology* 40, no. 1, 46–68, https://doi.org/10.1521/jscp.2021.40.1.46. Phil Reed, Tegan Fowkes, & Mariam Khela, "Reduction in social media usage produces improvements in physical health and wellbeing: An RCT," *Journal of Technology in Behavior Science* 8, 140–147, https://doi.org/10.1007/s41347-023-00304-7.

[10] W. Mischel, E. B. Ebbesen, and A. Raskoff Zeiss, "Cognitive and Attentional Mechanisms in Delay of Gratification," *Journal of Personality and Social Psychology* 21, no. 2 (1972): 204–218, https://doi.org/10.1037/h0032198.

[11] The link below leads to Kaczynski's essay. According to the Washington Post, "The author [the Unabomber] threatened to send a bomb to an unspecified destination 'with intent to kill' unless one of the newspapers published this manuscript. The Attorney General and the Director of the FBI recommended publication." "The Unabomber Trial: The Manifesto," Washington Post, September 22, 1995, https://www.washingtonpost.com/wp-srv/national/longterm/unabomber/manifesto.text.htm.

[12] David Garland, "Hating the Human Mind the Unabomber's Grievance Is Age-Old," *Roanoke Times*, April 28, 1996, https://scholar.lib.vt.edu/VA-news/ROA-Times/issues/1996/rt9604/960428/04290083.htm.

[13] Plato, *The Republic*, trans. Desmond Lee, 2nd ed. (London: Penguin Classics, 2007), 204–205.

[14] "Winston Churchill's Early Years," America's National Churchill Museum, accessed May 25, 2023, https://www.nationalchurchillmuseum.org/winston-churchill-early-life.html.

[15] Derek Sivers, "How to Start a Movement," TED video, https://www.ted.com/talks/derek_sivers_how_to_start_a_movement.

[16] Sivers, "How to Start a Movement," 2:08–2:24.

[17] National Park Service, "Frequently Asked Questions," Thomas Edison National Historical Park New Jersey, last modified March 31, 2012, https://www.nps.gov/edis/faqs.htm. Jacob Mullin, "Thomas Edison's recipe of ADHD: 'A Tremendous Ability in an Un-tremendous World,'" LINCS, October 31, 2012, https://community.lincs.ed.gov/group/29/document/thomas-edisons-recipe-adhd-tremendous-ability-un-tremendous-world.

[18] Mankell, Henning. The Fifth Woman. United States: New Press, 2000.

[19] Nicole Bitette, "Curse of the Lottery: Tragic Stories of Big Jackpot Winners," January 12, 2016, https://www.nydailynews.com/life-style/tragic-stories-lottery-winners-article-1.2492941.

[20] Plato, *The Republic*, 204–205.

[21] Ashira Prossack, "This Year, Don't Set New Year's Resolutions," Forbes, December 31, 2018, https://www.forbes.com/sites/ashiraprossack1/2018/12/31/goals-not-resolutions/?sh=69d1d893879a.

[22] You are reading this book, and hopefully, it has a positive impact on you. As you are reading, routinely ask yourself how this book is impacting you.

[23] I. B. Mauss et al., "Can Seeking Happiness Make People Unhappy? Paradoxical Effects of Valuing Happiness," *Emotion* 11, no. 4 (2011): 807–815, https://doi.org/10.1037/a0022010.

[24] Mauss et al., "Can Seeking Happiness Make People Unhappy?"

[25] Mauss et al., "Can Seeking Happiness Make People Unhappy?"

[26] *Oxford University Press*, s.v. "quality of wealth."

[27] Oxford English Dictionary, s.v. "principle."

[28] In Chapter 6 we'll talk more on the importance of self-awareness, how uncommon it is, and how you can use it to pursue purpose.

[29] J. M. Darley and B. Latane, "Bystander Intervention in Emergencies: Diffusion of Responsibility," *Journal of Personality and Social Psychology* 8 no. 4, pt.1 (1968): 377–383, https://doi.org/10.1037/h0025589.

# Endnotes

[30] "10 Percent of US Adults Have Drug Use Disorder at Some Point in Their Lives," National Institutes of Health, November 18, 2015, https://www.nih.gov/news-events/news-releases/10-percent-us-adults-have-drug-use-disorder-some-point-their-lives.

[31] Nic Rigby, "Benjamin Lay: The Quaker Dwarf Who Fought Slavery," BBC News, February 10, 2018, https://www.bbc.com/news/uk-england-essex-42640782.

[32] Benjamin Lay, (Philadelphia, Printed by Benjamin Franklin, 1737; Ann Arbor: Text Creation Partnership), http://name.umdl.umich.edu/N03401.0001.001.

[33] Marcus Rediker, "The "Quaker Comet" Was the Greatest Abolitionist You've Never Heard Of," Smithsonian Magazine, September 2017, https://www.smithsonianmag.com/history/quaker-comet-greatest-abolitionist-never-heard-180964401/.

[34] Marcus Rediker, The Fearless Benjamin Lay: The Quaker Dwarf Who Became the First Revolutionary Abolitionist (Boston: Beacon Press, 2017).

[35] Rigby, "Benjamin Lay: The Quaker Dwarf Who Fought Slavery."

[36] Ray Dalio, *Principles* (2011), 4, https://ia800403.us.archive.org/20/items/BridgewaterRayDalioPrinciples/Bridgewater%20-%20Ray%20Dalio%20-%20Principles.pdf.

[37] John Chester Miller, *Origins of the American Revolution* (Stanford: Stanford University Press, 1943), 170, https://archive.org/details/in.ernet.dli.2015.212021/page/n187/mode/2up.

[38] Marx, "Economic and Philosophical Manuscripts," in *Karl Marx: Early Writings*, trans. and ed. T. B. Bottomore (London: C. A. Watts, 1963), 59, quoted in Andrew Feenberg, "Realizing Philosophy: Marx, Lukács and the Frankfurt School," Simon Fraser University, accessed May 26, 2023, https://www.sfu.ca/~andrewf/Philosophy%20of%20Praxis%20preview%2025Jun14.pdf.

[39] Michael D. Higgins, "Speech at a Reception for Philosophy Ireland," November 19, 2016, Áras an Uachtaráin, Dublin, Ireland, transcript, https://president.ie/en/media-library/speeches/speech-at-a-reception-for-philosophy-ireland.

[40] Félix García Moriyón, "Matthew Lipman: An Intellectual Biography," *Thinking: The Journal of Philosophy for Children* 20, no. 1/2 (2012): 22–32, https://doi.org/10.5840/thinking2012201/24.

[41] Shahzad Tahmasebi Boroujeni and Mehdi Shahbazi, "The Effect of Instructional and Motivational Self-Talk on Performance of Basketball's Motor Skill," *Procedia - Social and Behavioral Sciences* 15 (2011): 3113–3117, https://doi.org/10.1016/j.sbspro.2011.04.255. Gary Lupyan, "Linguistically Modulated Perception and Cognition: The Label-Feedback Hypothesis," *Frontiers in Psychology* 3 (March 2012): 54, https://doi.org/10.3389/fpsyg.2012.00054.

[42] George J. Stigler, *Essays in the History of Economics* (Chicago: University of Chicago Press, 1965), 21.
[43] Ludwig Wittgenstein, *Tractatus Logico-Philosophicus*, 471st ed. (Mineola, NY: Dover Publications, 1998), 3.
[44] Ludwig Wittgenstein, *Philosophical Investigations*, revised English translation (United Kingdom: Blackwell, 2001).
[45] Albert Einstein, quoted in Jesse Weaver, "Life, Liberty and the Pursuit of Technology," Medium, August 27, 2018, https://medium.com/predict/life-liberty-and-the-pursuit-of-technology-745ff54778b1.
[46] Friedrich Nietzsche, *Twilight of the Idols* (Mineola, NY: Dover Publications, 2019), 2, https://www.google.com/books/edition/Twilight_of_the_Idols/gLKhDwAAQBAJ?hl=en&gbpv=0&safe=strict.
[47] J. Robin Moon, et al., "Short- and Long-Term Associations between Widowhood and Mortality in the United States: Longitudinal Analyses," *Journal of Public Health* 36, no. 3 (September 2014), 382–389, https://doi.org/10.1093/pubmed/fdt101.
[48] "The Life of Viktor Frankl," The Viktor E. Frankl Institute of America, accessed May 9, 2023, https://viktorfranklamerica.com/viktor-frankl-bio/.
[49] Viktor E. Frankl, *Man's Search for Meaning: An Introduction to Logotherapy*, 4th ed., trans. Ilse Lasch (Boston: Beacon Press, 1992), 87–88, https://www.google.com/books/edition/Man_s_Search_for_Meaning/K2AvZmco3E0C?hl=en&gbpv=0&safe=strict
https://www.google.com/books/edition/Man_s_Search_for_Meaning/K2AvZmco3E0C?hl=en&gbpv=0&safe=strict. All subsequent citations refer to this edition.
[50] Dalai Lama XVI, "Our prime purpose in this life is to help others. And if you can't help them, at least don't hurt them," Goodreads, accessed May 26, 2023, https://www.goodreads.com/author/quotes/570218.Dalai_Lama_XIV.
[51] Patrick L. Hill and Nicholas A. Turiano, "Purpose in Life as a Predictor of Mortality across Adulthood," *Psychological Science* 25, no. 7 (2014), https://doi.org/10.1177/0956797614531799. Aliya Alimujiang et al., "Association Between Life Purpose and Mortality Among US Adults Older Than 50 Years," *JAMA Network Open* 2, no. 5 (2019), https://doi.org/10.1001/jamanetworkopen.2019.4270.
[52] Members of the Adolescent Moral Development Lab at Claremont Graduate University, "The Psychology of Purpose," John Templeton Foundation, February 2018, 10, https://www.templeton.org/wp-content/uploads/2020/02/Psychology-of-Purpose.pdf.
[53] Koichiro Shiba, et al., "Purpose in Life and 8-Year Mortality by Gender and Race/Ethnicity among Older Adults in the U.S.," *Preventive Medicine* 164, (November 2022), https://doi.org/ 10.1016/j.ypmed.2022.107310.

# Endnotes

54 Barbara Kingsolver, *Animal Dreams: A Novel* (New York: Harper Perennial, 2013), 299.

55 Frankl, Man's Search for Meaning, 113.

56 Tasha Eurich, "What Self-Awareness Really Is (and How to Cultivate It)," Harvard Business Review, January 4, 2018, https://hbr.org/2018/01/what-self-awareness-really-is-and-how-to-cultivate-it.

57 "95% of leaders think they have this quality—but less than 15% actually do," EAB, January 24, 2019, https://eab.com/insights/daily-briefing/workplace/leaders-think-they-have-this-quality-but-few-actually-do/.

58 Eurich, "What Self-Awareness Really Is (and How to Cultivate It)."

59 Eurich, "What Self-Awareness Really Is (and How to Cultivate It)."

60 Erik Samdahl, "Top Employers Are 5.5x More Likely to Reward Collaboration," The i4cp Productivity Blog, June 22, 2017, https://www.i4cp.com/productivity-blog/top-employers-are-5-5x-more-likely-to-reward-collaboration.

61 Samdahl, "Top Employers Are 5.5x More Likely to Reward Collaboration."

62 Bob Kulhan, *Getting to "Yes And": The Art of Business Improv* (Stanford: Stanford University Press, 2017), 182–183, https://www.google.com/books/edition/Getting_to_Yes_And/as4ZDgAAQBAJ?hl=en&gbpv=0&safe=strict.

63 Keith Sawyer and Stacy Dezutter, "Distributed Creativity: How Collective Creations Emerge from Collaboration," *Psychology of Aesthetics, Creativity, and the Arts* 3, no. 2 (2009): 82, https://doi.org/10.1037/a0013282.

64 Draper Hill, *Fashionable Contrasts: Caricatures by James Gillray* (London: Phaidon Press, 1928), 6, https://rarebooksocietyofindia.org/book_archive/196174216674_10152262638611675.pdf.

65 "Extracts from the Manual of the Reich Chamber of Culture (1937)," German History in Documents and Images, accessed May 10, 2023, https://ghdi.ghi-dc.org/sub_document.cfm?document_id=1576.

66 Union of Writers of the USSR, Voronezh branch, "Rise" (1990), 48.

67 Oxford University Press, s.v. "art."

68 Brian Burrell, *Postcards from the Brain Museum: The Improbable Search for Meaning in the Matter of Famous Minds* (New York: Broadway Books, 2004), 300, https://archive.org/details/postcardsfrombra00burr/page/300/mode/2up?q=opts.

69 "The Top 20 Reasons Startups Fail," CB Insights, accessed May 26, 2023, https://s3-us-west-2.amazonaws.com/cbi-content/research-reports/The-20-Reasons-Startups-Fail.pdf, 11.

70 Steve Jobs, quoted in Gary Wolf, "Steve Jobs: The Next Insanely Great Thing," WIRED, February 1, 1996, https://www.wired.com/1996/02/jobs-2/.

71 Isaac Newton, *The Correspondence of Isaac Newton: 1661–1675*, ed. H. W. Turnbull, vol. 1 (London: Published for the Royal Society at the University Press, 1959), 416.

72 T. S. Eliot, *The Sacred Wood: Essays on Poetry and Criticism* (New York: Alfred A. Knopf, 1921), 114.

73 Karoline Aslaksen and Håvard Lorås, "The Modality-Specific Learning Style Hypothesis: A Mini-Review," *Frontiers in Psychology* 9, (August 2018), https://doi.org/10.3389/fpsyg.2018.01538.

74 The disfluency effect comes into play when someone is forced to process information slowly but also retains the information more because of it. For example, this book would be harder to read if all the pages were slightly printed off-center, but you may retain the information longer if you decided to still read it. You can find supporting studies in the chapter resources section.

75 R. Keith Sawyer, *Explaining Creativity: The Science of Human Innovation* (Oxford: Oxford University Press, 2012), 401.

76 Westby, E. L., & Dawson, V. L. (1995). Creativity: Asset or burden in the classroom? Creativity Research Journal, 8(1), 1–10. https://doi.org/10.1207/s15326934crj0801_1

77 "Average Number of Hours in the School Day and Average Number of Days in the School Year for Public Schools, by State: 2007–08," National Center for Education Statistics, accessed May 26, 2023, https://nces.ed.gov/surveys/sass/tables/sass0708_035_s1s.asp.

78 Ronald A. Beghetto, "Creativity in Classrooms" in *The Cambridge Handbook of Creativity*, ed. James C. Kaufman and Robert J. Sternberg, 2nd ed. (Cambridge: Cambridge University Press, 2019), 588.

79 Quentin Tarantino, in StudioBinder, "Quentin Tarantino Explains How to Write & Direct Movies | The Director's Chair," Youtube, July 29, 2019, https://www.youtube.com/watch?v=6V1Sm0WCtHU.

80 George Orwell, *Why I Write* (Amereon Press, 1946), 10.

81 Aaron Copland, *Music and Imagination* (Cambridge: Harvard University Press, 1980), 41.

82 Martin Luther King Jr., "I Have a Dream" (speech), August 28, 1963, Washington, DC, YouTube video, 6:20–6:46, https://www.youtube.com/watch?v=vP4iY1TtS3s.

83 Emma Dorothy Eliza Nevitte Southworth, *Capitola's Peril* (J. H. Sears, 1923), 201.

84 Abraham H. Maslow, *The Psychology of Science: A Reconnaissance* (Henry Regnery Company, 1969), 13.

85 Kim van Broekhoven, David Cropley, and Philipp Seegers, "Differences in Creativity across Art and STEM Students: We Are More Alike Than Unalike," *Thinking Skills and Creativity* 38, (December 2020), 10, https://doi.org/10.1016/j.tsc.2020.100707.

[86] Broekhoven, Cropley, and Seegers, "Differences in Creativity across Art and STEM Students," 10–11.
[87] "Lorne Michaels," Interview by Alec Baldwin, January 30, 2012. https://www.wnycstudios.org/podcasts/heresthething/episodes/182698-lorne-michaels.
[88] Abraham H. Maslow, *Toward a Psychology of Being*, 3rd ed. (Hoboken, NJ: Wiley, 1998), 132.
[89] "Ricardo Semler | Semco Style," accessed May 26, 2023, https://ricardosemler.com/.
[90] The information about Arnold Rothstein was collected from the following sources: "Arnold Rothstein," Jewish Virtual Library, accessed May 26, 2023, https://www.jewishvirtuallibrary.org/arnold-rothstein. *Encyclopedia Britannica*, s.v. "Arnold Rothstein." "Arnold Rothstein," Biography, May 27, 2021, https://www.biography.com/crime/arnold-rothstein.
[91] Biographiq, *Lucky Luciano: The Father of Modern Organized Crime* (Filiquarian Publishing, LLC, 2008).
[92] Lloyd Morris, *Postscript to Yesterday* (New York: Random House, 1947), 75, https://archive.org/details/PostscriptToYesterday/page/n1/mode/2up.
[93] "Alcohol Facts and Statistics," National Institute on Alcohol Abuse and Alcoholism, accessed May 11, 2023, https://www.niaaa.nih.gov/alcohols-effects-health/alcohol-topics/alcohol-facts-and-statistics.
[94] "Life Expectancy in the USA, 1900–98," accessed May 11, 2023, https://u.demog.berkeley.edu/~andrew/1918/figure2.html.
[95] F. Gino and D. Ariely, "The Dark Side of Creativity: Original Thinkers Can Be More Dishonest," *Journal of Personality and Social Psychology* 102, no. 3 (2012), 445–459, https://doi.org/10.1037/a0026406.
[96] Xin Liu et al., "In Line and Out of the Box: How Ethical Leaders Help Offset the Negative Effect of Morality on Creativity," *Journal of Applied Psychology* 105, no. 12, 1447–1465, https://doi.org/10.1037/apl0000489.
[97] Xin Liu et al., "In Line and out of the Box: How Ethical Leaders Help Offset the Negative Effect of Morality on Creativity," *Journal of Applied Psychology* 105, no. 2 (2020): 1463, https://doi.org/10.1037/apl0000489.
[98] Robert G. Evans, "Tough on Crime? Pfizer and the CIHR," *Healthcare Policy* 5, no. 4 (May 2010), https://www.ncbi.nlm.nih.gov/pmc/articles/PMC2875889/.
[99] "Accolades," Pfizer, accessed May 11, 2023, https://www.pfizer.com/en/about/careers/accolades.
[100] Liu, "In Line and out of the Box," 1462.
[101] The Me Too movement was started to combat sexual harassment, rape, and other forms of abuse experienced by woman, with a focus on the workplace.

[102] Hai Liang and Francis L. F. Lee, "Opinion Leadership in a Leaderless Movement: Discussion of the Anti-Extradition Bill Movement in the 'LIHKG' Web Forum," *Social Movement Studies* (2021), 20, https://doi.org/10.1080/14742837.2021.1989294.

[103] "2021 Presidential Historians Survey 2021," C-Span, accessed May 26, 2023, https://www.c-span.org/presidentsurvey2021/?page=overall.

[104] J. T. Duryea, Letter to Josiah G. Holland, undated, quoted in Allen G. Guelzo, "Holland's Informants: The Construction of Josiah Holland's 'Life of Abraham Lincoln,'" *Journal of the Abraham Lincoln Association* 23, no. 1, (Winter 2002): 53.

[105] Abraham Lincoln, quoted in *Golden Book Magazine*, November 1931, 306.

[106] Adam Grant, Francesca Gino, and David Hofmann, "Reversing the Extraverted Leadership Advantage: The Role of Employee Proactivity," *Academy of Management Journal* 54, no. 3 (June 2011): 528–550, https://doi.org/10.5465/AMJ.2011.61968043.

[107] Douglas Rushkoff, "Social Animals," chap. 2 in *Team Human* (New York: W. W. Norton & Company, 2021), 12.

[108] Greg Satell, "What Successful Movements Have in Common," *Harvard Business Review*, November 30, 2016, https://hbr.org/2016/11/what-successful-movements-have-in-common.

[109] Jordan Hughes, "The Art of Peer Pressure: Social Desires as Incentives to Join Students Protests in Jordan," Independent Study Project (ISP) Collection, 2826, (Spring 2018): 31, https://digitalcollections.sit.edu/isp_collection/2826.

[110] Information about Rosa's story is taken from Gordon Cunningham, "The Jambi Kiwa Story: Mobilizing Assets for Community Development," La Historia de Jambi Kiwa, https://coady.stfx.ca/wp-content/uploads/pdfs/JAMBIenglishfin1(1).pdf.

[111] Rosa Guamán, Iosphera, "Bajo la Influencia de la Luna / Under the Influence of the Moon / Sota la Influència de la Lluna," YouTube video, Apr 12, 2011, 5:39, https://www.youtube.com/watch?v=YBpVuCBOngI&t=140s.

[112] Robert K. Greenleaf, "Who Is the Servant-Leader?" in *The Servant as Leader* (Westfield, IN: Greenleaf Center for Servant Leadership, 2008), 6.

[113] John P. Kretzman and John McKnight, Building Communities from the Inside out: A Path toward Finding and Mobilizing a Community's Assets (Vancouver: Langara College, 2004), 6.

[114] Hanna Nel, "A Comparison between the Asset-Oriented and Needs-Based Community Development Approaches in Terms of Systems Changes," *Practice* 30, no. 1 (2018): 33–52, https://doi.org/10.1080/09503153.2017.1360474.

[115] R. M. Kanter, "Seven Truths about Change to Lead By and Live By," *Harvard Business Review*, August 23, 2010, https://hbr.org/2010/08/seven-truths-about-change-to-l.

# Index

ABCD (Asset Based Community Development)
  defined, 182, 183
  Rosa Guamán, 183
abolitionists
  Lay, Benjamin, 68
  Tubman, Harriet, 67
Age of Knowledge, 7, 33
ALS Ice Bucket Challenge, 102
American Tobacco Company, 1
Apple
  Steve Jobs, Woz, Tim Cook, 169
  store customer service, 50
Aristotle
  quote, 171
Arnold, story of
  creative, "fixer", 152
automatic thinking, 22
Bernays, Edward, 1
  quote, 1
Bird, Sue, 28
Black Lives Matter (BLM), 162, 164
*Black Panther*, 160
Bonaparte, Napoleon
  caricature of, 120–22
Boston Tea Party, 162
boundaries
  practicality and, 147
Brock Turner Case, bias, 52
*Building Communities from the Inside Out* (Kretzmann, McKnight), 182
Burrell, BD
  quote, 125
campaign
  defined, 102
*Capitola's Peril* (Southworth), 140

CB Insights
  startup failure, 126
Change
  defined, 12
  objections to, 13
Changemakers
  Candy Lightner, MADD, 18, 25
  Churchill, Winston, 16
  defined, 1, 4
  health, prioritizing, 39
  meaning informs priorities, 39
  questions to ask, 111, 112
  responsibility, 54
  unreliability of judgment, 9
  Wisdom as guide, 11
  Wisdom-led, 78
  Wisdom-led, five concepts leading to, 2
Chinese finger trap, 22
Churchill, Winston, 48, 78
  quote, 169
  work ethic, 16
cognitive empathy, defined, 57
collaboration
  ABCD and, 185
  breakdown of, 76
  collaborative emergence, 118
  control and, 173
  defined, 115
  distributed creativity, 114
  high-performance organizations and, 115
  improvisation and, 118
  Socratic method and, 87
collaborative emergence, 118
Common Man
  charisma versus principles, 78
  collateral damage and, 161
  defined, 15–16

misconceptions, 16–19
negative connotations, 15
Plato and the, 24
unreliability of judgment, 9
Common Sense
climate change study, 5
defined, 3
dueling, changing views of, 5
formed unconsciously, 185
issues with, 5
principles and, 92
progress and, 7
replace with Wisdom, 34
slavery, changing views and, 5
viral trends and, 102
vision and, 26, 185
Common Sense.
pushing boundaries, 148
Community
defined, 175
concepts, intimacy with, 36
cooperation
defined, 115
Copland, Aaron
creativity and self-discovery, 138
coyotes versus wolves, 100
creativity
dark-side studies, 153
purpose and, 119
studies of unethical, 154–55
unethical, 158
critical thinking
perspective, 52
Cross, Rob
quote, 115
Dalai Lama
quote, 99
Westby, Erik L.
student/teacher creativity research, 131
Dewey's Community of Inquiry, 86

DeZutter, Stacy and Sawyer, R. Keith, study, 118
DiCaprio, Leonardo
school trashing and, 130
diffusion of responsibility, 54
distributed creativity, 114
collaborative emergence and, 118
improvisation and, 117
study, 118
divergent and convergent thought balance, 148
divergent thinking
defined, 142
study, 142
divergent to convergent problem-solving, 147
diverse teams
traits, 146
diversity
qualifiers to creativity, 145
Doe, Kelvin, 168
Edison, Thomas
Common Sense changed, 4
overcoming limitations, 18
Einstein, Albert
Common Sense defined, 10
quote, 93
Eliot, T. S.
quote, 128
empathy
emotional versus cognitive, 57–59
*Endgame*
Tony Stark as Iron Man, 160
equitable change
path to, 186
ethical leadership
studies, 158
Eurich, Tasha
quote, research, 109
self-awareness in leadership, 109

# Index

external self-awareness
  defined, 111
faith
  defined, 106
  intimacy and, 106
*Fearless Benjamin Lay, The* (Rediker), 69
follower
  role of, 18
Foolish Genius
  blind dedication, 78
  defined, 11
  emotional empathy, 57
  leadership as control, 172
  seven signs of, 70–80
four I's of Change
  preparation to, 140
Frankl, Viktor
  Changemaker, 99
  quote, responsibility, 107
  *why*, 97–99
Franklin, Benjamin, as hero, 48
Gandhi, Mahatma, 171
Gee, Tim
  quote, 69
Gen-Zers
  social justice warriors, 66
Getting to "Yes And" (Kulhan), 117
Gillray, James
  Napoleon cricature and, 120
  perspective, 141
Beghetto, Ronald A.
  school uniformity, 135
Goebbels, Joseph
  Reich Chamber of Culture, 122
Graham, Billy, 59–60
Great Commission, 42
Greenleaf, Robert
  servant-first leader, quote, 180
Guamán, Rosa
  community, 178
  Estuardo Gallegos and, 180

Jambi Kiwa, 181
  philosophy, 179
Haitian Revolution, 67
happiness
  benefits of, 37
Higgins, Michael D.
  quote, 84
high-quality life, 38–40
Hitler
  creative expression, control of, 122
  obedience to authority, 74
Hong Kong protests, 163
  without central leadership, 164
hope
  defined, 105
IKEA
  good intentions, 21
  ignoring ignorance, 22
  Juneteenth, 21
Incarnation
  defined, 30
James, Lebron, 28
Jefferson, Thomas
  as uncompromising hero, 91
John Templeton Foundation
  purpose statement, 104
Judge Judy, perspective, 51
Juneteenth
  IKEA, 21
Kaczynski, Ted, 18
  Unabomber justification, 14
Kanter, Rosabeth Moss
  quote, change, 185
Keith Sawyer
  creativity and, 129
Khan, Genghis, as villain, 48
*Kill Bill*, 135
King, Martin Luther, Jr.
  "I Have a Dream" speech, 138–39
  as hero, 48
  charisma, 78

199

civil disobedience, jail, 4
Common Sense redefined, 4
critical thinking, 52
Martin Luther King Day, 21
orator, 16
Kingsolver, Barbara
   quote, 106
Kony, Joseph
   Kony 2012, 101
   viral moment, 101
Kulhan, Bob, 117
L'Ouverture, Toussaint, 82
Darley, John
   personal responsibility study, 54
Lay, Benjamin
   abolitionist, 68–70
   death penalty and, 69
   first vegetarian society, 70
leaderless protests
   without a hero, 162
leadership
   cycle of, 170
   eight misconceptions, 165
   extroverts as, 169
   hero-minded, 165
   introverts, 169
Lee, Francis L. F., 164
Lee, Opal, Juneteenth, 21
Liang, Hai, 164
LIHKG Web Forum
   Francis L. F. Lee and Hai Liang article, 164
Lincoln, Abraham, 168
Lipman, Matthew, 86
Locke, John, 83
Lorne Michaels
   quote on creativity and boundaries, 147
Luxemburg, Rosa, 82
*Man's Search for Meaning* (Frankl), 98
Mandela, Nelson, 82
   orator, 16

Mankell, Henning
   quote, 22
Marvel movies, 160
Marx, Karl, 83
   quote, 83
Maslow, Abraham
   quote on creativity, 149
   quote on perspective, 141
Kretzmann, John
   *Building Communities from the Inside Out*, 182
Me Too movement
   loss of respect, 161
Milgram, Stanley, 74–77
Miller, J. C.
   quote, 83
Mister Rogers, orator, 16
More Mindset, 23–24, 40
   hero's, 181
   problem versus process, 24
   school and, 23
Mothers Against Drunk Driving (MADD), 25, 176
Musk, Leon
   school trashing and, 130
National Center for Education Statistics, 132
Nel, Hanna
   study, ABCD versus problem-based approach, 182
Newton, Isaac
   eureka moment, 124
   quote, 128
Nietzsche, Friedrich
   quote, 96, 99
Obama, Barack, 78
Orwell, George
   introspection, 137
*Peter Pan*, 135
Philosophy for Children (P4C), 86
philosophy, search for truth, 84
Plato
   Common Man, 26

# Index

quote, 25
positive psychologist, 105
*Propaganda* (Bernays), 1
*Psychologist Experiences the Concentration Camp, A* (Frankl), 98
responsibility
  barrier to Wisdom, 40
  Candy Lightner as Changemaker, 25
  Great Commission, 42
  hope and faith and, 107
  Nietzsche, Fredrich, quote, 99
  personal defined, 107
  sense of purpose, 107
Ritz-Carlton, customer service, 51
Rousseau, Jean-Jacques, 83
Rushkoff, Douglass
  quote, 175
Salt March, 171
Santayana, George
  philosopher, 72
Satell, Greg
  quote, 176
schema
  adjusting, 50
  bias and, 145
school
  Churchill, Winston, 17
  convergent thinking and, 148
  creativity and, 139
  death of imagination, 139
  divergent thought and, 143
  focus and, 8
  issues with, 8
  lack of individuality, 135
  Lumiar School, 150
  More Mindset and, 23
  prescribed method, 143
  Taliban and, 167
  trashing, 130
Semco Style, 150
Semler, Ricardo

corporate democracy, 150
  Lumiar School, 150
  Semco Style, 150
seven pillars
  society influences, 42
Sharp, Ann Margaret, 86
Shaw, George Bernard
  quote on responsibility, 55
Simon Sinek, 105
situationships, 26
Sivers, Derek
  quote, 18
  Ted Talk, How to Start a Movement, 18
social movement
  defined, 102
  failure of, 108
Socrates, Socratic method, 87
Sojourner
  Truth, Sojourner, 67
Southworth, E. D. E. N.
  quote, *Capitola's Peril*, 140
Stalin, Joseph
  creative expression and, 122
  Socialist Realism, 123
Stigler, George J.
  quote, 88
strategies
  creating, 112–13
Tarantino, Quentin
  individuality, 135–37
*Team Human* (Rushkoff), 175
Thanos, 160
Thunberg, Greta, 167
Torrance, Ellis Paul
  Father of Modern Creativity, 130–31
tradition, negative impact
  Santa visits, 71
  tipping, 71
Twain, Mark
  on history, 72
Unabomber, 18

Foolish Genius

Vlad the Impaler, as villain, 48
Voltaire
   quote, Common Sense, 6
Washington, George
   as uncompromising hero, 91
West, Kanye
   creative genius and, 130
*what* questions
   purpose of, 110
*why* questions, 110
   purpose of, 110
Wisdom
   compassionately empathetic, 59
   concepts, inimacy with, 36
   defined, 10
   ego and, 41
   failure and, 40
   happiness study, 36–37
   humility and, 41
   leadership, means to serve, 172
   metrics, 56
   responsibility, 55
   true wealth, 38
Wisdom-led Changemaker
   defined, 78
   equitable change and, 185
Wise Society
   ABCD approach and, 185
   community development and, 177
   creativity, role in, 119
   defined, 37
   seven pillars and, 42
   three principles of, 94
Wittgenstein, Ludwig, 92
*Wolf of Wall Street, The*
   school trashing, 130
wolves versus coyotes, 99
Yellowstone National Park
   wolves versus coyotes, 99
Yousafzai, Malala, 167
Zuckerberg, Mark
   school trashing and, 130

# About the Author

David Mahan was born and raised in Columbus, Ohio, where, after speaking at a local conference on "How To Find Purpose," he wrote his first book, *Foolish Genius*, at the age of twenty-four. David finds joy in creating practical solutions from grounded concepts such as: wisdom, purpose, creativity, and community to serve leaders in nonprofits, startups, schools, and faith-based organizations.

David currently works in affordable housing development, serves on the board of a community development organization, and is the founding team member of a local church plant. Being a devout Christian, David believes that the loving nature of pure wisdom and justice point to the same source, One that perfectly embodies each of these concepts.

# Bulk Orders

Order **Foolish Genius** as a gift, thank you, or incentive for your friends, colleagues, and business associates. Order through your local bookstore or online (www.foolishgenius.com),

Use the form below to order directly from the author.

☐ Please send me _____ copies of **Foolish Genius** at a cost of $27.00 plus $1.57 tax, per copy, and free shipping for a total of $_____.

Note: Call for quotes on bulk orders of 50 copies or more.

Make check payable to: **Foolish Genius**

Charge my credit card:

☐Visa ☐MasterCard ☐American Express ☐Discover

Credit Card # _____

Expiration date (month/year) _____

Address information for credit card and shipping books:

Name _____

Organization _____

Address _____

City _____ State _____ Zip _____

Phone _____

Email _____

☐ Please send me information about David's Consulting, Speaking, and Educational Offerings

_____.

**Mail to:** David W. Mahan, 120 Hawkes Ave, Columbus, Ohio, 43222

# Collaborate with David

## In-School Leadership Mentoring

As the role of the school has increased, so have the expectations placed on school staff to be more than just educators. The Foolish Genius Mentorship Program works to activate the young leaders in your school to positively impact whatever community they are a part of, whether it be their family, their friend group, your school, or our nation. Regardless of the scale, your students will learn how Wisdom can guide their actions through the process of equitable community development.

## Organizational Consulting

Collaborate with David to discover how your organization can work under a shared purpose, one that advances the principles and ideals of a Wise Society.

## What else would you like to see?

The Foolish Genius brand is expanding quickly, and we'd like to hear from you on how we could best serve you! Please send your name, organization, and any suggestions you may have to the email below:

team@foolishgenius.com.

www.ingramcontent.com/pod-product-compliance
Lightning Source LLC
Chambersburg PA
CBHW070343010526
44119CB00029B/418/J